ˉ EDITION

SHED BY

RD, SHROPSHIRE

SBN 0 9537332 0 3

DESIGNED, TYPESET AND PRODUCED BY

RON BILLINGS, REARSBY, LEICESTERSHIRE

PRINTED BY SCOTIA PRESS, LEICESTER

KENNETH SANDFORD

DEDICATION

This book is dedicated to the memory of my dear friend,
United States Federal Judge,
The Honorable Robert S. Gawthrop III.

An ardent admirer of Kenneth Sandford, whose talent he aspired to emulate, he died before being able to make his contribution to these pages.

'Dear, dear, dear!'

KENNETH SANDFORD

"merely corroborative detail"

by

ROBERTA MORRELL

CONTENTS

ACKNOWLEDGEMENT

I would like to thank Pauline Sandford, Ron Billings and Martin Gude for their unstinting efforts in the preparation of this book and all those who made available the articles and photographs which appear in these pages. I am also indebted to my family and friends, without whose support and interest I may not have survived the trials and tribulations of the first-time author.

INTRODUCTION

Who's the fairy in the green velvet suit and blonde wig?',

I whispered.

'That's Kenneth Sandford'

came the admiring, hushed reply. Little did I know that the man to whom I referred so naively was to become a life-long colleague, friend and mentor.

How well I remember that trip to the Alexandra Theatre in Birmingham to see *Patience* – a 16th birthday present from my Godmother, it was my first experience of Gilbert and Sullivan and the D'Oyly Carte Opera Company. As a serious musician studying clarinet, 'cello and singing, I was something of a musical snob and rather surprised to find that I quite enjoyed my first taste of comic opera. Determined to continue the widening of my cultural experience, Aunty Doris took me to see *Ruddigore* the following year and I was, again, fascinated by the wonderful performance of Kenneth Sandford as Sir Despard Murgatroyd.

Five years later, following my training at London's Royal College of Music, I found myself on stage with this remarkable man. After all, joining the D'Oyly Carte for a year or two seemed a good way to get my Equity card before making my name as a serious singer! Looking back with amusement on the arrogance of youth, I realise how very fortunate, not to say privileged, I have been to learn my stagecraft from such a uniquely talented performer.

This biography of Kenneth Sandford is a tribute to one of the finest singer/actors that England has ever produced; a man of unfailing modesty, charm and good humour, whom I am honoured to call my friend.

Author:
ROBERTA MORRELL

Chapter 1

THE EARLY YEARS

'And, by the by, he was a little boy'

Invariably described by respectful commentators as 'veteran' for the last quarter of a century, it is hard to imagine the distinguished, white-haired Kenneth Sandford as a child or, indeed, as a young man. The arrival on the West End stage of an ordinary Yorkshire lad via the Royal Air Force and the Royal College of Art seems just about as unlikely as any Gilbertian plot, but his background and unconventional route into the world of theatre contributed significantly to his development into the great D'Oyly Carte performer so admired by Gilbert and Sullivan devotees around the world.

Born the second child of Fred and Bessie Parkin on 28th June 1924, baby Kenneth's arrival was registered in Godalming, Surrey. Given the fact that his parents and older sister, Eileen, lived in Sheffield, the mystery as to why his mother returned to her family, the Sandfords, for her confinement has always puzzled Ken, but he was told that as soon as mother and child were strong they returned to Sheffield. Home was the picturesquely named 'Rose Cottage' pub in Cricket Inn Road, where Fred's father was the landlord.

Fred and Bessie's wedding day in 1917

Notwithstanding the rigours of the 1930s economy, young Kenneth had a normal and happy upbringing, enjoying drawing as well as the usual pastimes of football and cricket. He liked school, but does recall with amusement the time when, as a six-year old, he was found wandering in the churchyard, having escaped from his infants' school. He loved his parents dearly, describing his mother as pretty, warm and adorable and his father as a hard-working man, who cut a distinguished figure and not above doing a 'turn' in the pub. Here, perhaps, was a suggestion of the theatrical genes which he, undoubtedly, inherited from someone. Fred, an electrician by trade, eventually bought a radio shop and the family was able to move firstly to a modern council estate and then to a large Victorian stone villa in Norfolk Road.

During these early years the young Kenneth showed an increasing talent for drawing and, at the age of 11, left his elementary school to enrol in the Junior Department of the Sheffield College of Art. Here, mornings were spent on normal academic subjects, whilst afternoons were devoted to drawing, design and craftwork. He was in his element and, at 14, it was a natural progression to the Senior Department where, under the inspiring tutelage of Eric 'Jonesy' Jones, he was introduced to the delights of architecture, anatomy and composition. It was around this time, as Ken fondly recalls, that his father wryly observed that he should move into the attic – if he was going to be an artist, he may as well live like one.

Whilst taking his studies very seriously, Kenneth retained his passion for playing football and also joined some teenage friends in the choir of the local Methodist church, where he enjoyed making music with his pals. He certainly had no aspirations to be a singer and chuckles at the recollection of the choir master suggesting that he should have some singing lessons:

'to do something about that loud voice'

He was duly despatched to a somewhat eccentric and colourful local teacher called Madame Skaife, but fails to recall the efficacy of her approach.

Conscious of the cost to his parents of art materials, he got a job cleaning out fire grates – at least getting up at 6 a.m. in mid-winter meant that he could pay for his own paints. His diligence was rewarded when he gained both the Certificate for Drawing and the Certificate for Painting and was awarded a scholarship to the Royal College of Art in London. Fred and Bessie were proud and delighted, viewing the scholarship as a passport to a secure teaching post and pension for their son. How wrong they were.

When Kenneth was 15, the outbreak of World War II brought many changes to his idyllic and sheltered world as an art student. Realising that there was every possibility he may eventually be called up, he joined the local Air Training Corps with a view to later joining the R.A.F. His duties included overseeing black-out requirements and the use of a stirrup pump designed to counter incendiary devices. His inexperience and over-enthusiasm caused him to burst the pipe of the pump and he laughs at the memory of his parents' horror when he arrived home with his head swathed in bandages, looking like the Invisible Man. Fortunately, the deluge of caustic soda from the pump caused only superficial wounds and he was soon able to resume his post as Drum Major of the Wing Band, twirling the mace and hurling it theatrically in and out of the overhead tram lines.

Rataplan, Rataplan, I'm a military man'

As the war dragged on and Sheffield's industrial heart was targeted by German bombers (Kenneth was in a basement studio of the College of Art when a bomb destroyed the upper floors of the building), it became clear that his scholarship to the Royal College of Art would have to be deferred until after the war had ended. He was bitterly disappointed by this, but it was an inevitability – everyone had to pay the price of war. In March 1944, the long-expected call-up came and he duly reported to Trafford Park in Manchester, before travelling to Aberystwyth in North Wales to commence initial training. Kenneth, known as Ken to his fellow servicemen never saw active service (he refuses to be drawn as to whether this was good luck or good judgement), always being destined for more advanced training; firstly as a bomb-aimer, then as a navigator. He relished every aspect of R.A.F. life

'A most intense young man' Ken joins up

and welcomed the opportunity to travel to Canada. He was stationed at Picton, Ontario, where he found low-flying exercises over Lake Ontario totally exhilarating. He was transferred to St. John's, Quebec and Halifax, Nova Scotia before returning to England for advanced training on Wellington bombers at Moreton-in-the-Marsh.

At the suggestion of a girl in every town Ken becomes cagey. He admits to having been a rather shy and intense young man, which is no surprise to those of us who know him well, but the characteristic twinkling eyes tell their own story as he gives a tantalising glimpse of the naïvely romantic young Parkin. Before his call-up to the R.A.F., he had been quite taken with the drum majorette of the Wing Band and promised to see her when on home leave. Anticipating that week-end passes might be none too plentiful, he showed an early flash of the theatrical genius to come in his D'Oyly Carte roles – he packed a disguise! Having progressed through the Scout movement to Rover Scout, he still had his uniform and knew that it could be easily carried

'I sing and I play and I paint' Sergeant Parkin off duty

with him. When denied a week-end pass, he simply changed into scout shorts and hat before catching the train back to Sheffield. He declined to comment when asked if she was worth the risk.

At last the war was over and Ken was sent to R.A.F. Cranwell in Lincolnshire to await discharge, his navigator's skills never put into practice – which was not a bad thing given his ability to get lost in his own back yard. This was to prove a significant and fateful period of his life. His official job was art instructor to the education department, but he can only ever remember having one student. With plenty of time on his hands, he filled the days painting to his heart's content.

However, the natural exuberance of young men released from the cares of the war years prompted a long overdue need to have some fun whilst awaiting demob and putting on shows proved popular on the base. Ken soon found himself painting scenery and learning lines for such extravaganzas as Terence Rattigan's *While the Sun Shines* and Ralph Reader's pantomime *Robinson Air-Cruso* – his first taste of the theatre. When it became known that he had done a little singing, Ken was invited to sing with the Cranwell R.A.F. Band at one of their regular concerts and, ironically, chose for his solo *'Take a Pair of Sparkling Eyes'*, a song he liked by Gilbert and Sullivan. Further guest spots followed his initial success and some of his pals, impressed by his lovely tenor voice, secretly entered him in a radio talent contest hosted by Carroll Levis. Despite his protestations, he was persuaded to have a go and, to his astonishment, was voted 'listeners' choice'. He returned three weeks later to sing '*Santa Lucia*' in Yorkshire-tinged Italian, amazed by his success. Ken can claim to be a 'Carroll Levis Discovery' and if you are familiar with that term, you know you are getting old.

When he was not painting, Ken found singing an enjoyable hobby and decided to take some lessons when home on leave, duly going to a distinguished Yorkshire teacher, Eva Rich. It is clear that, at this stage of his life, he was still determined to be a full-time artist, despite the obvious financial insecurity that such a future might mean. He was certainly no less fired with enthusiasm than when first awarded his scholarship before the war and the harrowing intervening years had failed to shake his resolve – painting was still his *raison d'etre.*

The eagerly-awaited demob came in May 1947 and Ken was, at last, able to look forward to his deferred art studies. The scholarship could not be taken up until September, so it was arranged that he would fill in the time by teaching at his beloved Sheffield College of Art whilst enjoying a few months at home with his parents.

'Oh, Art, we thank thee for this boon'

Having been forced to put all thoughts of his scholarship to the back of his mind during the war years, Ken entered his student life with great gusto.

The Royal College of Art football team 1947/8

Many of his fellow undergraduates were also ex-servicemen and, at 23 years old, they had great motivation to work hard and make up for the lost years – as it was, they were not going to enter the world of employment until 26 years of age. Although Ken loved every moment of the days devoted to art, he relished the social activities, too, proudly playing for the college football team. Most of his team-mates had served in the forces during the war and he recalls the infantile pleasure they felt on discovering that they had a fixture against the Army Officer Cadets at Sandhurst. It seems that the rather superior cadets were not too pleased to be on the receiving end of a thrashing from a bunch of scruffy art students!

As time passed, Ken also began to widen his social horizons outside the college. As a poverty-stricken student, he was fortunate enough to be able to live with his brother-in-law's parents in

Hammersmith and, looking for a chance to enjoy some singing, he joined the choir of the local church, St. Peter's. One of the choristers, a girl called Pauline Joyce, quickly caught his eye and their friendship soon blossomed into romance.

During a chance conversation at college, one of the other students mentioned to Ken that he had heard about a remarkable singing teacher, Jane Douglas, who lived close to their college in South Kensington. Seemingly, this inspired lady, knowing that young singers need to learn more than vocal technique alone, asked the students unable to afford her fees to instruct others in their particular field. To Ken this seemed like a wonderful opportunity and, after making some enquiries, he soon found himself taking not only singing lessons, but also classes in the basics of acting, movement and dance given by young performers anxious to 'pay' for their singing lessons. Ken sometimes paid for his tuition by performing at up-market soirées in private Kensington apartments, when he first discovered the delights of songs by Michael Head and Ralph Vaughan Williams.

It is interesting to note that Ken's tenor voice gradually deepened over the four years he spent in Jane Douglas' capable hands but, however much she nurtured his lovely voice, there remained the problem of his Yorkshire accent. The sage Madame Douglas duly despatched him for elocution lessons with two elderly and somewhat eccentric sisters, who lived in a cavernous mansion flat. Seldom comfortable with these strange maiden ladies, his embarrassment at the bizarre, cacophonous exercises they set him was all the incentive he needed to lose the offending brogue as quickly as possible.

By the age of 25, Ken's art studies and love of singing were totally absorbing but, as yet, he had not given too much thought to the future at the end of the 3-year course. Inevitably, the final few months at college focused his mind on how he was to earn a living and he found himself dreading a lifetime of teaching – he was first and foremost a painter and that was what he longed to do. But how could he possibly support himself, let alone contemplate marriage and a family? During a casual conversation about these worries, Jane Douglas, who had long recognised in Ken a real theatrical talent of which he himself was, as yet, unaware mentioned that auditions for the British premiere of *Carousel* were to be held as Drury Lane and that he should consider going along. He was completely taken aback – the thought of a career as a professional singer had never entered his head; that side of his life was purely for fun – wasn't it? After thinking long and hard about Jane's suggestion, he came to the conclusion that there could be no harm in going for an audition – if he failed, things would remain the same but if, by some remote possibility, he was accepted for the chorus of *Carousel*, he would have time to reassess his situation whilst earning some much needed money. He decided to have a go.

And so, the fateful introduction of Jane Douglas into the life of Kenneth Parkin and her subsequent enlightened tuition, led him to the threshold of his destiny.

Chapter 2

THE STAGE IS SET

'Therein is song and dance, too'

HAVING taken the momentous decision to audition for the chorus of *Carousel* in no way prepared Ken for the harsh reality of the actual event. He had rarely been to a West End theatre; an occasional visit to the Chiswick Empire and a memorable night at the Laurel and Hardy show pretty well accounted for his experience of theatrical entertainment, as art students were invariably too poor to see a show. So, it was with great trepidation and a feeling of complete ignorance that Ken arrived at the hallowed portals of the Theatre Royal, Drury Lane to attend what, in the business, is fondly referred to as a 'cattle call'.

The following few hours were to prove beyond anything he had anticipated or, indeed, could possibly have imagined in his wildest dreams. To begin with, he was astounded by the sheer number of hopefuls crowding the backstage corridors and staircases going through their various warm-up routines, seemingly oblivious to the world. Smartly-dressed men with Crombie coats draped around their shoulders and sporting flamboyant theatrical hats, warbled scales at the side of dancers in rehearsal clothes stretching their muscles in preparation for their auditions. Feeling decidedly like a fish out of water in his conservative clothes, Ken made a feeble attempt to warm up his voice and look as if he belonged in this strange new world. It had never occurred to him that the prospect of a job in a possibly long-running, prestigious new musical would bring out every out-of-work performer within spitting distance of London.

The second shock of the day quickly followed. He was expecting to be called, in turn, to sing his prepared song (which he cannot now recall) but, instead, found himself one of thirty men stretched shoulder-to-shoulder across the stage under the cold scrutiny of the audition panel which included the American producer, Jerome White, looking every inch the Hollywood Mogul. The idea that the initial selection process should be based solely on physical appearance seemed unbelievable and, as Ken waited whilst the unsuccessful candidates dejectedly left the stage, he was prompted to think that he must resemble someone in the Broadway cast.

Waiting his turn to sing, he took the opportunity of listening to the opposition, anxious to assess the vocal quality of the other auditionees and, on the whole, he found the standard surprisingly low. He had assumed, from snatches of conversation overheard in the wings, that he was up against seasoned professional singers. With confidence buoyed and a feeling that he could do better than many of the others, Ken strode to centre stage of the famous old theatre, sang his heart out and was immediately offered a chorus contract. Both surprised and delighted, he was ushered by the Stage Manager to join the other successful candidates chatting excitedly in a corner of the stage, where he was enrolled into Equity by the union representative present. On being informed that the weekly salary would be £7.10 shillings, a small fortune by his standards, the bubble of his elation suddenly burst as he was struck by an awful thought – rehearsals were due to start in May and his college course was not due to end until July. With admirable presence of mind, he smoothly told the Stage Manager that he needed to be certain that he could get replacements for several forthcoming engagements and asked permission to confirm his availability for *Carousel* the following day. This having been granted, he dashed to the Royal College of Art in an effort to resolve his dilemma. He need not have worried. His tutor, not wishing to have yet another destitute artist on his conscience, agreed that Ken could leave college on the understanding that he complete his thesis and the paintings for his exhibition – otherwise, he could not be awarded his diploma. Ken was ecstatic; his paintings were almost finished and he could surely write during breaks in rehearsals. Until then he would work like crazy at the college until his contract commenced – he was actually going to be a professional singer! Flushed with instant success, it suddenly occurred to him that his surname, Parkin, hardly rang with theatrical overtones and so, after careful consideration, he opted to take his mother's maiden name – Sandford. The rest, as they say, is history.

What a baptism of fire that rehearsal period proved to be. The intensity of the professional process was a new and exhilarating experience; he was expected to learn quickly or risk the wrath of a constantly-swearing Jerome White, whose responsibility it was to recreate the American production. Everything fascinated and impressed Ken, from the morning vocal warm-up, through the teaching of the stage business, to the opportunity of watching the amazingly-talented American principals – it was a world he never knew existed and he was entranced.

The excitement and nervous tension of opening night made Ken feel dreadfully inexperienced, to the point where he felt sure that the call-boy's shout of:

'Overture and beginners, please'

was aimed specifically at him! *Carousel* opened to great critical acclaim and he soon settled happily into the run of the show, sharing a dressing room with several experienced (or so they told him) West End choristers. Every performance was a chance to learn and the time flew by. After six months, the

American artistes were replaced by British performers and a new understudy was going to be needed for the leading role of Billy Bigelow. Having been summarily dismissed as:

'too young, son'

by Jerome White when the job came up at the beginning of the run, Ken, who by now was feeling much older and very experienced indeed, again asked to be considered. To his delight and the chagrin of the chorus baritones, he was given the cover and the pay rise that went with it – another ten shillings a week. That would certainly help offset the initial expenses of becoming a theatrical.

EXPENSES

Please note that I am on my first tour - consequently I have had to equip myself accordingly, particularly as the tour covers quite a large area, including Scotland.

Wardrobe Accessories

	£	s.	d.	£	s.	d.
Black shoes	4	5	0			
3 woollen vests	3	3	0			
Towels	3	1	9			
Shirts & Collars (Dinner shirts)	7	2	6			
Shirt & Collars	2	0	11			
2 prs. socks (black)		12	0			
Cardigan	2	5	11			
Dress Overcoat	9	10	0			
Dinner suit	15	0	0			
Rehearsing Jacket	2	10	0			
Cleaning		12	6			
Dressing gown for theatre use	4	15	3	54	18	10
Trunk				21	0	0
Suit Case				6	3	3
Make-up Box				1	1	0
Language Coaching				5	5	0
Music				20	0	0
Postage, telephone, telegrams, stationery				18	10	0
Taxis, tips for call boys, dressers, door men, etc.				40	0	0
Laundry of towels, make-up				17	10	0
Hairdressing & Chiropody				23	0	0
Singing Lessons 50 @ £1.1.0.				52	10	0 -
Hire of studio - aver.5 hrs. per wk @ 2/6d. per hour				32	10	0 -
Coaching accompanists - 46 hours @ 10/6d. per hour				24	3	0 -
Entertaining agents, press, tickets for shows, etc.				30	0	0
				346	11	1
Photo Repro.				3	10	6
Spotlight				17	4	0
				367	5	7

Working with the other understudies proved invaluable and Ken was particularly grateful to the Mr. Snow cover – a genuinely experienced performer who taught him much about stagecraft which would stand him in good stead for the future. Inevitably, the day dawned when he had to go on and, with the unstinting support of the principals, he accepted the enormous challenge of playing Billy Bigelow, acquitting himself reasonably well despite his understandable first-time nerves. It was the first of many opportunities to play what is, arguably, one of the most difficult roles for any singer/actor and, suddenly confident that he could make a good living in Show Business, he plucked up his courage and proposed to Pauline in the star's

Ken as Billy Bigelow

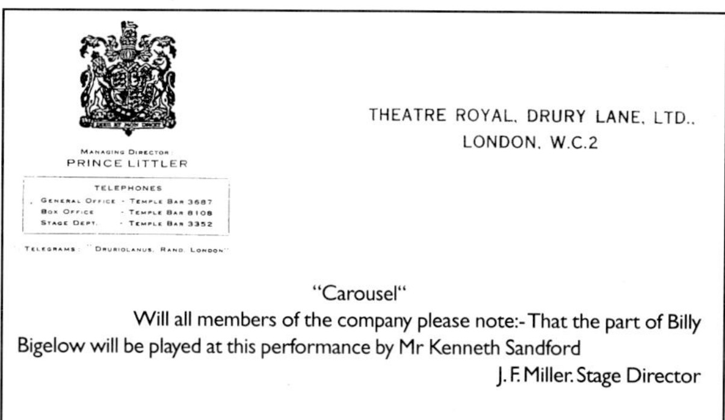

MANAGING DIRECTOR:
PRINCE LITTLER

TELEPHONES
GENERAL OFFICE - TEMPLE BAR 3687
BOX OFFICE - TEMPLE BAR 8108
STAGE DEPT. - TEMPLE BAR 3352

TELEGRAMS: "DRURIOLANUS, RAND, LONDON"

THEATRE ROYAL, DRURY LANE, LTD.,
LONDON, W.C.2

"Carousel"

Will all members of the company please note:- That the part of Billy Bigelow will be played at this performance by Mr Kenneth Sandford

J. F. Miller. Stage Director

dressing room following a particularly good performance. [After a career spanning 48 years, I think he was right to make that assumption.]

Ken's work had begun to attract some attention and he soon found himself represented on a three-year contract by the classy agency of Fraser & Dunlop, who had recognised the employability of a tall, handsome and young leading man. He was encouraged to continue his singing lessons and these led to a recital at the Wigmore Hall in London, where his programme included songs by Wolf-Ferrari, Rachmaninov and Medtner and his accompanist was the distinguished pianist, Ivor Newton. Not a bad way to spend a night off from *Carousel.*

'When I was a lad' Ken in recital mode

Although Ken speaks of this wonderful show in terms of its importance as a huge learning curve for him, he looks back with great affection on the people he came to know so well and the many hilarious moments they shared, both on and offstage. Two incidents in particular still stand out in his memory and, despite the intervening half-century, he relates these anecdotes so vividly that it is impossible not to join him in roars of laughter. The first concerns the lady (over whose identity he draws a considerate veil of anonymity) who played Nettie Fowler – an opera singer of considerable years and experience, whose long career on the boards had taught her to make the most of every offstage moment in which to relax. After giving a spirited rendition of *'June is bustin' out all over',* her routine was to retire to her dressing room, where she would undo the back of her dress, remove her false teeth and pour herself a purely medicinal measure of gin. This favoured indulgence was only disturbed by the knock of the call-boy for her next entrance. He only forgot her once, but that single occasion caused a panic-stricken Nettie to fly onto the stage, unable to turn her back to the audience, as she struggled to deliver her dialogue with a peculiarly muffled sibilance! It was a fine example of how to 'corpse' one's fellow performers and earned the call-boy a toothless reprimand.

Ken's other favourite story is bizarre to say the least. At the rise of the curtain it was immediately apparent to all on stage that a man in the stage-level box was attempting to conduct. Dressed in white tie and tails and flanked by two men in dinner jackets, he would sit attentively through the dialogue and then, at the appropriate cue, pick up his baton before standing to conduct every musical item. Now, as anyone who has ever appeared on a stage can testify, such audience eccentricities are not only distracting, but also totally riveting and it was, indeed, fortunate that the gentleman's conducting skills were sufficient to enable the performance to continue, as every member of the cast had their eyes glued to him! Ken is sure that the erstwhile Musical Director was very happy when, at the end of the act, he was escorted from the theatre.

Ken's enduring love of *Carousel* is hardly surprising – he owes it a great deal. It was a dream way to start a career in the theatre; fabulous music, wonderfully challenging characters and the chance to learn the business at the very highest level. Little wonder that he now derives as much pleasure from singing the famous 'Soliloquy' as he did nearly half a century ago and those of us who have heard his wonderful interpretation of it can detect a trace of that early tenor voice in his searingly emotional ending on a top B flat – the same B flat he first put in as an understudy, only to be told by the management never to do it again, as the principal could not get anywhere near it.

But it was time to move on. The year-long run of *Carousel* at Drury Lane was coming to an end and with it, the financial cushion that Ken had never previously enjoyed. What on earth would he do next? He and Pauline wanted to get married, but that would be impossible if he was out of work. It soon became clear to him, however, that his agents would not get their money's worth from him if he was unemployed and so he was on the audition circuit in no time – not like twelve months earlier, as an inexperienced prospective chorister, but as a principal with West End experience. No more 'cattle calls', watching the shifty technique of the rejected auditionee hanging around in the wings to miraculously appear just as the successful candidate rejected the financial terms of the contract. No waiting for hours to sing, but auditions with an appointed time and salary negotiations via his agent. He was beginning to recognise the sad theatrical reality that sets principals and choristers apart.

'Then hail O king'

Before very long, at the end of 1951, Ken was offered the part of Count Igon Staniev in Ivor Novello's show *King's Rhapsody,* starring Jack Buchanan, Zena and Phyllis Dare and Olive Gilbert. This was to prove another learning experience – a year-long national tour. Having lived in London for the previous four years, the prospect of finding accommodation in towns and cities, most of which he had never visited, was quite daunting. But, ever practical, he asked around the company members during the rehearsal period and was soon fixed up for the first few dates. Then there was the matter of travelling the length and breadth of the country; he certainly could not afford a car and must, therefore, resign himself to lengthy train journeys, most of which would be on Sunday, his only day off in the week. Still, he was young and enthusiastic and had secured work for another year – this time as a principal in his own right. Obviously he would miss seeing Pauline, but the regular income would bring their wedding day closer, so the end justified the means.

Having left behind the family atmosphere at Drury Lane, Ken found himself something of a loner in his new show. He was joining an established line-up of principals from the West End run and considered his colleagues to be decidedly precious after the earthiness of the *Carousel* cast. They were far too busy mourning the recent death of 'darling Ivor' to notice him and he found the floods of tears at every mention of the great man's name overly-theatrical and unconvincing – not the sort of thing that an ordinary chap from Sheffield was used to seeing. He was also conscious of the resentment shown him by one of the chorus baritones, who obviously felt that he should have been playing the Igon Staniev role and this created a slightly tense atmosphere unfamiliar to Ken.

Not that everything was gloomy on that long tour. There were many aspects of the show that he really enjoyed, not least because they added to his

The regal cast of 'King's Rhapsody'

accumulation of theatrical knowledge. *King's Rhapsody* not only boasted a vocal chorus, but also a full ballet chorus, which was required to do twice-weekly classes. On learning that the class was short of a man, Ken happily volunteered his services and could well be said to have 'leapt' at the chance to improve his dancing skills, the rigours of classical ballet disciplines inevitably benefitting his stage presence.

He also enjoyed coming to grips with a totally different theatrical style, realising how important it would be for his career prospects to be able to move comfortably between contrasting forms of musical theatre. *Carousel* was a typical American block-buster musical; extravagant, utterly extrovert and bursting with gritty, down-to-earth characters hewn from the hard rock of ordinary life. *King's Rhapsody* could not have provided a greater contrast, representing the typical English show of the era, which was neither operetta nor musical. An exercise in European elegance, light-weight and pretty, it required from Ken a complete change of approach – a challenge to which he rose splendidly, according to his agent. Having watched a performance at Birmingham's Hippodrome Theatre, Peter Dunlop wrote to Ken to congratulate him on his work, highlighting the specific scenes in which he felt that Ken had excelled both as actor and singer. However, like most theatrical agents of the time, he did offer constructive criticism, which he felt to be a part of his responsibility to his client, tactfully implying that Ken's make-up left something to be desired, commenting that:

> *'your nose looked too short and your face a little podgy'*

He recommended that Ken consult a make-up artist on his return to London. He must have done so, because his ability to create a total change of face in a few minutes has been inspirational to many a young D'Oyly Carte performer.

The *King's Rhapsody* run provided only one other lasting memory. Knowing that the company was to have a week's holiday and increasingly confident of his ability to earn a regular living as a singer, he and Pauline decided to tie the knot. They were married on 6th July 1952 at St. Peter's Church in Hammersmith, where they had first met in the choir, honeymooning in Guernsey.

'Ere Sol has sunk into his western slumbers'

With the tour hastening to its conclusion, Fraser and Dunlop set to work arranging for Ken to audition for another Broadway musical set to open in the West End – *Paint Your Wagon*. He was by now proving very employable and he was delighted to be offered the part of Sandy, with the understudy to the leading character, Julio. After a year in the provinces, he was thrilled by the prospect of being back at home in London and happily brushed up the American accent he had first acquired for *Carousel*.

The show, which starred Bobby Howes and his daughter, Sally-Ann, went out on a short pre-London tour before moving to His Majesty's Theatre, where it ran throughout 1953. Ken loved the virility of this vibrant American musical, with the enviable athleticism of the dancers standing out in his memory and dropping back into the broad 'western' style was no problem. Having spent a year in the refined atmosphere of *King's Rhapsody*, he enjoyed the company of the American performers, whose outgoing friendliness so highlighted the distant aloofness of his previous colleagues. Another bonus was his costume of scruffy trousers and raccoon-skin hat (which was completely threadbare by the time the show closed), it's casual comfort so different from the elegant, but stifling, uniforms of Count Igon Staniev. Nothing much has changed in that department – even at the age of 75 Ken is still happiest in a pair of blue jeans and battered old hat.

'Go West Young Man'

His memories of *Paint Your Wagon* are happy, but rather vague. He enjoyed the show and being at home with Pauline for the first time since their marriage, but specific anecdotes are in short supply with two notable exceptions. The first concerned the lady who played the part of Elizabeth Woodling. Sadly, her eyesight was not her greatest asset and she had a reputation for being a liability behind the wheel of a car; a fact that Ken was able to confirm after a hair-raising drive along the Strand. Alarmed by the repeated sudden application of the brakes, with the accompanying yell of:

'Get out of the way!',

Ken was unable to account for the invisible obstacles causing this eccentric behaviour, until it dawned on him that any car or pedestrian a hundred yards away appeared, to his visually- challenged chauffeuse, to be directly under the front bumper of her car. Thus educated and possessing a few more grey hairs, he made a mental note never to accept a lift with her again.

Then there was the American singer playing the role of Steve Bullnack. A huge, bearded man of 6ft. 6ins., who constantly managed to sing under the note, he passed Ken in the wings one evening and complained:

'Damned orchestra's playing sharp again'.

A few years later and Ken might well have replied

'That's so like a band'.

Another bonus of the lengthy period in London was the resumption of his singing lessons with Jane Douglas, when he was sometimes accompanied by the distinguished pianist, Viola Tunnard, who was well-known for her association with Benjamin Britten and the Aldeburgh Festival. During one lesson, she mentioned to Ken that she coached young singers at the London Opera School and suggested that he would benefit from studying there. Intrigued by the idea, he took her advice and enrolled as a part-time student, thus beginning his life-long love affair with grand opera. Inevitably, after such a happy year, it was a wrench when *Paint Your Wagon* closed and the search for work began again.

'The hours creep on apace'

Ken could never complain that Fraser and Dunlop had not looked after his interests, but there was nothing suitable on the musicals scene, so the next job they lined up for him was as different from his previous shows as anything he could possibly have imagined. True, he had turned down the chance to play Julio on the Australian tour of *Paint Your Wagon*, in the hope of getting work rather nearer home, but the offer of a part in a revue called *Half-Past Eight* would mean a complete departure from anything he had done before. There were two other drawbacks – the contract was only for six months and the show was in Glasgow, making it impossible for him to get home. Still, in the absence of any other offers, he had no alternative and, after talking it over with Pauline, he signed the contract and found himself thrown into the frenetic world of variety.

After rehearsals through the April of 1954, *Half-Past Eight* opened at the Alhambra Theatre in Glasgow, with Jack Radcliffe and a young character actor called Stanley Baxter heading the cast, supported by Ken with his singing partner, Lynette Rae (who was to marry the entertainer, Val Doonican) and the Cherry Willoughby Dancers. It was certainly different. To begin with, Ken was used to performing the same show every night for a year – a change of programme every two weeks was incredibly demanding, both on his repertoire and his stamina. On top of that, he was expected to take part in comedy sketches, so there was always new dialogue to learn. He was required to sing anything and everything that the director threw at him, whatever the vocal range, with solos and duets from simple Scottish songs to grand opera. Great fun, great experience it may have been, but Ken quickly recognised the dilemma he faced by constantly crossing over between tenor and baritone. Whilst enjoying the challenge of singing a duet from *Showboat* as a tenor, quickly followed by '*Largo al Factotum*' (delivered as he actually shaved a cast member) from *The Barber of Seville*, it was, quite literally, 'tough at the top'. The crunch came when he and Lynette were singing the ravishing duet from Act I of *La Boheme*. She was struggling vocally due to some kind of virus and, as they walked hand-in hand upstage, she asked Ken to take the top 'C' at the end of the number. Ever the gentleman, Ken naturally obliged – and made a mental note to become a baritone forthwith; reasoning that his voice would last a good deal longer if he was a baritone with a good top on the voice to be used sparingly, as opposed to a tenor with an over-worked high tessitura. For that one top 'C' in Glasgow, D'Oyly Carte devotees the world over are infinitely obliged.

The constantly-changing programme provided Ken with some decidedly off-beat moments in which to display his burgeoning talents and he never failed to be amazed by some of the daft things he was asked to do. During a casual conversation with the company pianist about the delights of Mussorsky's *Songs and Dances of Death*, the show's director happened by and enthusiastically suggested that Ken should include one in the next programme change and, despite his protestations that it was hardly suitable for inclusion between a comedy sketch and a high-kick routine, it was in! Then there was the bright spark who set words to Debussy's exquisite piano piece *'Au Clair de Lune'* for Ken to sing. He was dressed in white tie and tails with a full-blown ballet swirling around him, which paused just long enough for him to lift one of the ballerinas shoulder high in the bars when he wasn't singing. He always knew that the hours spent sweating in the *King's Rhapsody* dance classes would come in handy one day.

As a measure of how things have changed in the theatre during the past forty years, Ken relates that he and Lynette Rae were programmed to sing

'The consequence was he was lost totally . . .' Ken sings 'Au Clair De Lune'

a duet from *Porgy and Bess*. The lighting designer rigged a special lamp which, effectively, turned their faces black as they walked into its light – there was no such thing as political correctness in those days.

All-in-all, the six months of *Half-Past Eight* certainly pushed back the boundaries of his experience; it was exhausting at times, but a gratefully accepted chance to significantly increase his repertoire and, let us not forget, to make the fateful change from tenor to baritone.

'And so thou woulds't be a jester, eh?'

Grateful to be back in London after six months in Glasgow, Ken's first thought was to enjoy some time at home, but continuity of employment was essential and he was quickly in touch with Fraser and Dunlop again. He had sorely missed his studies at the London Opera School and was anxious to get back to some serious singing as soon as possible. Part-time tuition cost £2 per week; this was a big consideration when having to support two people and pay rent on their West London flat. Not much seemed to be happening on the musicals scene at the end of 1954, so he gladly auditioned for a new Jack Hylton show called *Jokers Wild*, which was due to open on 16th December at the Victoria Palace Theatre. A mixture of comedy sketches and music, it was created as a vehicle for the zany talents of the famous Crazy Gang and Ken's mandate would be to take part in sketches and vocal spots whilst the Gang had a short rest or change of costume. The experience gained in

Curtain call for the Gang, with Bud Flanagan, centre and Ken on the left

Half-Past Eight might prove invaluable – just as well, given that twice-nightly performances constituted uncharted waters. However, the prospect of not too many daytime rehearsals, leaving him free for the Opera School studies which he was longing to resume, was the deciding factor and he signed the contract.

Life with the Crazy Gang was certainly never dull – Ken was working alongside some very fascinating characters, with whom he developed a great rapport. Amongst the supporting acts were two names well-known to British audiences in later years. Peter Glaze (who was responsible for teaching Ken that 'Trex' cooking fat was wonderful for removing grease paint and considerably cheaper than Crowe's Cremine) and Peter Gilmore, alias Captain James Onedin, the eponymous hero of the successful television series *The Onedin Line*. The great Bud Flanagan he liked and laughs about the occasion when Bud tried to convince him that he would make far more money if he learned to sing like him! For readers too young to be familiar with Flanagan's unique vocal style, it might well be described as resembling the cry of a sheep on a roller-coaster and, forty five years on, he can still regularly be heard singing the title song to the evergreen television comedy *Dad's Army*.

Despite the happy-go-lucky atmosphere of the show, Ken was sharply reminded to stick to his own job when he made the mistake of responding to one of their practical jokes and he was left in no doubt as to who were the comedians. It seemed perfectly alright for them to interrupt his solo spot, when their quick change was completed early, by handing him a cup of tea mid-aria, or to place a large stage weight in the suitcase he was to use in a sketch; but woe betide if the same stage weight materialised in one of their suitcases – that was no joke. However, everything settled down well and Ken received favourable reviews in the London Press and claimed the dubious honour of having one of his lines cut by the Lord Chamberlain. In a brief sketch, in which he and his new 'bride' hurried to catch the train for their honeymoon destination, they had to struggle along the platform with their luggage as Ken breathlessly panted:

> *'Oh, darling, we've hardly had time to get our things together'.*

It survived for only one performance before being censored by the aforementioned venerable peer and provides an excellent example of how theatrical times have changed.

In April of 1955 the cast of *Jokers Wild* was invited to appear in a Royal Command Performance at the Blackpool Opera House. Although he remembers little of the occasion, except that he did not have a solo, he does recall the train journey back to London when one member of the Gang was seen running along the corridors stark naked, with little concern for the appearance of his large pot belly!

It would be easy to imagine that two performances of that unpredictable show every night

The Gang in the famous suitcase sketch, with Ken in the carriage door

would have exhausted any performer – but not Ken. His days were full, too, as he threw himself into his studies at the Opera School, where he was privileged to work with such top-class tutors as Peter Gelhorn, Vilem Tausky, Leon Lovett and the celebrated Joan Cross. As many of the college performances were given on Sundays, he was able to take part in productions of *The Marriage of Figaro, Iphegina in Aulis* and *Cosi Fan Tutte* – for which he received an excellent review in Music and Musicians for his role as Guglielmo. Another highlight was *Not In Front Of The Waiter* – an Offenbach pastiche arranged by his accompanist, Viola Tunnard, performed at Aldeburgh in the presence of Britten himself and the great German baritone, Dietrich Fischer-Dieskau. Interestingly, one of his fellow performers that night was a singer called Norman Lumsden who, in recent years, has become well-known as J. R. Hartley in the Yellow Pages television commercial.

As if he hadn't enough on his plate already (it was little wonder that one of his college reports noted that 'he frequently seems tired'), he was about to take on even more. In 1956 the musical *Kismet* opened in London, starring the famous American singer, Alfred Drake. Without a second thought, Ken asked Jack Hylton if he could understudy the great man as Hadj. The impresario felt that Ken's many commitments made this impractical but, nevertheless, invited him to attend the rehearsals. However, when Drake returned to America, Hylton contacted Ken and asked him to cover the new Hadj – which he did for three months. Adding to the demands of this terrifying schedule were the frequent sleepless nights occasioned by his baby daughter, Amanda, who had been born a few months earlier. Needless to say, he saw very little of her during this frantic period of his life.

Stamina-sapping it may have been, but this was a vitally important phase in his career and Ken was beginning to realise which direction he wanted it to take. Shows like *Jokers Wild* paid the bills, but more than anything else in the world he wanted to be an opera singer and he was determined to leave behind variety and the musicals for the ultimate challenge of grand opera.

'Time alone can tell'

As *Jokers Wild* ended after more than 800 performances, Ken was faced with a big decision; he had immediately been offered another six-month contract in Glasgow – this time in *Five-Past Eight*. He desperately wanted to try for the opera companies, but he now had his daughter to consider and, after much soul-searching, decided that the family's needs were paramount. So it was back to Revue. But this time, Pauline and Mandy would go with him. So, in May 1956, he rented a tenement apartment, where he took turns with the other residents in scrubbing the communal hallway and stairs and put his operatic ambitions on hold for a while.

Ken found *Five-Past Eight* to be disappointing after the success of the earlier *Half Past Eight* – the splendid sets and costumes unable to hide the fact that the show's content was inferior to that of its predecessor. The excellent Jack Radcliffe was back, but the brilliant character acting of Stanley Baxter was sadly missed and his replacement, Jimmy Logan, was no substitute. Gone, too, were the leggy Cherry Willoughby Dancers, to be replaced by a team of more modern dancers under the direction of an inexperienced young choreographer called Lionel Blair. His singing partner this time was a Joy Saxon, whom Ken describes as a good professional, but the whole experience was lacklustre and he was more than glad when October came and the family could go home to London.

'Give in to fate'

Happy to be home again after six uninspiring months in *Five-Past Eight,* Ken was certain of one thing – he was tired of variety and wanted his career to move on. He returned, once more, to the London Opera School, desperate to get back to some serious singing and was soon back in the groove, delighted to pick up several concerts, courtesy of his college contacts. He was not enamoured of his appearance with the Etruscan Choral Society at the Victoria Hall, Hanley, when informed by a patronising committee member that his presence was hardly necessary as they had a gold medallist amongst the choir's baritones!

The occasional concert was hardly enough to support his family and, with Pauline at home looking after Mandy, Ken had no alternative but to look for a more regular income, so it was back to Fraser and Dunlop. He was soon offered the part of Oggle, an American football player, in a one-off live television presentation of *High Button Shoes* by Jule Styne, Sammy Cahn and Stephen Longstreet. It was to star Alfred Marks, Maggie Fitzgibbon and James Hayter. Unused to working in front of cameras, Ken found it a nerve-jangling experience and remembers being horribly embarrassed by having to change his trousers behind the scenery – which happened to be in full view of the live theatre audience. He also recalls his astonishment on finding James Hayter doing handstands on a dressing room chair for no apparent reason.

A few more concerts followed, including rare visits to the world of oratorio – Mendelssohn's *Elijah* and, notably, Mozart's *Requiem* with the Jacques String Orchestra for the Imperial College Musical Society (Ken was indignant when I suggested that a former tenor might well have struggled with the bass notes of the *'Tuba Mirum'* of that great work). But nothing could change the fact that he wanted to sing opera and he decided that the time had come to go for broke. Fraser and Dunlop did not represent opera singers, so he set about writing to all the major companies for auditions. Having done the rounds, there was nothing for him at Sadler's Wells and, despite being recalled to sing for Rafael Kubelik, Covent Garden had no vacancies. Glyndebourne, however, offered him a place in the extra chorus, but the salary of £11 per week was so low that it could not possibly be considered. Disappointed and frustrated by his failure to break into the world of opera, he was left with the depressing prospect of going back to musicals and variety.

Then, on the morning of March 29th 1957, he opened a letter from Bridget D'Oyly Carte granting him an audition for her opera company. He was at a loss to know how she got the idea that, to a person or persons unknown, he had expressed an interest in auditioning for her. Later experience would teach him that the D'Oyly Carte management must always be seen to be doing their employees a favour. Ever the pragmatist, he could see that he had nothing to lose by attending the audition.

He knew little about the company other than that it specialised in Gilbert and Sullivan and that he had once appeared in a fund-raising concert in which several of their principals played a scene from *The Gondoliers*. He laughs ironically at the memory of them milking their applause, having ignored a plea from the show's director to keep their curtain calls as swift and slick as possible.

Unfamiliar with the Gilbert and Sullivan repertoire and unable to think of a suitable 'bright English song', Ken opted for the Count's aria from *The Marriage of Figaro*, duly presenting himself on 9th April. A few days later he received a letter asking him to return for a second audition, when he was promptly offered a contract to take over from Arthur Richards in the famous Leo Sheffield parts, at a weekly salary of £37.10 shillings. He was extremely surprised by the speed of events and needed time to think – it was not really what he wanted, he was an opera singer and Gilbert and Sullivan was a little light-weight for his taste. But it could not be denied that it was an established and historic company; it paid well and, in a couple of years, it could prove a spring-board into the world of opera. And so, on 1st of May 1957, Kenneth Sandford unknowingly submitted to his fate, signed the contract and became a member of the D'Oyly Carte Opera Company.

THE D'OYLY CARTE OPERA COMPANY LTD

Telegrams: Savoyard, London **1, SAVOY HILL, LONDON, W.C.2** *Telephone: Temple Bar 1533*

29th March, 1957.

Dear Sir,

It has been suggested you might be interested in an audition for this Company.

I shall be hearing some people sing on Tuesday, 9th April, and if you wish to be heard and will come along to the Savoy Theatre (Stage Door) at 11 a.m., arrangements will be made to hear you sing. Please bring a bright English song with you.

Would you kindly let me know whether you will be keeping this appointment and, if so, fill in and return the enclosed form.

Yours faithfully,

Kennet Sandford, Esq.,
146, Watchfield Court,
Chiswick,
W.4.

DIRECTORS: BRIDGET D'OYLY CARTE · HUGH WONTNER, M.V.O. · A. F. MOIR · WALTER HORE

The D'Oyly Carte Standard Contract

AGREED BETWEEN THE D'OYLY CARTE OPERA COMPANY LIMITED AND THE BRITISH ACTORS' EQUITY ASSOCIATION AND APPROVED BY THE LONDON AND PROVINCIAL THEATRE COUNCILS

AGREEMENT made this ......1st...................... day of ......May...................... 19.57.... between BRIDGET D'OYLY CARTE for and on behalf of The D'Oyly Carte Opera Company Limited, whose registered office is situate at 1 Savoy Hill, London, W.C.2 (hereinafter called 'Bridget D'Oyly Carte') of the one part and ......KENNETH SANDFORD.............. of .. 146, Watchfield Court, Chiswick, W.4. (hereinafter called 'the artist') of the other part.

Whereby it is agreed as follows :

ENGAGEMENT *One of these sub-clauses to be deleted

1. Bridget D'Oyly Carte engages the Artist to
   *(a) Rehearse, sing and perform such parts as Bridget D'Oyly Carte may call upon the Artist to perform ; or
   *~~(b)~~ Sing and ~~Perform as Chorister, and to rehearse, understudy, sing and play small parts as required.~~

PERIOD OF ENGAGEMENT *One of these sub-clauses to be deleted

2. The engagement shall be :
   ~~*(a) For the period of rehearsals and for a tour or season in the West End of London and/or the Provinces and/or the Suburbs terminating not later than .... such tour or season not to exceed fifty-two weeks.~~
   *(b) For the period of rehearsals and for an indefinite season in the West End of London and/or Provinces and/or the Suburbs terminable by either party giving to the other ....twelve.... weeks' notice in writing (not being less than four weeks), such notice to expire after the last performance on any Saturday.

OPENING DATE

3. (a) The tour or season shall commence on the ...1st.................. day of ...July..........19.57 or on some day not more than two weeks before or one week after that date at the discretion of Bridget D'Oyly Carte.
   (b) The period of rehearsal shall commence on a day to be appointed by Bridget D'Oyly Carte not being more than 5 weeks prior to the commencement of the tour or season.

SALARY

4. Bridget D'Oyly Carte agrees to pay to the artist :
   (a) During the period of rehearsal half salary to artists engaged under Clause 1 (a) hereof and full salary to artists engaged under 1 (b) hereof. A broken week at the beginning or end of the rehearsal period shall be paid for pro rata.
   (b) From the commencement of the run of the tour or season the sum of £37.10.0............... (not being less than £10) for every week of...7..or..8.......performances (not exceeding eight). Every perfomance over eight shall be an extra performance and shall be paid for at the rate of one-eighth of a week's salary per performance.

5. An Artist engaged under Clause 1(b) when required to play a part shall receive in consideration for such additional work an agreed additional sum over and above the minimum salary referred to in Clause 4(b), but this shall not apply if the Artist already receives an agreed additional sum inclusive in his salary.

SESSIONS AND REHEARSALS

6. (a) During the tour or season the weekly salary stated in Clause 4(b) above shall cover a maximum of thirteen working sessions, of which not more than eight shall be performances.
   (b) Should a working session, not being a performance or a dress rehearsal session, exceed three hours, then overtime shall be payable at the rate of 7s. 6d. per hour or part of an hour. The same rate shall apply to rehearsals prior to production in excess of six hours per day.

SICKNESS PAYMENT

7. The obligation to pay salary (less the amount due to the artist under National Health Insurance) during sickness as provided in Clause E of Schedule 1 of the Esher Standard Contract for Opera (annexed hereto), shall apply only to artists engaged under Clause 1(b) hereof and not to artists engaged under Clause 1(a) hereof.

EXCLUSIVE SERVICES

8. Notwithstanding anything to the contrary in Clause D(1) of Schedule 1 of the Esher Standard Contract for Opera (annexed hereto), the artist shall not accept an engagement which includes any item from the Gilbert and Sullivan Operas or from other Works controlled by Bridget D'Oyly Carte.

GENERAL PROVISIONS

9. (a) The artist shall not introduce into his performance any material not previously approved by Bridget D'Oyly Carte and shall not without such consent alter the music, words or business of the part which he is playing.
   (b) The Artist shall not go into the front of the theatre nor address the audience nor bring anyone not engaged in the theatre behind the scenes without the express permission of Bridget D'Oyly Carte.

ESHER STANDARD CONTRACT

10. Except insofar as they are expressly varied in this Agreement, the provisions of the Esher Standard Contract for Opera (annexed hereto), shall apply to this Agreement.

As WITNESS the hands of the parties on the day and year first above written.

FOR AND ON BEHALF OF THE D'OYLY CARTE OPERA COMPANY LTD.

Chapter 3

CULTURE SHOCK

'Produce them all at once and let me know the worst'

ALTHOUGH he had been a professional singer for seven years, no amount of experience would have prepared Ken for his introduction to the world of the D'Oyly Carte Opera Company. Presenting himself for his first rehearsal at a dismal studio in Central London, he was met by the lady responsible for teaching him the productions, Eleanor 'Snookie' Fancourt and the pianist, Stuart Nash, whom he was delighted to see as they had worked together in the Jane Douglas days.

Not a little intrigued by the prospect of having to learn seven productions in just four weeks, he was anxious to make a start – particularly as his only previous experience of Gilbert and Sullivan had been singing *'Take a pair of sparkling eyes'* with the Cranwell College Band. As the company was appearing in Oxford, prior to its annual holiday, he would be working alone with Mrs. Fancourt until joining his new colleagues for pre-tour rehearsals. How on earth was he supposed to relate to the other characters in such splendid isolation? That was shock number one.

The second shock quickly followed. Snookie soon made it clear that she knew best – there was no place for Ken's ideas, he must do exactly as she told him. The widow of the legendary Darrell Fancourt, she was a former small part player and stage director with the D'Oyly Carte who was considered to have all the virtues necessary to initiate him into the mysterious world of the traditional D'Oyly Carte style. Ken was soon to realise that this meant having to ignore nearly everything he had learned about acting and stagecraft during the previous seven years.

This was immediately apparent as they started work on his first role – Pooh-Bah in *The Mikado*. No sooner had he entered at the back, walked down to centre stage and uttered the immortal words *'It is'*, than she stopped him abruptly and, with a charming smile, said:

> *'No, dear, you are far too superior to look at Nanki-Poo and Pish-Tush. You must look at the audience – not at them'.*

She then insisted that he must make his mouth small and purse up his lips to create an upper-class voice. Astonished and not a little uncomfortable with this bizarre instruction, he politely enquired as to why it should be necessary.

'Because that is the way it has always been done' was Mrs. Fancourt's reply. How those words would haunt Ken during his lengthy D'Oyly Carte career. He still gets hot-under-the-collar whenever he thinks about the number of times that reason was trotted out to justify some piece of business which made no theatrical sense to him and it saddens him that this blind acceptance of so-called 'traditional' business has spilled over into much of the amateur Gilbert and Sullivan fraternity.

So the enormous task of absorbing and retaining seven operas in such a short space of time continued. He enjoyed working on the music with Stuart Nash, but found the process of learning his moves, amidst a crowd of invisible colleagues, most frustrating. As he worked his way through the roles, he became acutely aware that Snookie Fancourt could offer him nothing in the way of characterisation; her only concern being that he direct his music and dialogue straight at the audience with impeccable diction. What about the other performers on stage with him? He found it impossible to imagine that they never looked at each other – that made no sense at all.

On several occasions Ken excused himself mid-afternoon, on the pretext that he had reached saturation point. In reality, he was so bemused by some of the things he was told to do that he just wanted to escape and convince himself that he had not made a terrible mistake by signing the contract.

But, he reasoned, once he was rehearsing with his new colleagues, he was sure that the necessary interplay between the characters would follow quite naturally. Thus fortified, he dutifully worked his way through Pooh-Bah in *The Mikado*, Don Alhambra in *The Gondoliers*, Wilfred Shadbolt in *The Yeomen of the Guard*, The Sergeant of Police in *The Pirates of Penzance*, Private Willis in *Iolanthe*, Grosvenor in *Patience* and Sir Despard Murgatroyd in *Ruddigore*, ploughing his lonely furrow and eagerly awaiting rehearsals with the full company. (I can vouch for that feeling of isolation, having joined the D'Oyly Carte mid-tour as a replacement chorister. I, too, spent four weeks working alone with the Assistant Director, Jimmie Marsland, before being rushed into all eight operas in the repertoire.).

At last the annual holiday was over and an enthusiastic company reconvened in London for the two-week rehearsal period which preceded the next tour. Ken was the only new principal to join, but there were several choristers to be assimilated into the productions, so he was not going to be the only object of the existing company's curiosity. With the exception of joining an established cast for the *King's Rhapsody* tour, he had been used to being with a group of performers which created a show from scratch, the exhilarating process of learning music, lines and routines together being something he had relished. He sensed that this was going to be very different and so, it was with a mixture of anticipation and apprehension that he arrived for his first full company rehearsal.

It was a relief to meet his new colleagues that first morning – Peter Pratt, the principal comedian (Ken soon learned that the incumbent of these comic roles was known as the 'patter man'), Donald Adams, the bass baritone with a genial personality; Leonard Osborn, the rather aloof principal tenor; Jean Barrington, a sophisticated and charming soprano; Joyce Wright, the established soubrette (and wife of Peter Pratt), whose first remark to Ken was that she hoped he would be more conscientious than his predecessor; Alan Styler, an exuberant baritone and Ann Drummond-Grant, the rather formidable contralto who was the wife of the company's long-serving conductor, Isadore Godfrey and whom he always addressed as 'Miss Grant'. The Assistant Music Director was William Cox-Ife and the Director of Productions, Herbert Newby.

The formalities being over and feeling every inch the new boy on the block, Ken was glad to get down to some serious work. The following two weeks of rehearsals proved to be an unforgettable experience for him, following as they did a time-honoured formula which was still being strictly observed some twenty-four years later, as the company embarked on preparation for its final tour in August 1981. Eight shows had to be rehearsed, with costume fittings at Bermans and appointments with the wig-maker having to be squeezed in whenever possible. The fact that Ken was not in *HMS Pinafore* provided time to have alterations made to the costumes he had inherited from his predecessor, although his wigs were made to measure.

By now increasingly aware of the somewhat quaint methods of the D'Oyly Carte, he was totally nonplussed to find that neither props, with the exception of a fan for *The Mikado*, nor stage rostra would be available for the rehearsals, so he still had very little concept of the objects he would be required to negotiate in a few days' time. Someone managed to find a few photographs of the sets, but with seven operas to memorise, these were of little consolation. Even the ever-changing revues in Glasgow could not have prepared him for this minimalist approach to rehearsals. Each of the productions was prepared in one day, with the principals and chorus working separately in the morning sessions, before coming together for a full run-through in the afternoons. Isadore Godfrey constantly nagged them to watch the stick at all times – failure to do so would result in the frequently tetchy conductor putting down his baton to look around in feigned puzzlement as to where the offending singer was directing his gaze. Ken assures me that he often did this during a performance and remembers with great glee the occasion when the orchestra, uncertain as to why Mr. Godfrey had put down his stick, slowly ground to a halt, leaving the embarrassed maestro to pick up the musical pieces as the singers struggled on above him!

As the rehearsal period continued, Ken became increasingly concerned by the constant direction to deliver words and music towards the audience. It seemed both unnatural and unnecessary not to speak to the other performers on the stage and proved difficult for him to accept.

However, it was not questioned by his colleagues and so he had to get on with it. So much for his hope that full rehearsals would encourage the interaction of characters that he craved. Perhaps this was part of the fabled 'traditional style'? On enquiry, nobody could give him a clear definition and, some forty years later, he is still none the wiser. If it meant that this was the way in which W.S. Gilbert originally staged the operas, then why not say so? But nobody ever did – nobody seemed to know. Despite such minor irritations, Ken was slowly becoming more at home with his new artistic surroundings and eagerly looking forward to his debut as Pooh-Bah in *The Mikado.* He asked about the arrangements for the dress rehearsal, only to be told that the company did not have them.

Although his sense of panic was understandable, Ken did not realise, at this early stage, that the D'Oyly Carte did not have its own orchestra, touring only four or five section leaders. (Some years later the company employed its own orchestra, so that dress rehearsals became possible). This meant having to recruit local musicians in every town and city on the eleven-month tour. No wonder poor Mr. Godfrey insisted that every singer watch him like a hawk, it would be as much as he could do to keep pit and stage together and this did nothing to allay Ken's fears.

So, on the morning of 1st July 1957, one of the truly great Savoyards in the history of the D'Oyly Carte Opera Company prepared for his debut in less than ideal circumstances. Having gleaned that the orchestra would be working with Mr. Godfrey in the theatre, Ken arrived early in Southsea, brightening at the prospect of a chance to run through his music. Plucking up his courage, he poked his head through the stage curtain and asked if he might sing in at appropriate moments. A bemused Mr. Godfrey irritably replied:

'If I have time, Kenneth, if I have time'.

He did have time, giving the relieved Pooh-Bah a feel for the acoustics of the King's Theatre. Prior to the performance he was able to 'walk' the set, frantically trying to relate the stage business learned on a flat rehearsal hall floor to the scenery now confronting him.

He remembers little of that first *Mikado*, except that he survived it relatively unscathed, just grateful that his D'Oyly Carte career was at last under way. In point of fact, that first week in Southsea was nightmarish. Ken was used to performing eight times a week, but it had always been the same show and making his debut in a different show every night was asking a great deal.

Desperate to analyse and reflect on his first Pooh-Bah, he was forced to turn his mind to the following night's opera – *The Gondoliers* and his first effort at Don Alhambra. Try as it might to stay in Venice, his feverish brain kept returning to Titipu and he did not sleep soundly. Being aware of the schedule of a repertory company was one thing, when a typical week might be Monday *The Mikado,* Tuesday *The Gondoliers,* Wednesday two *Pirates of Penzance*, Thursday *Patience,* Friday The *Yeomen of the Guard,* Saturday *Iolanthe* twice, but actually having to face up to it was quite another and it was a frightening prospect. Nevertheless, the next morning he again attended the band call to sing through his Don Alhambra music. Struck by the indifferent playing of some of the musicians, it dawned on him that Mr. Godfrey's inflexibility with regard to tempi was born of the necessity to pull his scratch orchestra through a performance on one rehearsal – no mean feat, but a source of artistic frustration to Ken, who liked to indulge himself with the occasional rallentando.

The first week was eventually over and the new boy remembers only becoming numb to the pressure of successive debuts and the disapproving:

'tut, tut, tut'

from Mr. Godfrey at the way he delivered certain lines of the dialogue. How welcome was his Sunday off, giving him the chance to quietly reflect on the events of the week. The foundation stone of a distinguished twenty-five year career with the D'Oyly Carte was laid.

Peter Pratt and Ken in The Gondoliers

Chapter 4

ROME WASN'T BUILT IN A DAY

'And once embarked upon, there's no throwing it off'

HAVING survived the first nerve-racking few days, Ken looked forward to the opportunity of consolidating those initial performances, but he would not be able to do that until he had played the rest of his new roles in the second week. Despite the fact the he was acutely aware of how easy it was to slip, inadvertently, from one opera to another, he completed the set without mishap, but was then faced with the daunting prospect of returning to *The Mikado* after what seemed like an eternity but was, in reality, only a few days. He need not have worried, as the third and subsequent weeks passed without disaster and he became aware that the pressure was beginning to ease; relief at getting through a performance without mishap giving way to a calmer realisation that he was gaining in assurance every day. And he was beginning to enjoy it.

Dialogue in American musicals and revue was one thing, but W. S. Gilbert's words were quite another and Ken began to marvel at the brilliance of this master wordsmith, whose characters were going to offer him so much scope. But he had to be careful; he was very new to the D'Oyly Carte and most of his colleagues were well-established. He had no wish to discomfort them on stage and was relieved that his unhoned and undirected interpretation of the dialogue was accepted without comment by the other principals, although they must surely have made adjustments to accommodate him. He felt it necessary, therefore, to return the compliment and adjust his timing based on his observation of their requirements. He must have managed this reasonably successfully, because his early press reviews were good, particularly for a newcomer. An encouraging start maybe, but it was going to take time to do justice to his wonderful parts. Unbeknown to him, he was going to have plenty of time – twenty-five years, in fact.

There were adjustments to be made offstage, too. He had been used to the noise and cheerful camaraderie of modern musicals and the chaotic backstage ebullience of the Crazy Gang, but this company was unlike any other in his experience. There was an atmosphere of upper-class gentility pervading the D'Oyly Carte principals' dressing rooms – the sort of public school ambience which was totally alien to an ordinary fellow from Yorkshire. Apart from an occasional burst of hilarity from the mens' chorus room, he was often struck by the cloister-like quiet backstage, as if the company was taking part in some time-honoured ritual far too serious to warrant any light-hearted banter.

Sharing a room with Peter Pratt was hardly exciting, but at least it was peaceful. Onstage Ken describes him as a brilliant performer; a comedian capable of reducing an audience to helpless laughter but, offstage, it was a different matter. Peter took himself very seriously and, in the two years during which they shared, Ken never really got used to the prolonged and pedantic preparations for a performance which never varied night after night. On the surface, seemingly, devoid of humour, Peter was quite inscrutable and although they rubbed along together comfortably enough, he felt that he never got to know the real man. Thank goodness for Alan Styler's wicked sense of fun, both on and offstage. Boasting a huge repertoire of very risqué stories, his down-to-earth nature suited Ken and along with the affability of Neville Griffiths (the other principal tenor) and Donald Adams, he felt quite comfortable. Their acceptance of him was in sharp contrast to the distant politeness of Leonard Osborn and the dowager austerity of Ann Drummond-Grant. To him, many of the performers seemed to be totally untheatrical and it is interesting that the famous old D'Oyly Carter, Derek Oldham, observed this in an interview some years earlier, remarking that:

> *'The routine member of the D'Oyly Carte is not, or certainly was not, of a theatrical type'.*

Ken was very conscious of a distinct chill emanating from the baritone section of the chorus, one or two of whom made little effort to conceal the fact that they considered themselves better suited to the parts that he had been brought in to play. This did not worry him, but he could understand their suspicion of a performer known only for working in musicals and variety moving, without previous experience, into the unique field of Gilbert and Sullivan – he was going to have to earn his stripes with the chorus, too.

As that first tour flew by and Ken began to relax into his roles, he became more and more aware of the possibilities that W. S. Gilbert offered him as an actor. He was blessed with a wonderful variety of characters to interpret, from the suave sophistication of Don Alhambra to the red-nose slapstick comedy of the Sergeant of Police and although that form of humour did not come naturally to him, it was certainly an interesting challenge.

As far as the presentation of these colourful Gilbertian creations was concerned, he was left very much to his own devices; no advice, help or direction was offered and he could only assume that his work on stage was satisfactory to the management, as nothing was said to the contrary. He could appreciate that his fellow principals might find it awkward to offer any criticism, but he certainly expected guidance from the production staff. In his previous shows, the director had worked closely with the performers and it amazed him that any enquiry he made about his work was met with:

'Fine, Kenneth, fine'.

It is worth pointing out that anyone joining the D'Oyly Carte as a principal stepped into a block of parts, sometimes known by the title of one of the characters, e.g. The Pooh-Bah roles, or The Mikado roles. The newcomer was expected to play all the parts inherited from his or her predecessor, regardless of the fact that they may not be ideally suited to some of them. In Ken's case he was not comfortable playing King Hildebrand in *Princess Ida* or the Sergeant of Police in *The Pirates of Penzance*. The Sergeant required a bass voice and he was, of course, a high baritone best suited to higher tessitura roles such as Grosvenor in *Patience* and Doctor Daly in *The Sorcerer*. This somewhat eccentric method of casting was a cause of frustration to Ken, but that was the way it had always been done and he had little option but to get on with it. He had to wait five years before convincing the management that his understudy could take on the role of Sergeant of Police.

Little wonder that he looked for help, but the D'Oyly Carte's inability to employ a staff producer of any theatrical pedigree would persist until the company's closure in 1982. He recalls the occasion in the 1960s when Peter Goffin, who was mainly known as a designer, was brought in to re-work *The Yeomen Of The Guard*. Arriving for their first rehearsal, Ken and John Reed (Peter Pratt's successor) were told by Mr. Goffin to work out how they wanted to play their scenes and then he would tell them whether or not he liked it! There was one notable exception to the sorry procession of directors. In 1968 Anthony Besch was asked to prepare a new production of *The Gondoliers* and this proved to be a turning point in Ken's D'Oyly Carte career – but more of this later.

During his first two years with the company Ken worked tirelessly on his characterisations. Spurred on by his ever-growing admiration for Gilbert and, by now, fully aware that he could expect no help from the company's directors, he came to the conclusion that further thought about the timing of dialogue was the way forward. The reaction of the audience would surely guide him in the right direction; if there was no laughter at a point where Gilbert might have expected more than the odd chuckle, he explored possibilities by slowing down certain lines, or injecting more pace into them, or making longer pauses between them. By this process of trial and error he gradually educed a consistent reaction from audiences, becoming convinced that the key to unlock the door of timing was to be found in listening. This may not have been an original thought, but it certainly showed him the way ahead and, more than forty years later, Ken enthusiastically encourages inexperiened performers to have the courage to wait, allowing sufficient time to digest the meaning of a line before replying to it, rather than clinging desperately to a cue line and then, gratefully, getting rid of their response as fast as possible. This means that the audience, too, gets the chance to understand what might be unfamiliar words before the performer moves on to the next line.

'List and Learn' –
Ken inspires a group of amateur performers

He became certain that Gilbert's humour is best served by not trying to be funny but, rather, by assisting the audience to discover the humour for itself. He came to hate the delivery of funny lines directly to the audience, even when alone on stage he preferred to invite the listeners to share his private thoughts and emotions, as opposed to speaking to them directly. Unfortunately, his conviction that dialogue must be a conversation between characters on the stage which involves the audience in the exchanges was at odds with the D'Oyly Carte's policy of speaking directly out front and this inflexible production style was the great frustration of Ken's early years with the company.

Whilst he was thoroughly enjoying his immersion in the delights of Gilbert and Sullivan, he never lost sight of his ultimate goal to become an opera singer. Whenever the company played a London Season he would return to the Opera school where he was able to take daytime classes with Joan Cross and her talented staff. He particularly valued the coaching of Peter Gelhorn and the masterly accompaniment of Viola Tunnard, with whom he was delighted to renew his association. Such tuition was invaluable to his musicianship and stagecraft, to the inevitable benefit of his D'Oyly Carte performances and it is, incidentally, interesting to note that Miss Bridget D'Oyly Carte was a benefactor of the Opera School. The highlight of his time at that influential establishment was, undoubtedly, his appearance in Gluck's opera *Iphegenia in Aulis* in 1959. With the permission of the D'Oyly Carte management, he played the leading role of Agamemnon in the production staged at Morley College, under the baton of Leon Lovett, receiving an excellent notice in The Musical Times. Fortunately, the performance fell on one of his few nights off when *H.M.S. Pinafore* was being performed. He was also able to take part in a midnight Opera Gala to celebrate the work of Joan Cross, at Sadler's Wells Theatre, in which he sang a duet from *Eugene Onegin* with the distinguished soprano, Ava June. These brief forays into the world of opera gave him enormous satisfaction and enabled him to continue his bread-winning job with the D'Oyly Carte in good heart. This was now all the more important, as Pauline had given birth to their second child, Anthony, during a performance of *The Mikado* in 1958, giving Ken the opportunity to add a little more justifiable smugness than usual to Pooh-Bah's line:

> *'Consequently, my family pride is something inconceivable'.*

'A dark and dingy room in some back street'

The superficial glamour of theatrical life barely obscured the harsh reality of touring, but Ken's family responsibilities motivated him to endure the hardships that so many months away from home were bound to bring. To an itinerant thespian, home must be where the suitcase is unpacked and he knew from previous experience how important it was to feel comfortable in order to survive a forty eight-week tour. His year-long *King's Rhapsody* contract had enabled him to compile an extensive list of affordable places to stay, so he knew those to contact and, more importantly, which to avoid at all costs. In the 1950s, inner city areas were largely undeveloped as we know them today, consisting of a high street or commercial centre, surrounded by residential streets and so, most theatrical accommodation was within walking distance of the theatre. This was just as well, as most performers could not afford the luxury of a car, having to rely on trains to get them from town to town. Indeed, when Ken joined the D'Oyly Carte, the Sunday 'train call' was quite a feature of company life, with Miss Carte's young ladies expected to be elegantly dressed; hats and gloves being considered essential wear even in the hottest summer weather. But at least the ridiculous practice requiring principals and chorus to travel in separate carriages had gone by this time. Ken was grateful to be spared these lengthy train journeys, enjoying the independence afforded him by his small car; an expense he was only too glad to justify if it meant that he could drive home late on Saturday nights when the company was within striking distance of London.

By the 1960s he had acquired a network of good lodgings (usually referred to as 'digs'), to which he returned year after year and although he became fond of many landladies, there was only one Mrs. Leech. She and her husband each ran a small business, she a 'kitchen pot' shop and he the undertakers next door. The living space behind was spacious and comfortable, allowing them to take in TV personalities and theatricals on a bed, breakfast and evening meal basis. Ample-bosomed and homely, Mrs. Leech was a superb cook, as well as a surrogate mother to her guests and Ken welcomed the cossetting to be found nowhere else in the country. For £5 a week he enjoyed every home comfort and could not have been happier in a five-star hotel.

No wonder the company's annual season at the Manchester Opera House became his favourite date on the tour; it meant a return to the best digs in the land.

On one occasion, having vainly tried to start his car, Mr. Leech obligingly brought the hearse round to the front door and gave him a lift to the theatre. The bizarre spectacle of Kenneth Sandford arriving at the Stage Door in a, fortunately, coffinless hearse was witnessed by a handful of bewildered D'Oyly Carte fans, but he would have loved to have seen the expression on Miss Carte's face had she known that one of her leading performers had come to work in such an unseemly and eccentric mode of transport!

Sadly, people like Mr. & Mrs. Leech were few and far between, with the majority of landladies providing a basic service; so as long as the accommodation was clean and the food edible, Ken had to be content. There were, however, some awful places. Sometimes his preferred accommodation had no vacancies and it was necessary to take a chance on one of the addresses submitted to the company manager in advance of the D'Oyly Carte's visit to a town. Such horror digs were, invariably, encountered at night after a long and tiring journey, when it was far too late to make alternative arrangements. Ken could relate many such incidents, but prefers the classic story of the late principal tenor, Meston Reid, to illustrate the point; only wishing it could be told in the inimitable style of the witty Scotsman.

Arriving at their pre-arranged digs one Sunday evening, Meston and a colleague carried their suitcases up to the front door to find it ajar. Repeated ringing of the bell and calling out to the landlady bringing no response, they cautiously entered the house and made their way down a gloomy passage to the back kitchen, where they discovered their hostess in a recumbent posture obviously the worse for alcohol and mumbling repeatedly:

> *'I've lost the joint'.*

All attempts to introduce themselves were met by:

> *'I saw it earlier, but now it's gone'.*

Although horrified by her gin-induced stupor, they were more concerned about the hunger pangs occasioned by their long journey and immediately launched a search for the missing meat. Before long the joint of beef was discovered, nestling in a bed of uncooked potatoes, amongst the dusters and scouring pads in the cupboard under the kitchen sink, which just happened to be next to the oven. Rather later than anticipated they enjoyed an excellent dinner as the landlady snored contentedly beside them. The following morning they optimistically appeared for breakfast feeling quite sure that the hostess would have slept off her inebriation, only to find her, still slumped, in the armchair where they had left her the night before. After cooking their own bacon and eggs, they hurriedly packed their bags, left money for the night's lodging and made their escape. As they hurried up the garden path, they were cheerfully hailed by the next-door neighbour, who was clipping his hedge:

> *'You'll be off then? They always leave on a Monday'.*

During the 1960s most city centres underwent radical redevelopment, streets of terraced houses being demolished to make way for the high-rise flats and offices built alongside modern retail premises. Most theatres escaped the bulldozers, but theatrical digs and their surrounding communities did not, forcing company members to seek alternative accommodation. Hotels were out of the question for Ken and his colleagues, being far too expensive. Only visiting London management could afford that luxury! And so, as they looked for flats and small houses to rent, the trend towards self-catering began. The company manager placed advertisements in local newspapers several weeks before the D'Oyly Carte's arrival in a town and the resulting offers of suitable accommodation were handed out on a first come, first served basis. A number of artists opted for a novel solution to the endless problem of finding somewhere to stay, choosing to take their homes with them. Small caravans offered independence and privacy, also allowing animal lovers to have pets with them. This option did not appeal to Ken, who preferred to drive home to London whenever possible, but he frequently passed the D'Oyly Carte caravan convoy en route to the next destination, waving a greeting to John Reed with his boxer dog, Sheba and Peggy Ann Jones with Judy, the Jack Russell.

Ken was happy to look after himself and usually sought a small flat or bed-sitting room with cooking facilities. Though hardly a gourmet chef, he could certainly find his way around a kitchen, working on the principle that if he wanted steak and kidney pie for dinner he must learn how to cook it. Ingenuity was frequently the order of the day, as

'No thanks, I have dined'
Judy and Peggy Ann Jones

most rented flats provided an extremely basic range of utensils and it was with great pride that he informed everyone in the theatre one evening that he had successfully made a peach upside-down pudding in a colander lined with aluminium foil! His legendary love of home-made apple pie encouraged him to make one large enough to last several days as soon as he settled into his new abode, this being a sure way of making him feel at home and, in an emergency, he has been known to roll out his pastry with a full bottle of Coca-Cola. Occasionally, it was impossible to find a suitable flat to rent and Ken had no option but to stay in a small hotel or bed and breakfast accommodation. Hotels were expensive, but at least provided an evening meal, whereas B & B meant having to trail around town centres in any weather in search of somewhere to eat, with little choice between workmen's cafés and overpriced restaurants. Generally speaking, his memories of day-to-day living out of a suitcase are happy enough, but he is now very grateful that semi-retirement allows him to spend most nights in his own bed. Holidays do not interest him, the simple joy of being at home brings the contentment that only those who have spent more than a quarter of a century on the road can understand.

'A source of innocent merriment'

The physical and mental demands of life on tour, coupled with the lengthy periods of time away from his family, made Ken very conscious of the truth of the old adage about all work and no play. In the early days of his D'Oyly Carte career the pressure of getting to grips with so many new roles made it essential that he found time for relaxation whenever possible and, in later years, it became equally necessary to escape the restraints of day-to-day life in the theatre. He had always found sporting pursuits to his taste, a perfect complement to his undiminished love of painting, but felt that his football days were over. He was, then, delighted to discover that the company boasted a cricket team which convened for occasional matches against local club sides and, in particular, recalls the wonderful hospitality of the Clontarf Cricket Club in Dublin. The following extract from the Gilbert and Sullivan Journal of May 1960 eloquently describes this group of enthusiastic amateurs and, although Ken fancied himself as the D'Oyly Carte's answer to the great Yorkshire bowler, Freddie Trueman, it is significant that he was not mentioned in despatches.

> *'During the present season the D'Oyly Carte Cricket Club has arranged matches in Bristol, Oxford, Belfast, Dublin, Liverpool and Brentwood. Although the 1959 season was not memorable for matches won, it was nevertheless very successful both from the sporting and social angles. There was a glorious afternoon's cricket against Brighton College when, despite a fine 52 knocked up by Peter Pratt (the highest score in the book by a D'Oyly Carte player) and Glynne Thomas taking 5 wickets for 32, the team lost by 1 wicket. Another exciting finish was against Magdalen College Cygnets, when the clock forced a draw with only 2 runs needed to win. The star performer of that game was, undoubtedly, John Banks, who took 7 wickets for 23 runs, including the only D'Oyly Carte hat-trick ever remembered. Other enjoyable matches were played in Bristol, Bournemouth and Exeter, where the team played on the Devon County ground against the cathedral choristers. The season ended with a very pleasant match against a Brentwood School XI. Altogether six matches were played last season, of which two were won, three lost and one drawn. Norman Meadmore headed the batting with an average of 20.8, followed by Peter Pratt with 15.'*

The D'Oyly Carte and the Clontarf cricket teams. Ken, Leonard Osborn, Donald Adams and Peter Pratt are in there!

On discovering that several of his colleagues played golf, Ken acquired a set of second-hand clubs and began to play regularly. In a tradition which persisted until the company's closure in 1982, D'Oyly Carte golfers were offered the facilities of some local clubs in return for a free concert for the club members – a very happy arrangement for all. In general, most of Ken's free time was spent alone and he made regular visits to art galleries and museums in the large cities on the tour. His car was a godsend, enabling him to have his easel and paints with him and the many solitary hours spent in the company of canvas and oils were a constant solace when away from home. This artistic self-indulgence came to an abrupt end during the D'Oyly Carte's London seasons, when family responsibilities caught up with him and his rapidly-growing children demanded his attention. Needless to say, Pauline always had a long list of household jobs to be completed before his next disappearing act and he became quite the D.I.Y. man. He particularly enjoyed carpentry, learning to make built-in storage units when he was not hanging wallpaper or painting ceilings. He made a theatrical dressing table for his daughter, complete with appropriate lighting; a bookcase and a downstairs cloakroom – the last two being featured in The D.I.Y. Magazine. Quite often he was glad to go back to work for a rest, but nevertheless cherished his limited time at home and was grateful that Pauline supported him loyally in his continued studies at the Opera School. Ironically, it was the family's needs that prevented him from making the break from the D'Oyly Carte into the world of opera. In 1961 he was invited to join Glyndebourne and was thrilled that his long-held ambition was about to be realised. But, ever the pragmatist, he realised that Glyndebourne's short season would leave him out of work for some months and he needed, above all, to provide for the family. With great sadness he turned down that tempting contract and, thereafter, it was never the right time or the right financial deal to lure him from the security offered by Savoy Hill.

'There's a change in store for thee'

Having worked so hard to blend his characterisations with those of his established colleagues during his first two years with the company and just as he was beginning to feel comfortable on the D'Oyly Carte stage, he entered a period of change that was to last several years. In 1959, wishing to pursue a career as a serious singer and actor, Peter Pratt decided to leave the company. This was the start of a four-year period which also saw the departure of Ann Drummond-Grant, Joyce Wright, Leonard Osborn, Neville Griffiths and Jean Barrington. The break up of such an experienced team was, inevitably, going to bring changes for performers and audiences alike. Peter Pratt's understudy, John Reed, was asked to take over the patter parts, thus beginning a working relationship with Ken which was to flourish for twenty years. Although John had occasionally deputised for Peter Pratt, working with an understudy was very different from working with a new principal and Ken realised that it was now his turn to make the adjustments necessary to accommodate a newcomer. He had been in the company long enough to know that John's task was not going to be easy; the mystique traditionally associated with the succession of D'Oyly Carte patter men making Peter Pratt a hard act to follow, particularly as loyal audiences were known for their devotion to the established comedian. Who would envy the understudy sitting nervously in the dressing room, listening over the tannoy to the disappointed groans of the audience just informed that their beloved comedian was indisposed? By now, Ken had the experience and confidence to take a different interpretation in his stride, enjoying the challenge that John Reed's fresh approach provoked in their mutual scenes. Rather more of an extrovert than his predecessor, John was easy company in the dressing room, where they were joined in later years by his dog, Sheba.

With the natural grace and athleticism of a dancer, a pleasant light baritone voice and the God-given ability to make people laugh, John soon began to win over those convinced that Peter Pratt's departure would mean the end of their D'Oyly Carte world and, over the years, his scenes with Ken became the highlight of the evening for most audiences. In particular, the exchanges between Jack Point and Shadbolt in Act II of *The Yeomen of the Guard* and Bunthorne and Grosvenor in Act II of *Patience* were considered to be an object lesson in comedy timing and an inspiration to a generation of amateur performers. Together, they were never afraid to take their time with dialogue, sometimes using pauses where lesser actors would never consider them; the raising of an eyebrow or a prolonged glance sufficient to reduce an audience to helpless laughter, as witnessed by their exchange in Patience:

> *'Ah, Bunthorne! come here – look! Very graceful, isn't it?'*

The sight of Ken looking adoringly at himself in a hand mirror always started the laughter, which increased as John took the mirror from him to look at his own reflection on:

> *'Allow me; I haven't seen it'.*

The simple sincerity with which he then said;

> *'Yes, it is graceful'*

was enough to bring gales of laughter, which Ken cleverly used to stare disbelievingly at John, before retrieving the mirror on:

'Oh, good gracious! not that –'.

Most inexperienced performers would then have taken a quick look in the mirror before completing the line with *'this'*. Not Ken, who would take nearly three seconds before his sincerely delivered *'this'*, leaving John time to look suitably appalled by this show of myopia. In short, neither man played the words for laughs, but imbued their lines with such conviction that the audience revelled in their ludicrous simplicity. As Ken always says:

'The first twenty years are the hardest'.

Having successfully negotiated the transition from Peter Pratt to John Reed, he next had to face the changes forced by the retirement of Ann Drummond-Grant. This time, there was no obvious successor within the company, so auditions were held and a young contralto, Gillian Knight, was given the difficult job of following the great 'Drummy'. Tall and elegant, with a glorious voice, she was, nevertheless, very inexperienced and required a great deal of support from the other principals. Most of this responsibility fell to John Reed, but Ken, too, had to make considerable adjustments in the scenes which they shared – most particularly in Act II of *The Mikado*. The formidable Drummy's timing in the *'visiting card'* scene had been set in stone and the difference in Gillian's delivery meant that his responses as Pooh-Bah altered accordingly. His other important scene with her came in Act II of *Iolanthe*, in which he certainly enjoyed having a beautiful young Fairy Queen with whom to flirt. The departure of several other principals for pastures new affected Ken to varying degrees, depending how much he was involved on stage with their replacements. Several sopranos came and went, but only in *Patience* did he work closely with them and his scenes with the company's two tenors usually involved other characters. The exception to this was in Act I of *Ruddigore*, in which he shared a substantial scene with Richard Dauntless. Having become used to Leonard Osborn in this role, Ken was pleasantly surprised by the easy cheerfulness of his replacement, the charming Thomas Round. It proved to be a pleasure for him to work on the development of such an important and melodramatic sequence with a man who fell so naturally into the category of 'Matinee Idol'.

Without doubt, the greatest change for Ken came in 1962 when Joyce Wright left the company, to be replaced by Peggy Ann Jones. With Joyce's departure, in his opinion, went the last traces of the elite dynasty of principals which he called 'The Royal Family' and with whom he was never completely at ease. As in the case of her husband, Peter Pratt, Joyce was extremely popular with D'Oyly Carte audiences and she had been around for a long time, so Peggy Ann's job was not going to be easy. She was, however, a breath of fresh air; naturally funny and with an extrovert, sometimes zany, personality with whom Ken felt he could forge a dynamic new partnership. This indeed proved to be the case during the ten years in which they worked together, although the rapport took time to develop. Peggy Ann was a born comedienne as opposed to a comedy actress and their dialogue scenes offered Ken the chance to break free from the stultifying traditional style of the D'Oyly Carte. In his many scenes with Peggy Ann he was able to inject a feeling of reality and human warmth into his characters, knowing that her response would be equally intense. This was, at last, a real opportunity to delve beneath the thin veneer of characterisation engendered by the D'Oyly Carte method of acting. The relationship between Phoebe and Shadbolt in *The Yeomen Of The Guard* became much more credible, her hilarious efforts to hoodwink him with her female charms never obscuring the underlying desperation of her mission to secure the release of Colonel Fairfax. This new depth of characterisation gave a piquancy to their roles and those who have been priviledged to watch their Second Act sequence:

'But I have never given thee cause for jealousy'

will never forget the richness of the comedy. Ken's befuddled pauses, Peggy Ann's facial expressions and their mutual love of the scene combining to hilarious effect. Her sense of fun certainly shone through in her Pitti-Sing and Ken's Pooh-Bah could only benefit; her cheeky vivacity in perfect contrast to his lumbering pomposity. Whenever they worked together theatrical sparks would fly, but it was *Ruddigore* which produced their most memorable moments and the second act scene between Sir Despard and Mad Margaret was simply wonderful to watch. Having originally developed his character alongside the cleverly understated and rather fey Margaret of Joyce Wright, his reactions to Peggy Ann's less subtle interpretation needed to change quite radically and their timing, evolved over several years, produced, arguably, their finest work together. Nobody could say:

'Basingstoke'

quite like Peggy Ann and the prolonged laughter prompted by her lugubrious delivery of the famous word meant that Ken's reaction to it became equally prolonged. The disbelief, forbearance and sheer pity evident in his face proved far more eloquent than any words and was memorable in the eyes of anyone lucky enough to have seen them perform this famous sequence. It is but one example of how flexible performers have to be when faced with a new slant on familiar words and Ken certainly grew in stature as a result of such changes of nuance.

However, there was one change he could cheerfully have done without. It was the occasion of the first manned landing on the moon and the members of the D'Oyly Carte, along with the rest of the world, were buzzing with excitement at this historic event. The company's performance of *Patience* that night took a topical turn when Peggy Ann, playing Lady Angela, left Ken lost for words when she inadvertently enquired of him:

'But who is this whose god-like grace proclaims
he comes from outer space?'

The last three words should, of course, have been '*of noble race*', rendering Ken's eventual response somewhat incomprehensible. She was, understandably, mortified, but it remains one of Ken's favourite anecdotes and one over which, he feels sure, Gilbert and Sullivan would have shared a chuckle. After Peggy Ann left the company, he worked with three other soubrettes before the company closed; Judi Merri, Jane Metcalfe and Lorraine Daniels. All were very different in their style of performance, so that Ken was kept constantly on his creative toes.

'That is one of our blameless dances'
Ken and Peggy Ann Jones in Ruddigore

With the emergence in 1964 of a fine young soprano called Valerie Masterson and the blossoming talents of Gillian Knight and Peggy Ann Jones, the D'Oyly Carte enjoyed a golden era, following a period when the experienced male principals had tended to dominate their female colleagues. The hugely popular talents of John Reed, Thomas Round, Donald Adams, Alan Styler and Ken, himself, were now complemented by the ladies to the benefit of performers and audiences alike. By the late 1960s, however, the demands of touring life, professional ambition and the untimely death of Alan Styler had taken their toll and the company's personnel changed radically once more. Valerie Masterson and Gillian Knight went on to distinguished careers in opera, but it is significant that both ladies still look back on their time in the D'Oyly Carte with affection. Donald Adams, too, moved into the field of opera, his comedy skills, honed over long years in the company, making him a much sought after 'buffo bass' with many large opera companies.

By 1973, with the exception of John Reed and Ken, every principal had been replaced, some staying for only one or two seasons and the D'Oyly Carte certainly seemed to lack star quality for a time. One notable exception was Donald Adams' successor, John Ayldon, who had been understudying The Mikado roles for several years. Gifted with a rich bass voice and wonderful facial expression, he gradually developed all the comedy skills of a great Savoyard; a popular performer until the company's closure, he is still delighting audiences today with his marvellous characterisations. Ken, meanwhile, had become resigned to the fact that he was not destined for a career in opera after all. On one or two occasions he was invited to audition for Covent Garden, but it was invariably when he had just signed a new contract with the D'Oyly Carte. Fortunately, Anthony Besch's ground-breaking production of *The Gondoliers* in 1968 and the introduction of *The Sorcerer* into the repertoire in 1971gave him plenty of interest, the latter providing him with what many people believe to be his greatest creation, Dr. Daly, the love-lorn elderly vicar. Both operas broke the traditional mould in presentation, favouring a much more natural approach, rather than the inevitable straight lines, semi-circles and synchronised gestures of the chorus. But these belated attempts to modernise, along with re-workings of *Iolanthe, The Yeomen of the Guard* and *The Mikado* were too little too late – the company was beginning to drift aimlessly towards closure.

The last few years of the original D'Oyly Carte Opera Company saw numerous comings and goings amongst the principals, particularly the ladies, but only one stood out – Patricia Leonard. Having joined the chorus in 1972, she progressed from understudying to playing the minor mezzo soprano parts of Edith in *The Pirates of Penzance,* Peep-Bo in *The Mikado,* Leila in *Iolanthe* and Cousin Hebe in *H.M.S. Pinafore.* When Lyndsie Holland decided to leave in 1977, Patricia was persuaded by Ken and others to consider taking over the principal contralto roles. She auditioned successfully and began an all-too-brief partnership with her good friend, John Reed. She both sang and acted well but, above all, she was funny and their onstage relationship quickly bloomed, particularly as Katisha and Ko-Ko in *The Mikado.* From Ken's point of view she was terrific to work with, extracting every last ounce of humour or pathos from her scenes and he adored her outrageous flirting as the Queen of the Fairies to his Private Willis.

'You're a very fine fellow' Ken and Patricia Leonard

In 1979 the company was dealt a blow from which it never recovered; at the end of the Australian tour John Reed left. Audiences considered him irreplaceable and the task of his successor, James Conroy-Ward, was almost impossible. He was a talented and likeable man, with his own individual sense of humour, but the company's devoted followers never accepted him – John Reed was always going to be a difficult act to follow. After twenty years in tandem with John, it was a big shock to Ken's creative system to have a new patter man on stage, particularly one so different in style to his predecessor, but he always thought that, given time, James would have been a tremendous asset to the company. But by then, it did not seem to matter very much as the company was heading, inexorably, towards its demise.

The ever-mounting costs of touring so many operas could no longer be met by box-office receipts and, despite numerous promises of sponsorship deals and rescue packages, nothing was forthcoming – the famous old company was to be lost. Pilloried by the musical establishment as 'anachronistic', the company's performers were ridiculed as 'tired and wooden' and the Arts Council refused an application for funding. For the artists, it was incredibly hurtful to be on the receiving end of such biased and, on the whole, unjustified criticism. The D'Oyly Carte boasted some fine performers, experienced professionals doing the job required of them by the management. There was the rub; the D'Oyly Carte management had always known best. For years they had refused to face the need for stylistic change, maintaining the tradition was all-important and, to audiences now becoming used to less rigid and more imaginative productions of Gilbert and Sullivan, the limitations of the D'Oyly Carte style were becoming clear. It was significant that, soon after the company closed, many members featured in West End musicals and went on to enjoy very successful careers in the theatre.

During the final months before closure, hopes of averting the unthinkable were frequently raised by stories of possible financial support, only to be dashed as the rumours were quashed one by one. The reality of imminent closure forced Ken and his colleagues to face the worrying prospect of redundancy. It was ironic; Ken had always longed to be an opera singer, but family considerations had made it difficult for him to take that leap into insecurity. Now, when there was no alternative but to make a career change, it was too late to fulfil his ambition. And so, after twenty-five years of loyal service to the company, he faced an uncertain future.

It is almost impossible to describe the agony of the D'Oyly Carte's final performance on 27th February 1982. In some ways, Ken was lucky to be suffering from 'flu; he had a high temperature and struggled through the show in a haze induced by too many aspirins. Those of us whose memories are clearer can still picture Ken on the bare stage of London's Adelphi Theatre, standing in a spotlight, sadly reading the Arts Council's damning report on the company. As the spotlight symbolically faded to leave the stage in darkness, the emotion of the audience boiled over into clearly-audible sobs. Backstage, the atmosphere was hardly better as the awful reality began to sink in. Performers followed their usual after-show routines in an unnatural silence, automatically packing make-up boxes as if it was any other Saturday night. Emotionally drained and longing to get away from the tension, nobody really said goodbye – it was easier to leave the words unsaid, everyone understood. Having run the gauntlet of near-hysterical fans at the Stage Door, the members of the D'Oyly Carte Opera Company dispersed for the last time. The management's lack of care on that awful night was predictable. Although Dame Bridget and the company's board of trustees were present for the final performance, not one of them came backstage to bid farewell to the artists, or wish them good luck for the future. But, as Ken points out, it was not surprising; the management had never valued its greatest asset, its employees. Perhaps their attitude can best be summed up by the angry words of Bruce Worsley, the Company Manager for many years. During a heated exchange with Ken, who was at that time the principals' Equity representative, regarding the distribution of recording royalties, Mr. Worsley exploded:

'Damn it all, Kenneth, Miss Carte provides the theatre, the orchestra, the stage, the costumes, the scenery and the props – all you have to do is damn well go on stage'.

Chapter 5

THE D'OYLY CARTE ABROAD

'Over the bright blue sea'

THE popularity of Gilbert and Sullivan throughout the English speaking world is evidenced by the number of performing groups in Australia, New Zealand, South Africa and areas of Europe wherever ex-patriots have settled to live and work. Nowhere, however, is it more popular than in North America, where huge interest in the Savoy Operas has spawned hundreds of active amateur groups in the U.S.A. and Canada. This transatlantic love for the works of the Victorian Dynamic Duo dates back to their earliest collaborations, when it seemed that, no sooner had their latest show opened in London, than New Yorkers were whistling the most popular tunes and pirated versions sprang up as if by magic. Such was the alarm occasioned by these unauthorised productions, that the management took the unprecedented step of staging a single performance of *The Pirates of Penzance* in Britain to establish the copyright before the main company premiered the new opera in New York. Thereafter, the D'Oyly Carte Opera Company toured successfully in North America until 1978, thus nurturing an enduring love for Gilbert and Sullivan and the D'Oyly Carte style of production.

It is interesting to note that the world's oldest Gilbert and Sullivan Society is to be found in America, the Savoy Company of Philadelphia. Founded in 1901 with the blessing of W. S. Gilbert, it is still flourishing and this author can attest to its remarkable ability to draw young people into the Gilbert and Sullivan fold. As the company's Stage Director in 1995, I was blessed with a large and enthusiastic young cast, which viewed the Savoy Operas as an opportunity to have great fun on stage; an attitude that should be emulated by amateur groups in Great Britain which struggle for survival, unable to replace their ageing membership with fresh young performers. It is ironical that the future of such a quintessentially English institution as Gilbert and Sullivan should be in safer hands in the U.S.A. than in its homeland.

'Pack up at once and off we go'

The previous chapter detailed some of Ken's experiences touring the provincial towns and cities of Great Britain, but did not touch on what was to become a major part of his professional life, the overseas tour. Given the aforementioned love of Gilbert and Sullivan on the other side of the

Atlantic, it seems surprising that he had to wait for five years before embarking on the first of many North American tours. The organisation of the five-month trip fell to the D'Oyly Carte management and the legendary American impresario, Sol Hurok, with the performers having little to do but make sure that their passports were up-to-date and their suitcases packed with clothing suitable for both the heat of California and the bitter cold of the Canadian winter. Such practicalities kept Ken busy enough to take his mind off the impending separation from his family, the anticipation of such an exciting tour tempered by his understandable concern for the well-being of Pauline and the children in his absence. Still, the fact that they would be joining him for the New York season in November did much to alleviate such familial gloom and he made his preparations in good heart.

Whilst recently burrowing through twenty five years of accumulated D'Oyly Carte flotsam and jetsam stored in his attic, Ken happened upon the dog-eared pages of a diary written during the first few days of the 1962 tour. The immediacy of his journal provides such a vivid description of his emotions and impressions that it is worthy of a long-overdue airing, giving us as it does, a flavour of the early stages of his odyssey:

> *August 9th 1962*
>
> *I was determined to spend as much time as possible with my family, in spite of detailed instructions which seemed to make things difficult. It was ordered that baggage should be delivered to the Embankment entrance of the Savoy Hotel by 5.30 p.m. and then we would receive travel documents and dollars from the touring manager. I phoned the office and obtained permission to deposit my effects earlier in the day and to pick up my travel papers at 4 p.m. in order that I might return home and have a little more time with my family, before joining the main gathering of the company at 8 p.m. This all occured as planned – it was rather fun to see that both Mandy and Anthony made a hit with the Savoy door-keeper. It not only gave me more time with the family, but also enabled me to give last minute instructions to Pauline on how to, and how not to, put the car into the garage – something I had promised to do and had not. I have a feeling that the instruction might have been worthwhile.*
>
> *At 7 p.m. I said my goodbyes to my darlings and proceeded to the Savoy by way of taxi and tube, arriving there in good time. There were the usual crowds of fans and friends, including Sir Malcolm Sargeant, to wish us "Bon Voyage". Most of the office staff and friends took private transport to the airport to be 'in at the end', so to speak. We boarded two coaches and proceeded to the airport, arriving there at about 9.30 p.m. There was very little formality and we all then had a very good meal. The atmosphere in the café became rather heavy*

and a premature exit began about 10.30 p.m. I had slipped out between courses to ring my last goodbye to Pauline. We embarked on our plane, a piston-engined DC 7 of the Royal Dutch Airlines, K.L.M. So began a very uncomfortable and unnecessarily long journey to New York, relieved only by the kind attendance of the stewards and excellent food and wine. The proposed stop at Gander was cancelled because of strong headwinds. An alternative route over the north of Ireland was taken in order that the more advantageous northerly winds should be used. It meant that the whole journey to New York should be done without refuelling. I can only assume that it was because of this that the speed was only 225 Kts (ground speed).

The aircraft was obviously not of the newest design; seats were uncomfortable and the engine noise such that real sleep was impossible. Consequently, few of the company slept – I for only 2 or 3 hours, and that broken. 9.00 (GMT) we had a breakfast consisting of ham, cheese, an egg dish, currant bun, roll, butter and marmalade – a most extraordinary meal, but nevertheless well done and well served. At about 11 champagne and caviar, again nicely presented, but much too near our previous meal and, as it turned out, much too near the commencement of the aircraft's descent. I had quite a few odd moments during the bumpy passage through cloud. We landed at Idlewild airport at 8 a.m. local time, having already had breakfast and lunch! The Customs proved a little difficult insofar that most members of the company had to present each piece of baggage unfastened. By the time all had gone through, tempers were a little frayed. They were even more tested when we learned that we had to wait until 1.45 p.m. before taking off to Los Angeles. I wrote an airmail letter to my dearest, saying that at least half the journey had been completed without mishap. I was a trifle indignant when I found that to obtain 20 cents worth of stamps from a machine cost me 25 cents. How lucky we are in England to get a threepenny stamp for threepence!

The long flight to the west coast was to be by astro jet (the very latest in jet travel) and we were delighted by the prospect of a short journey. It was a truly lovely aircraft stewarded, naturally, by a bevy of American beauties. The journey was quite a dream. In no time we were at 35,000 feet, travelling at more than 400 m.p.h. There was not a trace of vibration and the only noise from the rushing of air over the structure of the craft. What a contrast to the 14-hour ordeal of a few hours before! I could hardly conceive ever finding my way around Los Angeles and, now that I've been through, I don't want to. On the coach journey from the air terminal to Pasadena I have never seen traffic like it. The roads are quite fantastic, almost Jules Verne in their conception. Flyovers fly over one another from every conceivable angle and the poor driver has to contend with four lanes! I had considered hiring a car but, until I learn a little of California's peculiar Highway Code, I think I'll remain a walking visitor!

Our hotel in Pasadena is quite superb, although the locals consider it past its best. It was at one time **the** *place. Anyway, my room is all I could wish for; large and airy, with two single beds, writing desk, comfortable chair and my own bathroom and dressing room. I overlook a courtyard filled with trees, palms and a very welcome swimming pool. The latter should be a wonderful boon to us after playing the shows. If all the hotels of the tour are equal to this I shall have no cause to complain. Although I was quite tired, I decided to see at least a little of the town before going to bed. I thought that I might get to know where we were situated in relation to the Civic Auditorium, where we are to appear. I was delighted to find that the theatre was only two blocks away and I did go into a rather large store for some soap powder; it was as large as the average Woolworths at home and there might have been four assistants – I didn't get my soap flakes! I retired about 10 p.m. but slept very badly and was wide awake by 4 a.m. Had a swim in the pool at about 7.30 a.m. It was quite lovely at that time in the morning. I was joined by quite a number of the company who had evidently experienced sleepless nights due, no doubt, to over-tiredness and the unfamiliar heat. Most of the day was spent exploring the shopping area of the town and I was surprised at the prices of goods – usually pleasantly surprised, except for shoes, which I noted were in the $25 plus range for shoes of English quality. I continued my search for eating places and discovered a delightful coffee shop, where I breakfasted with other members of the company on orange juice, two eggs, fried potatoes and toast – for 85 cents! I returned for lunch, which cost only $1.05, and discovered that when meat is involved, the meal prices really rise, and one gets into the $2.50 range.*

Sol Hurok was kind enough to invite us to a performance of Gershwin's music at the Hollywood Bowl that evening – a very pleasant surprise. A bus arrived for our party and, once again, we set off on the nightmarish journey along the freeway, arriving at the Bowl around 7p.m. The performance didn't start until 8.30p.m. so Philip (Potter), *I and a few more company members decided to find a café for a meal, eventually finding a drugstore off Hollywood Boulevard for hamburgers followed by ice cream. The entrance to the Bowl was quite a long way from the auditorium and it would have entailed quite a climb but, of course, the Americans, unable to use their cars, have installed a long moving ramp, which does a very good service. The auditorium is really vast and I estimated the distance from the stage to the back must have been over 300 yards. We were at least 200 yards away. It was all most impressive – hills all around us in a sort of glorious technicolour, towering above the stage and a pool of water in front of the stage where fountains played. It was all quite wonderful to see, but the presentation dwarfed the content. Instead of listening to the music, I found myself marvelling at the acoustics of the place, the situation and the very fact that I was there. Anyway, I wouldn't have missed it for worlds."*

Sadly, that all-too-brief extract is all that remains of Ken's diary, but it is more than sufficient to illustrate his wonder at all things American, which was to increase as that long first tour unfolded. Within four days of the D'Oyly Carte's arrival in California, the jet-lagged company was back in harness, opening the Pasadena season with *The Mikado,* followed by the other shows in the repertoire: *The Gondoliers, Iolanthe* and *The Pirates of Penzance.* Ken was delighted that his work-load was not too onerous, due largely to the fact that, after five years of trying to convince the powers-that-be of his unsuitability for the Sergeant in *Pirates,* he had been relieved of the role. Not that the management had taken pity on him, of course, but Sol Hurok had insisted that, in the event of illness, a principal must be replaced by another principal. Consequently, Ken's understudy, George Cook, was promoted to Sergeant and he would cover George. At long last he was free of a part to which he knew himself to be vocally unsuited.

As mentioned in the extract from his diary, Ken was not impressed by Pasadena and what he saw of Los Angeles, being irritated by the ridiculous notion of having to cross the street on a traffic light when there were no vehicles in sight. Jay-walking indeed! It wouldn't have happened at home. Nor was he amused when accosted, whilst taking a stroll, by an American man who somehow pin-pointed him as Pooh-Bah.

'Do you still accept the bribes with your hand behind your back?'

he abruptly enquired. Ken replied that he did not, whereupon the peeved soul retorted:

'Then I shall not be coming to see you'

before stalking away in high dudgeon.

The next date on the tour was San Francisco and Ken was captivated by the beauty and vibrancy of the famous city. Along with his colleagues, he happily took in the sights and particularly enjoyed riding the cable car to Fisherman's Wharf, revelling in the panoramic views of Alcatraz and the bay. It was certainly an exciting time and his pleasure was completed by a meeting with one of his theatrical heroes, Alfred Drake. By coincidence, *Kismet* was playing in the Geary Theatre, right next door to the Curran Theatre where the D'Oyly Carte was appearing and Ken was unable to resist the temptation of introducing himself to the great star, on the pretext that he had almost understudied him in the 1956 London production. After five years as a principal of the D'Oyly Carte Opera Company, he was used to the admiration of devoted fans, but Ken describes his nervousness when knocking on Drake's dressing room door as that of a tongue-tied teenager. His trepidation was unnecessary, as he found Alfred Drake to be charming, unassuming and only too happy to meet a fellow professional, chatting about *Kismet* in London as if they were old friends.

From San Francisco the company travelled through spectacular scenery up the west coast to Seattle, where the World Trade Fair was in full swing. Ken remembers being impressed by the awe-inspiring tower, built to mark the occasion, which dominated the skyline of the city – the same tower now so familiar in the title sequence of the cult American sit-com *Frasier*. After a time, the crowded city became oppressive so, on one of their free days, Ken and Tom Round hired a car and set off for Mount Hood. Driving through petrified forests up to the snowline they marvelled at the scenic beauty of the area and contentedly agreed that being so far from home had its compensations. Having travelled on by train through more fascinating landscapes to Vancouver in Canada, the company had by now settled into a comfortable routine and Ken was totally absorbed both at work and at play. He was struck by the fact that touring in North America was completely different from touring in Britain. For one thing, he and his colleagues were constantly thrown together. During the previous five years he had hardly ever met most of them outside of the theatre and suddenly they were always in each others' company. Staying in the same hotels, taking the same planes and buses and eating in the same restaurants made him very much aware of the diverse personalities which made up the D'Oyly Carte personnel. Inevitably, cliques formed and Ken quickly learned that the only way to survive the enforced togetherness was by tolerating the irritating little foibles of others, in the hope that they would return the compliment.

Another difference was the number of formal social functions they were expected to attend. The company's arrival in a city always provoked great interest and there were numerous civic receptions, as well as private parties thrown by wealthy individuals – almost unheard of back at home. As far as Ken was concerned, they were a mixed blessing. On a day when *Pirates* was being performed, he was glad to escape from his hotel room and

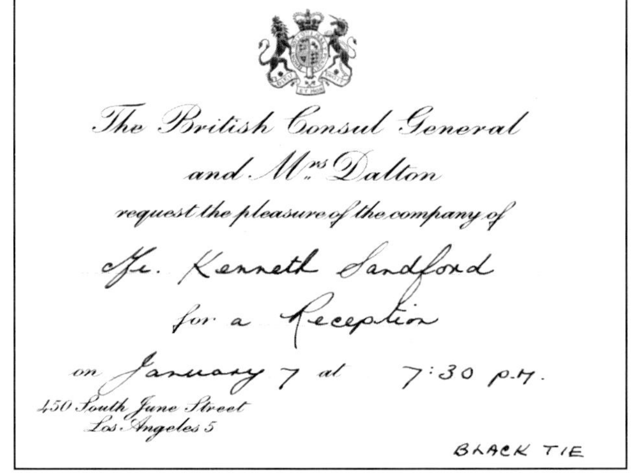

The British Consul General
and Mrs Dalton
request the pleasure of the company of
Mr. Kenneth Sandford
for a Reception
on January 7 at 7:30 p.m.
450 South June Street
Los Angeles 5
BLACK TIE

Ken, Bridget D'Oyly Carte, Isadore Godfrey, John Reed and Valerie Masterson at an official function

enjoy a little company but, after two *Mikados*, he was not so keen to be out socialising, preferring to quietly watch television before getting an early night. Sometimes it was easy enough to turn down an invitation but, on other occasions, the management expected a full turn-out, particularly if the host happened to be the British Ambassador or Governor General.

Perhaps the area of least upheaval during this vibrant period of his career was at work. Once inside the theatre, life was much the same as in England and his only problem involved getting used to the American sense of humour, which in the early part of the tour, took him somewhat by surprise. Certain lines, which at home guaranteed a laugh, were received in silence, but when he least expected it, a burst of laughter would quite unsettle him. He cannot now remember a specific example to illustrate the point, but is certain that it didn't

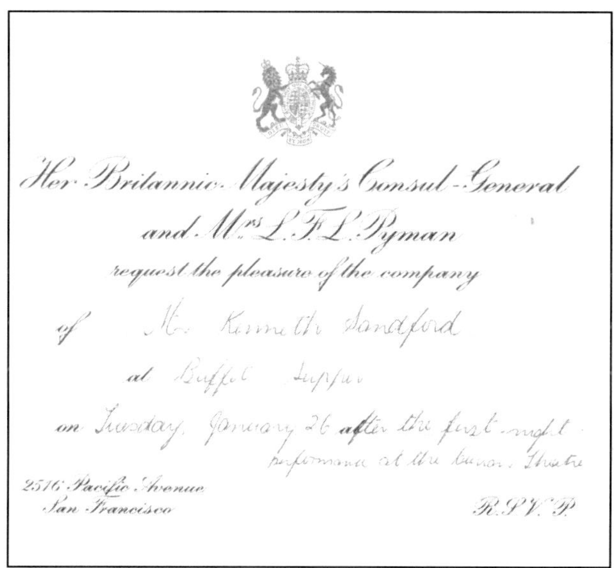

Her Britannic Majesty's Consul-General
and Mrs L. F. L. Pyman
request the pleasure of the company
of Mr Kenneth Sandford
at Buffet Supper
on Tuesday, January 26 after the first night performance at the Curran Theatre

2516 Pacific Avenue
San Francisco

R.S.V.P.

take him very long to adjust his timing in order to bridge the humour gap. Despite such minor difficulties, Ken was astonished by the Americans' appreciation of Gilbert and Sullivan; he had expected the Canadians to be enthusiastic, given their strong ties with Great Britain, but American audiences were a real surprise to him and he found them a delight to entertain.

The season in Vancouver went well enough, but was rather frustrating in terms of sightseeing, a persistent mist spoiling any chance to enjoy the scenery. Fortunately, the journey to the next port of call, Edmonton, more than made up for any disappointment. The company left Vancouver on a train which was to take them on an unforgettable journey through the Rocky Mountains, an experience which obviously remains vivid in Ken's memory as he describes the mountains, lakes and rivers which left him speechless with wonder. After sampling the crystal clear air of Jasper, he found the dreary surrounds of Edmonton to be a complete anti-climax, but he was there to do a job and that job had taken an ironical turn for the worse. The unfortunate George Cook had been struck down by appendicitis. Having waited for five years to escape the drudgery of the Sergeant in *Pirates*, Ken's sympathy for George's illness was tempered by his own depression at having to resume playing a role which made him so uncomfortable. Although he had to play the Sergeant for the rest of the tour, he fervently hoped that George would resume when the company returned to England. The management said nothing about it, so Ken said nothing about it, George just assumed and everyone was happy. Ken never played the part for the D'Oyly Carte again.

Ken's lot was certainly 'Not a happy one'

As the cold Canadian winter set in, the D'Oyly Carte moved on to Winnipeg via Saskatoon. They saw nothing of the latter city, because they only stayed long enough to give one performance. The train carriages occupied by the company were uncoupled and put into a siding, whilst the performers checked into a hotel for the day. As soon as the evening show was over, they reboarded the train and continued on to Winnipeg. As Ken points out, it is hard to imagine such a thing happening today. Despite the many fascinating new experiences which filled his days, Ken was beginning to really miss his family and counted the days until the New York season when they were due to join him. He regularly received letters from Pauline which kept him up-to-date with matters chez Sandford and wished he could make more phone calls home, but they were a luxury he could afford only occasionally. Most of his salary was paid into his bank account in London, the remainder being his allowance in dollars, so he was on a tight budget.

After several weeks in Canada the company returned to the U.S.A., where the first date was in eminently-forgettable Minneapolis. Then it was on to Washington and Ken's first visit to the beautiful American capital. He loved the art galleries and museums of the Smithsonian Institute, their delights filling his leisure time so that the days flew by, leaving only the Boston season before Pauline and the children arrived in New York. Soon he was greeting them and marvelling at how much the children had grown in three months. It was a happy reunion and, with so much to see and do in such a pulsating city, the daily performances were the only thing to spoil a happy family holiday. Ken was understandably low after they returned to England, but Chicago was the final date of the tour and he would soon be going home.

He found Chicago to be a wonderful place, but it was bitterly cold and he soon began to understand why it was known as the 'Windy City', the icy blast coming off Lake Michigan making venturing outdoors an unpleasant experience. Tiredness at the end of such an arduous tour was taking its toll on everyone in the company and Ken was grateful that, within a few days, they would be returning to England, but not before he had spent a low-key and cheerless Christmas Day away from home and family.

'Here we are once more on the scene of our former triumphs'

Some eighteen months later, Ken once again found himself packing his suitcases for a coast-to-coast tour of America. As he joined the others at the Savoy Hotel, he was aware of the difference in his emotions this second time around. The previous mix of excitement and apprehension had been replaced by a calm acceptance born of the experience gained on his first tour. He knew that the next five months would bring some memorable moments to alleviate the tedium of many long journeys, lonely hotel rooms and the lengthy separation from his family; so he boarded the plane in philosophical mood, knowing such tours to be a normal part of his job.

The 1964 tour opened in Boston on 19th October, the first stop of a much-changed itinerary which took the D'Oyly Carte to Philadelphia, San Diego, St. Louis, Cleveland, Bloomington, Indianapolis, Detroit, Toronto and Montreal as well as return visits to Washington, New York, Chicago, Los Angeles and San Francisco. Ken certainly did not miss the dreary mid-Canadian cities, but did enjoy his first visit to Ontario since his training days in the R.A.F. His routine soon fell into a familiar pattern with new cities to explore, art galleries to visit, the inevitable round of social functions and freezing winter conditions interrupted by a month of Californian heat. The weeks passed pleasantly enough and, as long as he could keep his laundry under control, he was quite content. His only regret was that Pauline and the children would not be joining him this time. It was a costly business and they did not wish to disrupt Mandy's and Anthony's education, so the decision was reluctantly taken for them to stay in London. At least he was able to thoroughly enjoy his work; having learned from his earlier experience of American audience reaction, there were no shocks in that department and he felt completely at ease on the stage.

The five-month tour threw up a number of unusual happenings to keep the company amused and although Ken did not keep a journal of events, his memory serves him extremely well. His only unpleasant recollection was of having to chase a porter who tried to steal his suitcase from outside the hotel in Washington. Not an aggressive man, Ken was, nevertheless, angry enough to give chase, only slightly manhandling the reprobate responsible for trying to abscond with his belongings. Looking forward to his first visit to the historic city of Philadelphia, Ken was to experience a theatre like no other. On arriving at the Stage Door of the Forrest Theatre, he was intrigued by the long subterranean route to his room. On enquiry, he was told that the architect responsible for the theatre's design had failed to recognise the importance of dressing rooms and had not included any! Fortunately, the building across the street was for sale and once this small oversight had been noticed, the theatre management acquired the property. Dressing rooms were provided therein and linked to the backstage area via a corridor constructed under the road. (I was inclined to treat this unlikely story as a typical D'Oyly Carte myth, the exaggerated result of too many tellings. However, its verity was unexpectedly confirmed by an architect whom I met whilst directing in Philly in 1995.)

In Cleveland, the company members were astonished to find a circus in full swing in the adjoining theatre and that many of the performers were staying in the same nearby hotel. Ken says that he soon got used to riding the elevator with the clowns, who made-up and dressed in their hotel rooms, but he never quite became accustomed to the roaring lions and trumpetting of elephants which punctuated his dialogue scenes, nor the startling faces of the clowns peering down from the fly gallery above the stage if he happened to glance upwards! Perhaps his favourite story of the 1964 tour came from Chicago where, once again, the company would spend a very quiet Christmas. The Opera House boasted a cavernous orchestra pit which dwarfed the small band of D'Oyly Carte musicians, wide open spaces separating the desks of players. During a performance of *The Mikado* the conductor, James Walker, inexplicably decided to take a stroll during a lengthy section of dialogue in Act I. As the next musical number drew ever closer, Ken and his colleagues realised that the itinerant Assistant Musical Director, who was quietly chatting to one of the violinists, was not going to make it back to the podium in time to start the music. With their attention riveted on his progress, they had little alternative but to slow down the dialogue to a funereal pace in the hope that a quick sprint would see Maestro Walker back to his baton in time to avert disaster. Happily, the prolonged sentences from above alerted him to his situation and he was able to crank up the orchestra just in time. This story may well stretch the bounds of credulity, but Ken swears that he has not exaggerated the facts of one of his best-loved moments on the stage. Overall it was a very happy tour.

After another eighteen-month gap, the D'Oyly Carte undertook its third major North American tour in four years and Ken, by now an old hand, can offer little in the way of anecdotes, except that Christmas of 1966 was spent in the singularly unattractive city of Detroit. He admits that much of his initial enthusiasm for such tours had begun to wane and that the prolonged periods away from home were hardly good for family life. It remains one of his greatest regrets that he missed so much of his childrens' early years and realises what a difficult task fell to Pauline, who was left to cope with the responsibility of everyday problems for months at a time.

The news that the company was to make two separate trips across the Atlantic in 1968 was greeted with amazement by a travel-weary Ken. He had expected the normal eighteen-month period before another tour, but an unexpected visit to Central City in Colorado, where the D'Oyly Carte had been invited to appear at the Opera Festival, filled him with consternation. His initial concerns about being away from home more than ever were quite understandable, but that brief few weeks in the Rocky Mountains proved to be one of the happiest experiences of his career. The company flew to Denver on 17th June, to be greeted by a band playing on the tarmac. This happy overture quickly gave way to a matter of serious concern, as Customs officials took issue with the large quantity of Scotch whisky being brought into the country by D'Oyly Carte members. This potentially serious matter could have been made worse by the wag who tried to convince the bemused officers that the offending spirit was essential for singers as a gargle to keep the vocal chords in good condition!

The gold-mining town of Central City was a twenty-mile drive from Denver and the altitude of 8000 feet required a few days' acclimatisation. Accommodation was in houses built for the early miners, which had been beautifully restored by the University of Colorado. Meals were taken at the Teller House, a hotel built in the typical western style of the 1850s, where everything possible was done to make them feel at home. The tiny Opera House, built in 1878, proved delightful – the last thing one might have expected in a frontier town and Ken was enchanted. As a devotee of cowboy movies he felt completely the part in his newly-acquired stetson and even tried his hand at gold prospecting, although the few grains he found hardly indicated an early retirement from Show Business.

The Opera House season opened on 22nd June with a performance of *The Mikado*. It was preceded by such colourful activities as square dancing, marching bands, a vintage car parade, Pony Express race and the 'Ceremony of the Bell', which officially opened the season. So exciting were the preliminaries that Ken finds it hard to believe that any of the performers managed to concentrate on the job in hand. The repertoire also included the staple American diet of *The Pirates of Penzance*, *H.M.S. Pinafore* and *Iolanthe*, but the inclusion of

The Yeomen of the Guard was a welcome change for Ken. Much as he loved his roles, he did get a little bored with only Private Willis to interrupt the constant flow of Pooh-Bahs and he still had plenty of free time to thoroughly enjoy exploring the local mountain terrain and paint to his heart's content.

The social life, too, was great fun; the idea of the same group of sedate members of the D'Oyly Carte joining the Red Bandana Club at the local pub in Britain would be impossible to imagine. The colourful local characters took them to their hearts and many Anglo-American friendships were formed. It was all so unlike any other visit to the States and, at times, seemed almost surreal; from the theatre ushers marching along the main Street singing ditties about how much more talented they were than the British singers appearing at the Opera House, to the sight of John Reed gulping lungfuls of oxygen from a cylinder at the side of the stage, after the rigours of singing the 'Nightmare Song' at such a high altitude. Where else would members of the audience follow the same ushers back along the Main Street after the performance to take part in the nightly square dancing? It was an idyllic five weeks, capped by an amazing party given by an eccentric millionairess at her mansion in Denver. On a glorious summer day the company travelled by bus from Central City to the home of their hostess, Elli Weckbauer. Enjoying the freedom of the gardens and swimming pool, plied with fine food and drink, it was little wonder that they failed to notice Elli's absence from the festivities until her late entrance. In a touching, if faintly ridiculous, tribute to the D'Oyly Carte Opera Company, she made her appearance dressed in Japanese costume and full kabuki makeup, riding in a rickshaw pulled by her servants, who were also dressed in Japanese outfits. It was a memorable day and a memorable season, which ranked high in Ken's list of happy times.

'Art and nature thus allied' – Ken takes time out to paint local scenery

Within three months and following an all-too-short time at home, the D'Oyly Carte flew back to America for an exhausting tour which saw them play fifteen cities in twelve weeks. The demanding schedule included many two- or three-night stands which, when followed by a long journey and performance the next day, left very little time to rest, relax, attend to laundry or shop for everyday necessities. If the Central City season had been a delightful romp, this was very much the opposite; the only respite being a two-week stay in Los Angeles over Christmas. It is possible that the extensive tours of the previous six years had given the American public its fill of Gilbert and Sullivan for the time being but, whatever the reason, the D'Oyly Carte's lucrative American market collapsed and it was to be another eight years before they returned. With his children growing up rapidly, Ken was grateful to be able to devote more quality time to them; he had missed much of their childhood and was anxious to be on hand during the critical period of their secondary education. Although Mandy had won a scholarship to The Godolphin and Latymer School, Anthony was at the expensive St. Paul's School, so continuity of employment was more vital than ever and Ken never seriously considered leaving the company. Much as he loved opera and still cherished ambitions to move in that direction, he knew that the financial security he enjoyed was all-important and as long as he derived artistic satisfaction from his work with the D'Oyly Carte, he would put his family first and personal ambition second.

'Gone abroad! His address'

'Denmark! Denmark'? Such was the incredulity with which the D'Oyly Carters reacted to the management's announcement that the company would be paying a week-long visit to that country in the autumn of 1970. To say that Ken was surprised and delighted is putting it mildly; he knew that there were no immediate plans to tour America and this short trip would provide a welcome change to the tedium of provincial touring. It has proved impossible to discover the reason behind the invitation to perform in Denmark, but it is a reasonable assumption that nobody minded the whys and wherefores – they were just pleased to be going. The repertoire would be *The Mikado* and *H.M.S. Pinafore*; the company's concerns that Danish audiences would not be able to understand Gilbert's words lessened by management assurances that many Danes spoke English and that *The Mikado* was well known in its Danish guise, *Mikadoen*.

On 11th October the D'Oyly Carte company flew to Copenhagen to give four performances, the first *Mikado* being attended by Crown Princess Margrethe and her husband, Prince Henrik, after which the world-famous brewers, Carlsberg, hosted a glittering party. Then it was on to the city of Aarhus for two shows. Audience reaction was enthusiastic and press reviews excellent, although it was something of a surprise that *Pinafore* was better attended than *Mikado* in both venues. In Aarhus, the success of *Pinafore* owed much to the fact that the NATO fleet was in town; the large contingent of British sailors cheering like a football crowd making it a memorable evening in the theatre. After the show, the officers threw a party aboard their destroyer of which, sadly, Ken remembers very little except that most of the company, himself included, got rather tiddly! It was a splendid week and his only regret was that the visit had been so brief. It was never repeated.

'Or perhaps Itali-an'

Some four years after the Danish adventure, the company packed its collective bags for another unlikely European destination – Rome. The idea of taking English operetta to the home of Grand Opera seemed like madness and Ken could hardly wait to find out how Italian audiences would respond to Gilbert and Sullivan. He had never been to Rome and the prospect of visiting the Vatican museum was thrilling indeed. For many company members (myself included) this was to be their first taste of touring abroad and excitement was high as they boarded the plane.

Iolanthe and *The Mikado* were the shows to be performed and it would be the first time that Ken had been scheduled to take part in every overseas performance, the decision not to take *Pirates* and *Pinafore* being most unusual. Attendances were disappointingly low and audience reaction mixed, the Romans making little sense of *The Mikado*, although they seemed to enjoy *Iolanthe* – probably because it seemed more typically British. It was certainly not a conventional week for the D'Oyly Carte; performances commencing at 9 p.m., if the audience was punctual and usually it was not, made for late nights and, with the early-morning horn-honking of Roman drivers, sleep was at a premium. This, coupled with the fact that every available moment of the sunny November days was spent taking in the sights, made for a fascinating, but extremely exhausting week. Ken was in his artistic element, the chance to see some of the world's greatest works of art seized with enthusiasm as he marvelled at the Sistine Chapel in particular.

The season was not without its little problems, not the least of which was the inedibility of the hotel food. The D'Oyly Carte management had arranged evening meals, but they were so ghastly that Ken and the others were forced to go to restaurants and pay for dinner from their modest allowance. Another difficulty arose when a transport strike forced the cancellation of a performance of *Iolanthe*. The addition of an unscheduled matinee to make up for this caused great disappointment amongst company members, who felt deprived of a valuable afternoon's sight-seeing time. Still, it was a wonderful experience and one which made Ken very grateful to be paid to go to such a place. O.K., it was a hard way to earn a living, but it certainly had its little perks. The eventful week came to a bizarre conclusion when the fatigued company arrived at the airport to fly home. Caught in the middle of a serious security problem, they were escorted to the plane by a posse of heavily-armed police. Arriving at Gatwick airport late on Sunday evening, the weary Savoyards made their way, in a blizzard, to Yorkshire, ready to open in the somewhat less eternal city of Bradford the following evening. It was not one of their more exuberant performances.

'And to that end we've crossed the main'

The news that the D'Oyly Carte was to make a long-overdue return to North America was greeted with great delight by the members of the company who had only heard about such tours from their seasoned colleagues, but who had yet to experience transatlantic touring for themselves. After such a long time, even Ken was happy to undertake another American tour and could not help wondering how different it would prove to be. To begin with, it was a much-changed company. Since 1968 there had been many departures and arrivals in all departments. Isadore Godfrey, who had seemed to be a permanent fixture, had retired to be replaced by James Walker who, in turn, made way for Royston Nash as Musical Director. Gone, too, were Valerie Masterson, Gillian Knight, Donald Adams, Philip Potter and Peggy Ann Jones; so, with the exception of John Reed, Ken himself and a few long serving choristers, American audiences would be seeing a very different cast. Now filling the principal slots were new names including Julia Goss, Lyndsie Holland, Jane Metcalfe, Meston Reid, Geoffrey Shovelton, John Ayldon and Michael Rayner. The impresario responsible for the tour was James Nederlander and Ken was relieved to find that the three-month trip would take place in spring and summer, with fewer venues and longer seasons replacing the frequent two- or three-night stops and lengthy journeys in the dead of winter, to which he had become accustomed in the 1960s.

On 3rd April 1976, the company set off via the Savoy Hotel and, as Ken settled into his seat on the ultra-modern 747 'jumbo' jet for the seven-hour flight to Toronto, he could not help smiling at the comparison with the horrendous fourteen-hour journey across the Atlantic which began his first tour in 1962. In fact, the whole experience was to prove much less frenetic and demanding; the younger, more open performers providing a congenial atmosphere both in and out of the theatre. With Mandy and Anthony now grown up, Pauline was able to join him for the Los Angeles season and Ken remembers their concern when, on phoning home, he was answered by a foreign gentleman wanting to know who wished to speak to Amanda. She had taken advantage of her parents' absence to invite several university friends to stay, leaving Pauline to worry about the state of their home on her return!

It was certainly interesting to return to many of the large cities and observe how much, or how little, they had changed in the intervening years. In many instances they played in different theatres from those of earlier tours, some of which proved to be quite a talking point. The magnificent new Opera House, one of three performing spaces which made up the John F. Kennedy Center in Washington D.C., provided a glittering example of the best in modern architecture; its plush scarlet interior and breath-taking crystal chandeliers making performing there something very special indeed. In Chicago, the enormous Arie Crown Theatre on the shore of Lake Michigan presented quite a challenge. A spectacular new building seating 4000 people, it hardly provided the intimate atmosphere in which Gilbert and Sullivan operas thrive. From the back of the auditorium the stage looked like a postage stamp and Ken, along with the other principals, realised that the unfamiliar amplification system was essential if dialogue was to be heard at the back of the house. That was not the only disadvantage of such a massive theatre; every aspect of stagecraft had to be adjusted to accommodate the distant audience. Dialogue delivery needed to be slowed down and gestures enlarged – a subtle glance or raising of an eyebrow were of no artistic value if they could not be seen. It was a fascinating experience, but not one which Ken enjoyed as an actor who relished the understatement.

Only one venue of the tour was new to him, Saratoga Springs in New York State. The small country town boasted a delightful outdoor theatre set in quiet woodland and provided a refreshing change to the clamour of the big cities they had visited. Overall, Ken had never enjoyed a tour as much as this one, the relaxed schedule making it easy to rest and keep fresh for the nightly performances.

Two years later another American tour followed. Under the same management, the format was similar, but this trip included a welcome return to San Francisco and Denver for Ken and a first visit to Long Beach, California, where the company were given the opportunity to stay on the Queen Mary if they fancied pampering themselves. It was ten years since Ken had last been in San Francisco, but he found it as exciting as ever and he was particularly pleased to be staying in a small apartment, the cooking facilities enabling him to get back to the serious business of baking apple pies! The highlight of the season was, undoubtedly, the publicity cruise around San Francisco Bay on a 19th Century sailing ship. With the company dressed in *H.M.S. Pinafore* costumes adding to the romance of the occasion, the press launch certainly got plenty of photo opportunities as they sailed around Alcatraz and under the Golden Gate Bridge. Accompanied by the San Francisco Fire Boat and Coastguard helicopter, it was a memorable voyage and the only thing to spoil the day was the look of anguish on the Wardrobe Mistress' face when several of the chorus men lost their sailor hats overboard. Such was their regret on leaving that favourite of American cities that, as the plane taking them to Los Angeles took off over the Golden Gate Bridge, the company broke into a spontaneous and emotional rendition of *'I left my heart in San Francisco'*. It was a moment to treasure.

For a seasoned campaigner like Ken, it was a pleasure to share the excitement of his younger colleagues experiencing for the first time such Californian delights as Disneyland and Universal Studios. There was enough of the child left in him to enjoy return visits to these attractions and he particularly liked staying in the Hollywood Hills, as opposed to downtown Los Angeles. To add to the enjoyment of this easy-going tour was a happy return to Central City. The D'Oyly Carte's successful season ten years earlier had gone down in company history and although the date in Denver was for just one week, those who had heard the stories of Central City were determined to see it for themselves. Ken couldn't wait to go back and, having toured the bijou Opera House and had a drink at the famed Teller House, he volunteered to guide a few hardy souls along the out-of-town trails where he had so enjoyed painting the spectacular scenery. Needless to say, the former R.A.F. navigator got a little lost, with the result that the overheated and exhausted party of explorers missed the bus back to Denver and had to fall on the mercy of a passing truck driver to take them back to the city! It took Ken a long time to live down that embarrassing episode and he still insists that the paths must have been altered.

It was certainly the tour for memorable occasions and two more spring readily to Ken's mind. During the Washington season the company members were invited to a party at the apartment of a senior political adviser to President Ford. On emerging from the Kennedy Center, the D'Oyly Carte revellers noticed that a crowd had gathered to see who would be riding in the fleet of stretch limos parked outside the theatre and were astonished when they realised that the government cars were their transport to the party. Feeling very important indeed, they duly waved to the disappointed, not to say confused, crowd of onlookers as they drove away in style! It would be hard to imagine that the tranquil environs of Saratoga Springs would be the setting for one of the most famous days in modern D'Oyly Carte history, but such was the case. Having travelled from New York, those members of the company who had decided not to stay on in the Big Apple for their day off needed something to do by way of entertainment. In such a quiet town this presented quite a difficulty, until someone had the novel idea of holding a sports day. The extensive motel grounds and swimming pool provided a perfect setting for the first and, thankfully, last D'Oyly Carte Olympics. The innocent pleasures of the egg-and-spoon race, three-legged and wheelbarrow racing, tug-of-war across the pool and five-a-side football match belied the competitive edge of the contestants. The resulting broken arm (Stage Manager), cracked ribs (Assistant Musical Director) and sundry sprains, strains and muscle pulls told their own story, but the greatest shame fell upon our hero, Kenneth Sandford. Struggling with a long-standing achilles tendon problem, he was consigned to goal-keeping in the

The D'Oyly Carte olympians

'Oh, shame – shame upon you!'

football game and was red-carded by the referee for moving the goal posts closer together when he thought nobody was looking! The ridiculously serious closing ceremony and prize-giving, when Company Manager, Herbert Newby, presented the trophies, was followed by an impromptu party to round off a day of never-to-be-forgotten camaraderie which typified the family spirit of this D'Oyly Carte Opera Company.

Within a few weeks of that hilarious day, the happiest of Ken's American tours came to an end. It was the last the company was to undertake.

Away we go to an island fair that lies in a southern sea'

Having enjoyed their annual holiday after the 1978 American trip, the company began the autumn provincial tour amidst increasing speculation that the rumoured tour of Australia and New Zealand might actually happen. It was an intriguing prospect, but Ken would only believe it when he boarded the plane and his colleagues felt the same wariness of the management's optimism that such a ground-breaking visit could be arranged. It was little wonder that, after weeks of speculation, they could hardly believe it when an announcement was finally made that a contract with the Australian impresario, Michael Edgley, had been signed for a three-month tour commencing in May 1979. Ken was tickled pink – he had never expected his D'Oyly Carte career to take him to the other side of the world but, like other married company members, he was conscious of how hard it would be for the husbands and wives left at home so soon after the American tour. Salary negotiations proved difficult; with so little money on offer it would certainly not be possible for Pauline to share the experience, so it was just one passport to be dusted off. During his discussions with the General Manager, Frederic

Lloyd, regarding contractual details, Ken was asked to play the role of Captain Corcoran in *H.M.S. Pinafore* for the Australian tour. This was a part he had always wanted to take because of its suitability to his vocal range. With *Iolanthe* and *The Mikado* also in the repertoire, it would mean having to do eight performances a week. Unbelievably, he was offered the same salary whether he played it or not and so, as a matter of principle, he turned down the opportunity to play a role he had always admired. It was another example of the management's inability to recognise the value of their top artists and, after twenty-one years of loyal service, he felt the insult keenly. Despite his understandable annoyance, he was determined to enjoy the forthcoming tour; after all, he was well used to an overseas diet of Private Willis and Pooh-Bah.

As with American tours, the shows going to Australia had to be dropped from the provincial tour several weeks in advance of the company's opening in Canberra; the logistics of transporting three operas to the other side of the world requiring a great deal of detailed planning. The scenery, costumes and properties for *Iolanthe* and *Pinafore*, along with the set of *Mikado*, were loaded into huge containers ready for shipping and each member of the company was allowed to send one suitcase with the advance effects. As the D'Oyly Carte possessed several *Mikado* sets, it was possible to continue playing the perennial favourite in England, its costumes and props travelling with the company some weeks later.

And so, on 7th May 1979, following the traditional gathering of the clan at the Savoy, the D'Oyly Carte Opera Company set off in high spirits for its unique tour of Australia and New Zealand. It was an exhausting journey, making Ken's first transatlantic flight in 1962 seem like a short pleasure trip. The question of a stop-over had never been mentioned and the 26 hours in transit seemed interminable, the depressing four-hour refuelling stop in Bombay convincing Ken that he did not wish to return to India. Having witnessed the grubby airport terminal and its resident ferocious-looking hawks, the shanty towns at the edge of the runway filled him with horror and he was glad to leave such human misery behind. The next leg of the journey was to Brunei, where they were not allowed to leave the plane, but were forced to while away several hours as best they could.

Ken was luckier than some in that he was able to fall asleep to order, but he still felt completely drained when they eventually touched down in Sydney after what seemed like a week in the air. After a delay of two hours, an increasingly irritable and weary band of Savoyards took the short flight to Canberra before, thankfully, crashing out in their comfortable hotel. Fortunately, the first performance was not until the 14th and Ken needed every moment of the free days to acclimatise, the jet-lag making him feel physically and mentally disorientated.

By the time of the opening night he was beginning to feel more like his normal self and was grateful that *Iolanthe* allowed him a gentle return to work. The performance at the Canberra Theatre Centre was well received and the ensuing champagne reception was the first of many given by the tour's sponsors, Benson & Hedges. The idea of a cigarette manufacturer sponsoring an opera company seemed quite shocking to the abstemious, but the company's smokers, Ken included, gratefully accepted the packs of 200 of the wicked weed, which were freely available until the end of the tour. There was not a great deal to do in Canberra. Ken was struck by the quiet, small town atmosphere of the Australian capital, but the glorious autumn weather made for enjoyable exploration of the surrounding countryside. In particular, the Tidbinbilla National Park offered beautiful woodland scenery and his first sighting of a kangaroo! The only other memorable moment of that first two weeks Down Under provided him with a story on which he dined out for years. During a live radio interview with a presenter whose knowledge of the Savoy Operas was matched only by his inability to do basic research, Ken was rendered speechless when asked:

'What are Gilbert and Sullivan doing now?'

After a low-key start to the tour the fun really began when the company moved on to Sydney. With so much to see and do, the days flew by very happily and his only regret was that the famous Opera House was deemed too small to be financially viable as a venue for the D'Oyly Carte. The barn-like interior of the dreary Regent Theatre certainly held more people, but it was hardly inspiring. Still, the performances during the three-week season were well attended and received with enthusiasm by and large, but everyone regretted not being able to say that they had played at the Sydney Opera House, particularly after attending a reception there, hosted by Australian Opera.

In such a sophisticated and exciting city it was inevitable that free time would be rather more interesting than usual and Ken remembers two events with particular pleasure. Almost a year to the day after the fantastic cruise around San Francisco Bay, the company found themselves donning *H.M.S. Pinafore* costumes once more, this time to sail around Sydney Harbour. At the invitation of international yachtsman and wine maker, James Hardy, they enjoyed champagne and sunshine all the way, marvelling at the spectacular vista and singing choruses from *Pinafore* to entertain their host at the wheel. It was a thrilling trip; the evening's performance suffered little from the excesses of the day and this time no hats were lost. A few days later, two of the chorus ladies gave a party to celebrate their birthdays. When separated from home and family for long periods of time, colleagues fell into the role of surrogate family and birthdays were always marked as special occasions. Given the large size of the apartments in the Sydney hotel, Sue Cochrane and Liz Denham decided on a fancy dress party to which the whole company was invited. The creativity and ingenuity of the party-goers was admirable, the judges having a difficult task in deciding the prize winners, but their choice in the category of 'Best Dressed Female' was met with thunderous applause as Kenneth Sandford stepped up to collect 'her' prize – a string of glass beads! His brilliant portrayal of Dame Edna Everage had not been achieved without much preparation and many misgivings. Having suggested the idea as a joke, he was carried along by other peoples' enthusiasm as Beti Lloyd-Jones provided his dress and gloves, someone else loaned him a wig and one of the men's chorus pitched in with white *Iolanthe* shoes. All he had to do was make the elaborate trademark frames to attach to his spectacles. The sight of a reluctant Ken sitting in the bathroom being made up with borrowed lipstick by James Conroy-Ward would have astonished his many fans, but any ideas he might have had for a second career as a drag artist quickly vanished after a humiliating encounter with several butch Aussie men in the hotel elevator.

'There is nothing like a dame'

Their hilarity and bawdy insinuations made Ken most uncomfortable and his feeble, high pitched *'Goodnight boys'* only made matters worse. On exiting the lift he vowed never to dress up as a woman again.

The next port of call was Brisbane, where the hot, sunny weather made it hard to believe that it was wintertime. It was Ken's first taste of a sub-tropical climate and, with a group of friends, he enjoyed driving in the Queensland countryside. On days off, many of the company made their way to Dickey Beach, a beautiful and unspoiled stretch of sand on the Sunshine Coast, some 100 miles north of the city, where they enjoyed picnics and swimming in the warm sea. Ignoring the locals, who sarcastically remarked that only the crazy 'Poms' would take a dip in winter, Ken and the others made the most of their opportunity. On a trip to a nature reserve he was happy enough to cuddle koalas and hand-feed kangaroos, but drew the line at snuggling up to a python and the sight of Meston Reid draped in a 12-foot monster was quite enough to tighten his vocal chords. So far, it had been a wonderful experience – it was too good to last.

'Ye South Pacific island viviparians'

Having left behind the delights of Queensland, the D'Oyly Carte wagon rolled on to New Zealand, the company making its debut at Auckland's St. James Theatre on 26th July.

Suddenly it was really winter, the leaden skies doing little to brighten the city's bleak architecture – and did it rain! Day after day of torrential downpours were not only depressing, but also made sight-seeing impossible. Everyone hoped that it would clear up for the planned trip to the world-famous geysers and hot springs of Rotorua, but it did not. The short bus ride was abandoned due to land-slides. It was a bitter disappointment, so near and yet so far. *'Why damme, it's too bad'*. In fact, the only bright spot in that dreary two weeks was Ken's 55th birthday party, when James Conroy-Ward and Meston Reid, both brilliant mimics, gave hilarious impersonations of Leonard Osborn, who had returned to the company as Director of Productions, to the delight of all present. It was certainly a case of having to make one's own entertainment – whoever said that they had been to New Zealand and found it closed was not joking. By the time the nightly performance was over, bars, restaurants and even television had shut down so, at the instigation of Beti Lloyd-Jones, a poker school was formed which convened on a weekly basis for the rest of the tour. Playing for pennies, Ken and his colleagues enjoyed a convivial and relaxing couple of hours after work and, with so many actors around the table, it was hard to tell who was bluffing.

The week in Wellington was somewhat brighter and Ken remembers that many of the company members were tempted by the large store devoted exclusively to sheepskin products. Coats, rugs, boots, hats, gloves and bedcovers were purchased and shipped back to England, prompting Michael Edgley's representative to sarcastically remark:

> *'We must be paying them too much'*.

After 20 years Ken still laughs helplessly as he remembers Patricia Leonard making a terrible *faux pas* in the aforementioned emporium. Surveying the single and double-skin rugs she decided that she and her husband, Michael Buchan, needed something larger and politely enquired of the sales assistant:

> *'Do you have a four-skin?'*,

To which the gentleman impassively replied:

> *'Yes, madam, I do have a selection of quad skins'*.

She has never been allowed to live down her embarrassment.

The week in Christchurch was certainly the highlight of the New Zealand leg of the tour and, after the disappointment of Auckland, everyone was determined to see as much of the stunning South Island as possible, particularly the mountains. One phone call to Mount Cook Airlines was all that was required to hire a six-seater plane (and pilot) to carry Ken and five of his colleagues to heaven and back. In brilliant sunshine, the little aircraft bobbed and weaved through the snowy peaks, over glaciers and around the summit of Mount Cook, before skimming low over the Canterbury plains back to Christchurch. He would never forget that wonderful flight and was left to reflect on his good fortune in being able to see the world and get paid for it.

Returning to Australia, the company played a three-week season in Melbourne, a city which Ken found to be bustling, yet relaxing. He was thrilled to be able to attend a dress rehearsal of Australian Opera's production of *Don Giovanni*, starring Joan Sutherland and James Morris. He was captivated by the talents of the latter and was astounded to learn that James was a great Kenneth Sandford admirer, who had listened to D'Oyly Carte recordings as a youngster at home in America. Indeed, during a performance of *The Mikado* he sat cross-legged on the floor in the wings watching Ken as Pooh-Bah, much to the delight of our hero. His lowest point of the tour provides a perfect example of the difficulties encountered by itinerant theatricals in need of medical attention. Whilst taking a shower, he was shocked when a crown on one of his front teeth fell off and headed in the direction of the plug-hole. Having retrieved the offending incisor, he was faced with the dilemma of finding a dentist who would replace the crown in time for the afternoon performance. If not, he must contact his understudy who would need to be notified as quickly as possible. Having found an obliging dental surgeon, he had to pay from his own pocket and then claim from the D'Oyly Carte's insurance; a hassle he could well have done without.

The tour had flown by and, on 12th August, the company moved on to Adelaide, which was to be the final date for Ken and Philip Potter. Apart from cooking a rabbit stew and visiting the wine-producing region of the Barossa Valley, only Beti Lloyd-Jones' somewhat eccentric birthday party remains clear in his mind. Having been told by the management to pack evening clothes for formal functions, no opportunity had arisen to unpack them, so Beti sent out formal invitations to her black-tie party, meaning that long frocks and dinner jackets could be given one airing at least. With glittering tiaras much in evidence, the other residents of the simple motel looked on in amazement at the antics of the Poms. It was a happy end to a happy tour for Ken, who was now looking forward to going home. Only *Pinafore* was to be played in Perth, so he and Philip flew back to England early at the end of what had proved to be an exhilarating experience.

It was the final overseas tour undertaken by the D'Oyly Carte Opera Company before its closure.

Though it may seem that the many foreign trips in Ken's long career with the company resembled paid holidays, he never forgot the purpose of such tours; to present the works of Gilbert and Sullivan to those who rarely had the opportunity to see the Savoy Operas performed at the highest level. Always the consummate professional, his days revolved around the performance; sight-seeing, day trips and socialising confined to his free days. The monotonous diet of *The Mikado* and *Iolanthe* he viewed as an opportunity to continually develop and hone his characterisations, with the result that the name of Kenneth Sandford still represents the highest standards wherever in the world Gilbert and Sullivan is appreciated and to which other performers will always aspire.

By arrangement with D'Oyly Carte Opera Trust & Dame Bridget D'Oyly Carte D.B.E.

Derek Glynne & Michael Edgley Proudly announce -

The first ever Australian Season of
the entire D'Oyly Carte Company, 1979

23rd August, 1979

Mr Kenneth Sandford
c/o Festival Centre
ADELAIDE

Dear Ken,

Here is your ticket which takes you back to England, together with $20 to pay for your exit visa ($10) and another $10 which I hope will cover your taxis.

I hope you have a safe journey home, and will soon be re-united with your family. I also hope that you will take back some happy memories of your Australian and New Zealand Tour.

Warmest regards,

Derek Glynne

Chapter 6

SOME YOU WIN, SOME YOU LOSE

'Paragraphs got into all the papers'

FOR any performer, amateur or professional, the theatre critic is an inescapable fact of life and it is certainly true to say that no artist likes to receive a bad review, but is always delighted by a good one. Human nature dictates that everyone humiliated by public criticism is elated by public praise, regardless of the theatrical credentials of the reviewer. The brickbats and bouquets handed out by the respected professional critic of a national broadsheet cause hardly more pain or pleasure than those dished out by the sports reporter drafted in to cover an amateur show for his small provincial weekly paper. The public has a tendency to believe what it reads and the consequences of a review may either cause a stampede for tickets or leave the Box Office idle. It is a subjective business and boils down to the opinion of the individual journalist, an opinion which may be at odds with the view of the audience of which he is a member. The critic carries a great weight of responsibility, his written summation capable of making or breaking a show, not to mention the confidence of a performer whose reputation is at the mercy of the reviewer. Most professional performers have a jaundiced view of critics, whom they perceive to be lacking in understanding of the hard-acquired technique and expertise necessary for an actor or singer to appear on the stage. They find it difficult to accept criticism from someone who probably cannot do the job themselves and yet, the same performers gladly quote favourable comments in their CVs.

After nearly 50 years in Show Business, Ken is philosophical about press reviews and has learned to take the rough with the smooth. He has been lucky insofar that the vast majority of his 'crits' have been glowing, the few bad ones usually courtesy of American and Canadian critics. Always prepared to accept constructive criticism if he feels it to be justified, he has, nevertheless, developed the facility to laugh off the barbed comments of self-serving journalists whose reputations thrive on acid comment. Any compliment regarding his use of dialogue, characterisation or timing he finds quietly satisfying, but effusive generalisations he dismisses out of hand.

An amusing incident on the 1976 North American tour gives an insight into Ken's attitude to newspaper reviews. Knowing that the Toronto theatre critics had a reputation for vitriol, the principals ran a book as to who would receive the worst notice. Several of them were in contention by the end of the week, but it was unanimously agreed that Ken had fared worst at the hands of one William Littler and he was duly awarded the ten-dollar prize. Whilst much amused by the fun of the competition and certainly not upset by the bruising comments, he had to agree with the opinion of the aforementioned reviewer of *The Mikado*, who remarked to the effect that if Kenneth Sandford had given nearly 2000 performances of Pooh-Bah, he had given nearly 2000 mediocre performances! The additional jibe that *'like Old Man River, he just keeps rolling along'* caused much merriment in the dressing rooms of Toronto's Alexandra Theatre, but left Ken feeling that there was some truth in it. It is indicative of the man's constant search for the truth of a character that he now wishes he could turn back the clock and have another opportunity to explore the possibilities of a role for which he became so well-known, but which always left him feeling dissatisfied by his efforts. As he points out, given the demands on a performer appearing night after night for 48 weeks, there were inevitably occasions when he felt unwell or extremely tired and he knew that he had not been at his best on the stage. Singers are human beings, not machines and times of underachievement were bound to occur now and then; if the press reported as such, so be it. As far as Ken is concerned, be a crit flattering or damning, the artist has to go on for the next performance, so his advice is to take nothing said in print too seriously, but to concentrate on extracting as much as possible from the words and music. After such a lengthy career he knows how hard the theatre business can be and acknowledges that if you are in the front line, you may well get shot down. Surviving uninformed opinion is part of the job, but learning from informed opinion should be every artist's aim.

In Ken's experience, it was generally the case that press reviews in small provincial towns on both sides of the Atlantic tended to be favourable, whilst those in the newspapers serving major cities were more critical – sometimes justifiably, sometimes not. However, it was significant that many North American theatre critics took issue with the D'Oyly Carte style of production. As early as 1962, 20 years before the company's closure, many reviewers saw the need for change, considering the shows to be rather stale and musty. Though not advocating extreme stylistic change, they called for a fresh approach in order for the Savoy Operas to maintain their deserved popularity. Of course there were exceptions, the occasional critic raging at the slightest departure from strict tradition and many who were more than happy with what they saw, but Ken is convinced that the D'Oyly Carte management should have taken notice of the calls for a re-think. Even when the British press advocated a change of staging style some years later, the company elders refused to admit that it might have a point.

Like every other performer, Ken hopes that a journalist reviewing a show is a conscientious professional who takes pride in what he writes for public scrutiny. Bearing in mind his power to encourage or discourage audience attendance, his readership should be entitled to fair and accurate comment. Sadly, this is not always the case and it is little wonder that artists cling to the view that many critics spend Act I in the bar, before leaving at the interval clutching a programme from which to construct their report. This cynical attitude is unfair to the many theatre journalists who ply their trade with integrity, but it cannot be denied that, on too many occasions, carelessness and a lack of basic knowledge of Gilbert and Sullivan contribute to the performers' mistrust of those sitting in judgement on them. The following selection of reviews and articles about the D'Oyly Carte in general and Ken in particular, contains several glaring examples of journalistic incompetence, most notably the frequent misspelling of cast members' names. Throughout his career Ken has been plagued by hacks who refer to him as Kenneth Sanford and, in one case, he was down as Sandford in the cast list included with the review, but called Sanford in the report itself. Such poor work does not inspire confidence and Ken doubts the worthiness of the critic who thinks that the Tower of London is populated by a solitary *Yeoman of the Guard*.

He considers press reviews to be a two-edged sword; sometimes providing a glowing addition to a biography and welcome boost to the ego, sometimes giving depressing food for thought. But on the whole, he believes that they should be taken with a pinch of salt, as the next performance is all that is important.

THE CRITS

GAY FESTIVE FARE IN CITY THEATRES

IF King's Rhapsody does not break upon the Edinburgh scene with the freshness of an unheard of novelty, it is none the less welcome as a Christmas and New attraction at the Empire Theatre.

Here indeed is the ideal avenue to festive season escapism – Ruritarian romance in the Ivor Novello grand manner. Fourteen scenes, indeed, and all of them flashing with gay uniforms and lovely dresses, reflecting a period when men dazzled with sartorial brilliance and women loved elegance in their fashions.

Olive Gilbert sings, with beautiful expression and her sparkling "Take your Girl" is as joyous as it is unexpected. Muriel Barron and John Allen both play well and there is some fine singing by Kenneth Sandford.

Edinburgh Evening Despatch, 19 December 1951

NOVELLO'S CAPTIVATING "KING'S RHAPSODY"

IT is easy, and I think unfair, to dismiss (as the highbrow critic is apt to do) Ivor Novello as a purveyor of sugary sentiment and singable songs.

There was far more than that in his make-up and in "King's Rhapsody," his last big romantic musical, which reached Oxford's New Theatre last night, after a very long London run, we have the Novello magic, the Novelle, craftsmanship at its best.

The principals are given excellent backing by the huge supporting cast, among whom Kenneth Sandford's singing is worth special mention.

Oxford Mail, 1 June 1952

RADIO TIMES 1954

Light Programme

1,500 m. (200 kc/s) 247 m. (1,214 kc/s)

FEBRUARY

FRIDAY 26

MORNING AND AFTERNOON

9.0 a.m. **Big Ben NEWS**

9.10 a.m. HOUSEWIVES' CHOICE
David Jacobs
introduces your request records

9.55 a.m. **FIVE TO TEN**
A story, a hymn and a prayer

10.00 a.m. **GREENWICH TIME SIGNAL**
WILLIAM DAVIES
At the BBC theatre organ

10.30 a.m. **MUSIC WHILE YOU WORK**
Harry Leader and his Band
(Harry Leader and his Band are appearing at the Astoria Dance Salon, London)

11.00 a.m. MRS. DALE'S DIARY
Script by Basil Dawson
(Yesterday's recorded broadcast)

11.15 a.m. MELODY MIXTURE
A programme of light music
arranged and played by
Jack Byfield and his Players
with
Frederick Curzon at the organ
and Kenneth Sandford (tenor)
(Kenneth Sandford is appearing in "Paint Your Wagon' at Her Majesty's Theatre, London)

VICTORIA PALACE
"JOKERS WILD"

MUSIC AND LYRICS BY ROSS PARKER; PRODUCED BY ALEC SHANKS

No modern comedians are more redolent of the old music hall than the Crazy Gang.

They are at their best when they dress themselves up as women railway cleaners and concentrate on nothing. If one of them attempts concentration, he is at once broken up by the rest. But a remarkable sense of timing creates unseen connections between one preposterous joke and another. Bud Flanagan is one person; Teddy Knox is, one would say, a very different person; but for the purpose of suggesting the general awfulness of women railway cleaners they are but limbs of the same mischievous entity, and Nervo and Naughton and Gold are other limbs not less expressive.

Their mockery of television's parlour game, "What's My Line?" quite misses fire; but the gentle drollery of the monkish bell ringers passing from sleepiness to skittishness will be great fun when practice has given it a smoother rhythm and the same may be said for the burlesque of "The Scarlet Pimpernel". The rest of the show is more spectacular than choral, and the John Tiller Girls are its dominant figures. One dance lifts well drilled regimentation into a sort of beauty. Mr. Kenneth Sandford is the most tuneful of the singers and an evocation of spring provides him a charming background. The music is suitably rumbustious, and Mr. Alec Shanks, the producer, has done an excellent job of work.

The Times, 17th December 1954

RECITALS OF THE WEEK

Mr. Kenneth Sandford wisely selected a light-weight, drawing-room programme to sing at Wigmore Hall on Friday, presenting it with some imagination, though he gave the impression on more than a few strained top notes that he was either singing in keys too high for him or else that his pleasantly lyrical tenor voice was very tired.

The Times, 9th April 1951

Bright "Gondoliers"

LIKE an apple tree, Gilbert and Sullivan's "The Gondoliers" flourishes and blossoms.

It starts slowly, almost too slowly, but the second half is a riot.

I thought that the D'Oyly Carte production at the New Theatre, Cardiff, last night rather reflected that.

But for me the highlight was that magnificent quartet "In A Contemplative Mood," sung with great spirit by Neville Griffiths, Alan Styler (Giuseppe), Joyce Wright (Tessa) and the fine voiced Jean Hindmarsh (Gianetta).

A word too, for the "Grand Inquisitor", sung beautifully by Kenneth Sandford.

South Wales Echo, 1st August 1957

Highlights in the show, but –

THE "Half-past Eight" show at the Alhambra, Glasgow, last night, had its highlights, although marred by over-elaborate production.

Jack Radcliffe twinkled, Stanley Baxter spread his own warm glows – too seldom – and Molly Urquhart also dazzled less than she might have done. But Kenneth Sandford, the tenor, shone.

Glasgow Mail, 21st August 1954

'ST. PAUL' A TOP-RANKING PERFORMANCE

West Middlesex Musical Society

PERFORMANCES by the West Middlesex Musical Society have become landmarks of musical activities in the district. The presentation of Mendelssohn's "St. Paul" at Ealing Town Hall on Saturday last added another jewel to the crown of their achievements.

St. Paul was given a sincere interpretation by Kenneth Sandford. His voice is powerful and has a dark smoothness of tone which made his singing of the role very effective. His rendering of "O God, have mercy" was very moving. He was well supported by William Bailey, notably in the duets.

Middlesex Observer, 20th April 1957

City goes Gilbertian again

JAPAN has invaded Cardiff – but only on the stage of the New Theatre Cardiff. The D'Oyly Carte Opera Company are here again and open a fortnight of Gilbertian spectacles with the ever popular "Mikado."

As far as the solo parts are concerned it may be that "When A is happy B is not." since many hold strong views on how Gilbert and Sullivan should be sung, but the Chorus work would undoubtedly have gained even the approval of one of those early critical Edwardian audiences.

Charming Yum-Yum

The story of the Town of Titipu, where flirting is capital, needs no introduction, though several of the singers do. Maureen Melvin makes a charming Yum-Yum, tripping about and singing brightly with a roguish lilt in the eye which is lost occasionally in a downward demure cast.

Also the company's new Poo-Bah, Kenneth Sandford. He looks a tremendous swell, in his Lord-High - Everything - Else's yellow robes.

Western Mail, Cardiff, 5th August 1957

A TOWER THAT FEW CAN RESIST

THE Tower of London is rather old. The story of a romantic prisoner and the lovesick maid who engineers his release is also rather smitten with age.

But mix the two together, add a background of brilliantly-clad yeomen giving voice to stirring melodies, and you have that mixture of sentiment and ceremonial against which few Britons are proof.

Foolish suitor

Peter Pratt (as Jack Point, the strolling jester) was light of foot and successfully garrulous in a part which called for an equal measure of prancing and garrulity.

One of his main foils was lumbering Wilfred Shadbolt, head gaoler and assistant tormentor, played by Kenneth Sandford. This swarthy denizen of the Tower sang the foolish words of a foolish suitor, but how good they sounded in his fine baritone.

Western Mail, Cardiff, 30th July 1957

Transformation by Sandford

Bristol Hippodrome: "The Gondoliers" by Gilbert and Sullivan. The D'Oyly Carte Opera Company.

What would the current D'Oyly Carte Company do without Kenneth Sandford?

Already this 'veteran' of a company liberally laced with newcomers has given us a roundly comic Pooh-Bah, and a pathos-dominated Wilfred Shadbolt. Last night his august Grand Inquisitor saved "The Gondoliers" from foundering on the rocks of a disappointing launching on the Venetian canals.

Both in voice and presence he is an artist in the true Savoyard tradition, and his first entrance transformed a lack-lustre production into a true reflection of the G. and S. genius.

Happily, the challenge he threw down was eagerly taken up by the other principals and the sparkle of the second act performances was matched only by the colourful cavalier costumes.

Thanks to the inspiration of Kenneth Sandford, the D'Oyly Carte triumphed again.

Western Mail, Bristol, 5th May 1960

SINISTER SANDFORD PUTS IT RIGHT

BY CHARLES REID

Ruddigore – Savoy Theatre

WITH Sullivan's deft parodies of Weber and Verdi well cared for by Isidore Godfrey (conductor) and orchestra and chorus responding spiritedly, I was reasonably happy in a musical sense, from the word go.

It must be said, however, that as drama, the opening scene limped and halted. It was not until the entry of the wicked Sir Despard Murgatroyd that the proceedings began to quiver with true operatic current.

To this role Kenneth Sandford brought assets which fiercely matched his red and green habiliments. His vocal line was rancorous but true, his facial play simian and sinister, his gesture freezing and calamitous.

Daily Mail, 9 January 1962

MIDNIGHT OPERA TRIBUTE

LILTING PASTICHE OF OFFENBACH

From Our Music Critic

THIS week the National School of Opera is finally, after 15 years' struggle, to close down. Not because it has failed, but because it has succeeded so well that an officially sponsored school, the London Opera Centre, has been brought into existence to extend and intensify the good work which Miss Joan Cross and Miss Anne Wood have done and, in the new organisation, will continue to do.

At midnight on Friday their friends, admirers and ex-pupils gathered at Sadler's Wells for a miscellaneous operatic programme in which those on either side of the footlights showed, each in the appropriate manner, just how valuable the Opera School has proved itself to all of us.

The pièce de résistance was doubtless the lilting Offenbach pastiche, *Not in front of the Waiter*, which Mr. Colin Graham (producer of the whole programme) had devised for the occasion.

There was plenty of distinguished singing to be heard earlier in the evening (or should we say morning?): from Miss Rae Woodland in the sextet from *Lucia di Lammermoor* (curiously dressed in Victorian costume), and Miss Janet Baker, a superb Dido, in the garden scene from *The Trojans*, and Mr. Kenneth Macdonald, elegant and mellifluous, in both these excerpts; from Miss Marie Collier as the chief *grisette* of Maxim's in Lehar's *Merry Widow*, and as Puccini's Manon Lescaut; from Miss Pauline Tinsley as an exceptionally musical Susanna and Antonia; and from Mr. Kenneth Sandford as Tchaikovsky's Onegin – we hope this talented singing actor will not remain forever in Savoy opera. Finally, there was Sir Tyrone Guthrie to express what we all felt and to hand Miss Cross and Miss Wood their farewell presents.

The Times, 29th July 1963

D'Oyly Carte Players Pull Biggest Audience

IT was a great night for the local Savoyards (the Gilbert & Sullivanites) – the first visit to Minneapolis of the one and only D'Oyly Carte Company, creator and caretaker of the G & S tradition, playing to the largest audience – 4,800-plus – that the famous London troupe has ever encountered in its travels.

Also, and moreover, Monday night's event in Northrop Auditorium marked the first local professional performance, so far as anyone can remember, of "The Gondoliers," Gilbert and Sullivan's last collaboration. An orchestra of about 30, mostly Minneapolis Symphony men, played in the pit, conducted by James Walker.

"The Gondoliers" is generally a gentler and slower opus than its more familiar predecessors, more lyric and less given to the satire and nonsense found in the earlier works. The first act suffered from poor projection into the monster hall, and took some time to get off the ground.

The two gondoliers were sung by Thomas Round and Alan Styler, and their deserted wives by Jean Hindmarsh and Peggy Ann Jones. Comedy was mostly in the hands of John Reed as the duke, a sprightly and impecunious nobleman who incorporates himself to improve his fortunes, and he had a skilful assist from Kenneth Sanford as the pompous Grand Inquisitor

Minneapolis Star, 9 October 1962

Spirited 'Gondoliers' by the D'Oyly Carte

By STANLEY EICHELBAUM

I HAVE always had a special fondness for "The Gondoliers" – that delightfully insane and melodic charade about royalty, which is perhaps the most polished and cutting of all the Gilbert and Sullivan satires.

It was presented at the Geary over the weekend by the D'Oyly Carte Opera Company and I cannot remember when I have enjoyed it more.

Though the mood of 'The Gondoliers" is mock 18th century Venetian and Spanish (with a story that's utter madness), the humour is strictly Victorian English and George R. Foa's direction made the most of all the foolishness but with gem-like British restraint.

Thomas Round and Alan Styler were admirable as the two republican-minded gondoliers who are abruptly raised to the dual rank of king. And Jean Hindmarsh and Peggy Ann Jones made them deliciously bouncy Venetian wives.

But the piece-de-resistance was offered by Kenneth Sandford, a baritone whose exquisite sense of humour had the sting of a serpent's tooth in the role of a Grand Inquisitor who equips his torture chamber with illustrated daily papers.

San Fransisco Examiner, 3 September 1962

'THE GONDOLIERS'

Tarnished Tradition

TRADITION is a fine and glorious thing in the theatre, but even the ageless charm of Gilbert and Sullivan can become a bore unless it is brightened and polished and made to look new – which is probably why the D'Oyly Carte Opera Company's Friday night presentation of "The Gondoliers" was such a curious combination of a quaint, old-fashioned charm and outmoded mustiness.

If Gilbert and Sullivan are to remain a treasure, then the operettas must be staged with all the brightness and gaiety and skill that the modern theatre can offer.

Despite being touted as a "new" production, Friday night's show was amazingly dull in alarmingly long stretches.

Nobody wants or demands a jazzed-up, frantic version of these beloved classics, but not even the most sacred of traditions is worth keeping if it just doesn't work any more.

Working within the spirit of Gilbert and Sullivan, it is still possible to put on a production that looks newly minted and the sooner the D'Oyly Carte company learns this, the better off they and their audience will be.

Chicago Daily News, 22nd December 1962

Iolanthe Redeems D'Oyly Carte's Honor

The D'Oyly Carte Opera Company, which last week-end presented a thoroughly bad production of "The Gondoliers" at the O'Keefe Centre, last night, redeemed its honor with "Iolanthe."

This company is, of course. the home team for Gilbert and Sullivan operas. As such, it sticks by Gilbert's outdated stagings as canons of the faith. But except for that staging, Peter Goffin's very bad sets and the odd weak voice, "Iolanthe" was as good, as "Gondoliers" was bad. Indeed, at three points the performance struck memorable high notes.

Gillian Knight, the contralto who sings all of Gilbert's ugly-old-lady roles (last night she was the Queen of the Fairies) has adopted a uniform vocal style and personality for all her parts. It is the highly artificial style – foggy-edged timbre, eccentric character – made familiar by countless church basement productions of G. and S.

This is objectionable, but less so than exhibiting no character at all, which is the choice of most of the minor female soloists. Their approach is, however, largely forced on them by Gilbert's staging, which places the chorus in a line or a semi-circle, all waving the same finger at the same time like traffic cops in training.

It is almost as bad as his custom of placing every solo, duet or quartet centre, with the singers playing straight to the audience rather than to each other.

Toronto Daily Star 2nd January 1963

D'Oyly Carte's "Mikado" Thrills Capacity House

by Louis R. Guzzo

Arts and Entertainment Editor, The Times

Gilbert and Sullivan dead? Nonsense. They Live – and uproariously – in the spirit of the fabled D'Oyly Carte Opera of London. The British troupe opened its World's Fair engagement with "The Mikado" last night at the Opera House, and a capacity audience displayed its pleasure repeatedly with applause and laughter.

It is an elegant production, visually and vocally. The sets are intentionally synthetic, offering commentaries in themselves on Gilbert's displeasure with the Japanophiles of his day. The costumes are grandly correct and the make-up authentic, the minor exceptions purposely promoting exaggeration.

Kenneth Sandford's Pooh-Bah was a model of excellence, the kind of portrayal Savoyards dream about. The essence of Gilbert's satire, Pooh-Bah is the ideal bureaucrat in the restrained interpretation Sandford gives him.

A few instances of faulty coordination, in which the orchestra fell behind the singers, marred the opening, but the ensembles – particularly the second-act madrigal – were hauntingly beautiful.

It's a thrilling production by the handsomest of companies.

Seattle Times, 1962

'The Gondoliers' Static, Dreadful

LAST night the D'Oyly Carte Opera Company of London presented "The Gondoliers" at the O'Keefe Centre. Even if Toronto audiences did not have last summer's excellent, Stratford version of this Gilbert and Sullivan opera as a standard of comparison the performance could only be ranked as dreadful.The debacle was partly – only partly – the result of poor singing, weak acting, static and unimaginative staging, timid and capricious conducting, lack lustre orchestral playing, a mumbling, frozen chorus, amateurish dancing, colourless costumes, old-fashioned sets and irrational lighting.

The remainder of the blame lies with the inhuman schedule set by impresario S. Hurok and the Centre. Last night's performance was the company's fifth in 48 hours. Five of the soloists sang major roles in every one of these performances. It's a wonder they could stumble on stage, let alone act or sing.

The biggest fault of all, however, is in George Foa's staging. Foa has broken the Gilbertean mould slightly, but has apparently not bothered to invent action to keep the stage interesting during the many dull spots in Gilbert's book. For that matter, even Gilbert's best moments are hardly utilised.

Far Behind Stratford

Principal comedian John Reed and Kenneth Sandford were, by Stratford standards, uninventive, characterless and dull. Mr. Sandford was a couple of notches below Mr. Reed, and both of them far, far behind Stratford's Douglas Campbell and Jack Creley.

Toronto Daily Star, 29th december 1962

On the Aisle

Unseasoned D'Oyly Carte "Mikado" is opened in din of Opera House

NOT too much can be said for the return of the D'Oyly Cartes in "The Mikado," which launched a brief engagement in the Civic Opera house Tuesday night. Settings and costumes were fresh and bright, a few of the performances had a salty tang in the general air of unseasoned amateurishness, and if the impeccable Isidore Godfrey in the pit was haunted by memories of greater days his conducting gave no sign.

John Reed's Ko-Ko and Kenneth Sandford's Pooh-Bah came closest to the point in a troupe badly in need of a director with authority and a style with spine. Mr. Reed is small, alert and crisp, with feet that seem to hang in the air as if suspended from the knees. They are funny feet in the Charleston image, and he has flair. His problem is that he has no idea when to stop and his stage business grows interminable. Mr. Sandford has the well oiled baritone, the unction and the air – should think time and a surer skill would do the trick.

Aside from Donald Adams, the Mikado of older days, most of the others seem incurably provincial. Thomas Round is no Nanki-Poo even when he finds the pitch, Jennifer Toye's amplified "The Moon and I" is torture to the unprotected ear, and Gillian Knight's Katisha is rather like a caricature of Turandot – which is not such a bad idea.

But a dab of this and a dash of that get you nowhere in a D'Oyly Carte realm once so amusingly authoritative. Few things are more futile than satire ineptly done.

Chicago Daily Tribune, 20 December 1962

D'OYLY CARTERS LAY AN EGG

CUBA, Rome and Greece have been joined by the D'Oyly Carte. The dismal news this morning is that the greatest Gilbert and Sullivan company of the lot has gone to pot.

Last night's performance of "The Mikado," opening a two-week stay further including "The Pirates of Penzance," "The Gondoliers" and "Iolanthe," was utterly miserable. I had so looked forward to denouncing recent companies we have seen of the Savoyards, but what happens? Along comes the hereditary group, under management of granddaughter, Bridget D'Oyly Carte, and "The Mikado," of all things, lays an egg!

Yielding to no one in his undying passion for all the works of Gilbert and Sullivan (infinitely superior to the sold out novelty of "Mr. President"), I must confess I was struck speechless by the listless, amateurish, deadly performance of this most popular of the Gilbert and Sullivan pace-setters.

Everything about the overture was all wrong and when the Principals came on, matters were worse. These players have a certain ability to sing (a fair novelty) but in the style of a genial shire's volunteer choral society. This talent was confused by, I hope, conductor Godrey's unfamiliar musicians, but worse than that, it was hopelessly uninspired, bored. To be bored by "Mr. President" is one thing, but to be bored by something infinitely wittier, more timely (despite its 77 years) is unforgivable.

The fault, I think, lies not with the comfortable principals and chorus, but with management which permits a guaranteed sure thing to go down hill as quickly as the, once, august D'Oyly Carte company.

How can this sort of outrage occur? One had noted with interest the anticipation of the London press for the productions which were to follow expiration of the D'Oyly Carte copyright last year. One gleaned, most reluctantly, of productions of the Savoy operas from such as Sir Malcolm Sergeant and Sir Tyrone Guthrie that they did not come up to expectations. Still, one had the feeling that the true Savoyards would conquer younger generations.

But - how miserably short-sighted is management! Instead of employing a full-scale orchestra, instead of giving us rich, full, finely enunciated voices, the D'Oyly Carte gives us a thin, under-trained, orchestra (Oh for the Hudson River Day or Night - Line), amateur voices, mediocre diction and the most irrelevant playing. Surely these gifts could have been found and could have been afforded, they are not here.

Instead, we have the worst, habits of amateurs - one almost can hear the cast count for its laughs - and we have a wholly uninspired performance of a musically brilliant, verbally alive work. Of the company I could find only a sparkle from Jennifer Toye, not, at all well costumed, but at least ALIVE.

I hope to be a Savoyard till I die. I think Gilbert and Sullivan among the wittiest collaborations ever I have seen or heard. But I heartily resent what an obviously unknowing management, the founder's granddaugher, has done to a once stimulating, richly amusing, marvellous company, So amateurish have some of our own companies been that I imagine some will find enjoyment in this production.

But the what-might-have-been is heartbreaking. the present D'Oyly Carte company is inexcusable. How marvellous this group once was! How cynical its flat, dull efforts now seem! How depressing it is to hear these lovely numbers limp by without any desire whatever for that once treasured thing, an encore!

The Washington Post, 16th October 1962

G & S GONDOLIERS WERE KIND OF TIRED

And now consider, class, the word "new."

A simple enough word, you'd say, solid, sturdy, compact. And yet this strange little word enjoys amazing elastic qualities which enable it to be twisted and stretched to startling lengths.

For instance, we speak of the "new" moon, but it's the same old moon playing coy. And Detroit turns out what it calls all "new" cars, which are the same old cars with the chromium shifted around. For a time there was the "new" look for women, but that turned out to be the same old look with some of the lumps tucked out of sight.

And, finally, there are what the D'Oyly Carte Opera Company calls "new" productions, which strangely look and sound exactly like the old ones.

This, indeed, promised to be a new production. But last night it turned out to be a very old one. Not just old in words and music– after all, there'll be no tampering with the masters' work while there's still a single D'Oyly Carte left on guard – but old in concept and execution. Here are the same gestures, movements, inflections, groupings and bits of business as usual, And, worse yet, there's an old and tired rhythm to the production that, makes The Gondoliers plow along as sluggishly as a garbage scow.

Now it's unfortunate, perhaps, that just this summer at Stratford we had the opportunity to see The Gondoliers mounted with youthful imagination and invention by the keen young Canadian, Leon Major. And we certainly don't expect the same irreverent hi-jinks from D'Oyly Carte.

But there can be no excuse for such a sorry lack of vigour, of pace, of grace and of enthusiasm. Why, even the second act dance, the Cachucha, the most obvious opportunity for a little display of spirit, looked like round-up time in the stockyards.

The D'Oyly Carte may consider this a "new" production, but then some people still call this hemisphere the New World – 550 years after its discovery.

EVANS SUMS IT UP . . .
It's old wine . . . in an old bottle

The Telegram, Toronto, 29th December 1962

Gilbert's ridicule lives on

By EMRYS BRYSON

"Patience" probably went down better last night than anything the D'Oyly Carte Opera Company have done at the Nottingham Theatre Royal this week. Maybe it struck a chord which yearns for the same ridicule to be poured on the junk that frequently passes for art nowadays, on the meaningless, ingrown bosh that clings like a thick fuzz to painting, poetry, music and sculpture. Would "Patience" have lasted so long if Gilbert had stuck to his original plan of satirising the Church?

In floppy bow tie, peg-top trousers and wilting postures, John Reed glided beautifully along his mystic way – a path which hilariously crossed that of the massive Lady Jane (Christine Palmer, formidable as ever), there was a splendid milkmaid Patience from Ann Hood, the epitome of commonsense and firm vocal tone. And Kenneth Sandford added another of his relaxed, superbly-timed portraits as the narcissistic Archibald, doomed to have every woman fall in love with him.

Nottingham Evening Post, 13th May 1967

AUDIENCE HAILS 'PATIENCE' HERE

By DONALD DIERKS The San Diego Union's Music Critic

TWENTY days after its first two performances here this season, the D'Oyly Carte Opera Company returned for a final performance with its powers of musical and humorous persuasion undiminished. Thursday night, for an anything but full house at the Civic Theater, the Savoyards presented Gilbert and Sullivan's "Patience."

The players in principal roles were the same as those that were seen in "The Mikado" and "The Pirates of Penzance." They go from one role to the next with apparent ease, great skill and large amounts of zest.

From the vocal and musical standpoint, however, the fact that these same singers sing each performance causes its inevitable toll of voice fatigue. Voices can not always be fresh, rested and in top form with such a schedule of performances – and they were not last night.

Kenneth Sandford in the part of Archibald Grosvenor, an Idyllic Poet, did much to make the operetta the success it was. It is a grateful part and one he made the most of comically and vocally. The other poet, Reginald Bunthorne, was played by John Reed, with scarcely less success.

San Diego Union, 21st March 1967

G and S hit a low note

BY DAVID GILLARD – *Utopia Limited, Gilbert & Sullivan. D'Oyly Carte, Royal Festival Hall*

'UTOPIA LTD.' was G & S's penultimate collaboration and had not until a couple of month's ago, been professionally revived since its first performances in 1893.

One can see why, in truth, it is a pale contrived yawn-inducing shadow of its predecessors.

The person responsible for the production remains, wisely, anonymous while the singing and diction do no justice at all to the high standards once set by D'Oyly Carte, though there are some keenly judged performances by such stalwarts as Kenneth Sandford and John Reed.

Sadly, the evening adds neither prestige nor distinction to the company's centenary celebrations.

Daily Mail, 18th July 1975

Daft yet adorable, that's Ida

IN Ida's never-never land, she's created a ladies' university where the male in all his forms is rigorously excluded (even cock-crow is celebrated by a singularly accomplished hen). But Ida (Barbara Lilley) was espoused at one year of age, in one of those quixotic Gilbertian turns of plot which turn up more than once in the G & S repertoire, to Hilarion, son of belicose King Hildebrand, who 20 years later is determined to enforce the match.

Now there's a daft and adorable plot for you. But you forgive it when it provides such opportunities for Kenneth Sandford, as Hildebrand, and John Reed, as the heroine's disagreeable old pa, King Gama.

Sandford has spent so long playing in grandiose costumes that he does it to the life (catch a glimpse of his stately stride off-duty and you'll see what I mean!). And with this particular costume – mythical Atlantis visualised by the designer of "Up Pompeii" – he cannot and does not fail. Great stuff, great comedy. Though the repeatedly low-pitching of some of the king's songs does give his high baritone some minor difficulties, damping down the vocal clarity and projection of which he is normally a master.

Eastern Daily Press, 1977

Enjoyable lustre to 'Ruddigore'

THE chief pleasures of this production are the Sir Despard of the excellent Kenneth Sandford, in the guise of the Bad Baronet; and as "reformed character" with Judi Merri's outstanding Mad Margaret.

Mr. Sandford has been a G & S principal for something approaching 20 years. Yet he is so fresh, so inventive in his every performance, that one could believe he was delighting in his material for the very first time.

His Bad Baronet is a joyful nonsense of flashing eyes, marvellously exaggerated gestures, and syncopated movement which seems to dictate the music rather than the other way round. His "reformed being," on the other hand, is a mock-righteous figure like a house-trained curate beyond Miss Austen's imaginings!

Surely no one could better his supreme timing and swooping voice (a sort of basso profundo parallel of Dame Edith Evans' "...a handb-a-a-g?") in his thunderous threat to give his family pictures to the nation so that "no one will ever look upon them again".

Eastern Daily Press, June 1974

Going for a song

MEET a man who sings for a living and paints for a hobby – Kenneth Sandford, who is principal baritone of the D'Oyly Carte Opera Company and is pictured here with a portrait he painted of another member of the company, John Reed. The D'Oyly Carte is currently presenting a season of Gilbert and Sullivan operas at Sadler's Wells Theatre, and visitors to the theatre can also see an exhibition of paintings by Kenneth Sandford in the dress circle bar. Mr Sandford is pictured at the opening of the exhibition, which runs until February 29.

Islington Gazette, 30th January 1976

Sadler's Wells Theatre

The Gondoliers

by ELIZABETH FORBES

IT is very difficult to be objective about the D'Oyly Carte productions of the Savoy Operas. Most of the regular audience is so passionately partisan that to criticize makes one feel like the subject of a Bateman cartoon, "the spectator who did not like Gilbert and Sullivan." Monday's performance of The Gondoliers, however, was not of the kind to raise anybody's temperature much above normal. Anthony Besch's straightforward production, and John Stoddart's pretty sets could certainly offend no-one, even if they have not the originality of, say, Tyrone Guthrie's superb *Pirates of Penzance*.

The performance was dominated, musically and dramatically, by the Grand Inquisitor of Kenneth Sandford, who exuded authority in every word, note, and gesture. John Reed was also an excellent Duke of Plaza-Toro, with Christine Palmer (the Duchess), Julia Goss (Casilda) and Colin Wright (Luiz) completing the Spanish contingent. The four Venetian lovers, who have some of the finest music that Sullivan ever wrote, in the finale of the first act, were all more than adequate. Ralph Mason and Thomas Lawlor, as the two Gondoliers both sang well, and achieved a perfect togetherness during their short joint reign as King of Barataria. Linda Anne Hutchison made a pretty Gianetta, though her voice was dangerously uncovered at the top. Pauline Wales sang Tessa with lovely creamy tone, and a nice sense of mischief.

The orchestra was a section of Philomusica of London, conducted with spirit by James Walker, especially in the Cachucha, which went with a real swing. This was one of the moments, when the performance seemed about to take wing, but somehow it never quite managed to get off the ground, except when Don Alhambra del Bolero (aptly named) was on stage.

Financial Times, 16th December 1970

THE D'OYLY CARTE CLINGS TO CUSTOM

By HERBERT WHITTAKER

In this day of long-haired youth and Beardsley revivals, one admits to approaching Patience seeking a new pertinence, hopeful that its satire on the Esthetic Movement will find a new echo in today's happenings. But, of course, one is wrong to expect the rock of the D'Oyly Carte to be affected by the passing of Beatles.

And so it turned out. The D'Oyly Carte Opera Company, which opened a week's engagement at O'Keefe Centre Monday night with Patience, remembers that its strength lies in its unchanging devotion to tradition. Enough that it should be forced by progress to perform in large auditoriums bringing with it scenery more portable than persuasive. The important thing is not to yield.

However, the pendulum swings for all of us and there is no escape. One must put Yorkville out of one's mind when gazing on the grandeur of Kenneth Sandford as Archibald Grosvenor. But the reward is immediate, for this singer is fully in control of his idyllic nonsense. With his entry upon the drab cemetery which is Bunthorne's Castle, the scene brightened and his first solo with Ann Hood's sprightly Patience was as delightful in artificiality and ease of style as in its solid musical accomplishment.

Daily Star, Toronto, 1968

Yeoman is Finely Wrought

BY ARLYNN NELLHAUS

CENTRAL CITY, Colo. – Fine voices and incisive characterisations marked the D'Oyly Carte Company of London's finely wrought Yeomen of the Guard (occasionally too much so) which opened this weekend a the Central City Opera House.

She Deserves Better

First there's Phoebe, who helped Fairfax escape because of her love for him. Peggy Ann Jones in the role is fresh-faced, sassy and mellow-voiced. You wish better than what she gets – Wilfred.

She's resigned, almost, to marrying the leaden, morose jailor and assistant tormentor. Kenneth Sanford's Wilfred is a man who comes to life with enthusiasm only when he considers the torture chamber or marriage to Phoebe. (But not for the same reasons.) When Phoebe, while she's wheedling his jail keys, puts her hand on his knee, he dissolves into blubber.

The Denver Post, 8th July 1968

Why the Yeomen got a raw deal

by CHRISTOPHER GRIER

THE D'Oyly Carte Company, now in residence at the Sadler's Wells theatre, is feeling pretty miffed. It has been torpedoed by the Arts Council and subjected to disobliging comments. There are counter charges of prejudice.

These I believe to be justified. An inverted snobbery about Gilbert and Sullivan undoubtedly exists in musical circles. More damaging, the company itself is sometimes dismissed as a guardian of ossified tradition and casual standards.

It presides, so it is claimed, over a sort of cosy, homely tribal rite, more suited to woollen-ears north of Watford than to sophisticated southerners.

This is an old and large reproach which D'Oyly Carte has learned to live with, it not to love. Unfortunately, there is something in it. The problem is pointed up by The Yeoman of the Guard.

Pretty to look at, decently acted and declaimed with fruity, stylised assurance – Patricia Leonard doing her Edith Evans bit as Dame Carruthers is not to be missed – it falls down on musical values. How come, in so restricted a repertory, that coordination between stage and pit should be so hard to achieve? Why do the strings sound so thin and the chorus so raw by normal professional standards ?

These are technical matters distinct from the slightly subdued flavour of the whole show – understandable enough under the circumstances.

On the credit side were Kenneth Sandford's Shadbolt, James Conroy-Ward's nimble Jack Point, Lorraine Daniels's spirited Phoebe, Jane Stanford's appealing Elsie and a most mellifluous account of that brave bounder Colonel Fairfax from Geoffrey Shovelton.

Such artists deserved better backing.

London Evening Standard, 21st December 1979

What a how-de-do on opera liquor

From DONALD McLACHLAN . NEW YORK, Tuesday

THE high school band played Rule, Britannia. At the foot of the aircraft steps the Mayor waited for his distinguished guests . . . and waited.

It was a Gilbert and Sullivan situation. As they said in *The Mikado* : 'Here's a how-de-do.'

For inside the plane that had brought the D'Oyly Carte Opera Company to America, the Customs men were on to something big.

Visitors to Central City, Colorado, are not allowed to import drink.

And on the 'little lists' of the 45 members of the company were 61 bottles of hard liquor.

Phillip Potter, principal solo tenor, said glumly: 'Last time we came to America we were allowed to bring six bottles each.

'So most of us stocked up at the duty-free shop before take-off at London.'

Joker

One or two on board tried to jolly the Customs man along: 'We use it as a throat spray,' a voice called from the back of the plane.

For Customs men there was 'no possible shadow of doubt.' But they unbent enough to call the director for advice. He decided to permit one bottle each.

Anne Sessions, an understudy, said: 'Don't get this wrong. The reason we brought out all this liquor is not that we are great drinkers – it's because it was so cheap.' (£1 2s. 6d. for whisky.)

After the bottles were all shared out among the company, the remaining, 16 were taken away by the Customs men.

Then the big tarmac reception went ahead.

In Central City, where the company will stay for six weeks, Mr Stanley Knight, the company, manager, said today: 'I brought a bottle like almost everyone else. The Customs men were very nice about it, but quite firm. It is the law, after all.

Daily Mail, 19th June 1968

ELLIOT NORTON WRITES:

D'Oyly Carte Players Perfect In Opening 'Patience' Opera

THE D'OYLY CARTE OPERA Company is back in Boston and better than ever. At the Savoy Theater on Washington St., the Savoyards of London gave a perfect performance of Gilbert and Sullivan's "Patience" Tuesday evening. The word is perfect.

Yes, there were occasional faults and lapses. Yes, some of the singers were occasionally less lucid in the elaborate lyrics than others. But the faults were tiny, minor, miniscule, the production was brilliantly sung, beautifully played in the high dry mock-comic style performers have always possessed and which is so exhilarating to watch. Call it perfect.

Kenneth Sandford, as Archibald the All Right, is more than All Right; he is magnificent. Coolly handsome, comically elegant, sighing with near gale force, he praises himself and his beauty with jaded acceptance and wishes dolefully that he were somehow not quite so wonderfully well endowed in beauty, in wisdom, in wit and in all the graces.

King-of Comical Cockneys

Mr. Sandford parades the exquisite follies of Archibald without so much as a single misplaced emphasis. His fooling is as broad as buffoonery and at the same time as elegant as a minuet, And when he finally, under threat of a curse, turns himself into a very common fellow in a bowler hat, he is a king of comical Cockneys.

Boston Record 1968

Gilbert and Sullivan and John Lennon

PATIENCE ceased to be headline material long ago and I don't for a minute buy the argument, found in the D'Oyly Carte souvenir program, that parallels exist between teenage worship of the Beatles and 20 love-sick maidens fawning over the "fleshly poet" – Reginald Bunthorne. On second thought, maybe I do.

Bunthorne is a composite caricature, combining Whistler's eyeglass and hair-style, Oscar Wilde's kneebreeches and mannerisms and the high-flown literary style of Swinburne. A John Lennon, perhaps?

Patience is palpably silly to modern eyes and lovable for that very reason. In the whole of the modern musical theatre we find nothing to surpass the sight of that monumental dowager, Lady Jane, mournfully standing beside her massive cello as the sun rises. And when was the last time we heard an exchange to match this one:

Bunthorne. "Tell me, girl, do you ever yearn?"

Patience: "I earn my living.'

Such lines can only be spoken by the pure of heart and the hollow of head. They can only be played absolutely straight. Save in a few instances, where the desire to milk an extra laugh overcame the discipline of stylisation, the D'Oyly Carte cast did the right thing.

In H.M.S. Pinafore and Iolanthe, Donald Adams stood out as practically the only one who did the right thing.Not so this time. His Colonel Calverly was a wonderful portrait of military bluster but Kenneth Sandford gave us a characterisation equally free from hardening of the nuances, by parlaying an utterly bland demeanor and a clerically detached speaking tone into a precis of priggishness.

Globe and Mail, Toronto, 23rd November 1968

D'Oyly Carte Opera Company Offers Tale of Delightful Phonies

The D'Oyly Carte Opera Company offered "Patience" last night at City Center. Possibly, overreacting to the goblins in the air, the reviewer went home with the distinct feeling of having attended an amusing party in a haunted house.

The amusing parts of "Patience" can be laid at the feet of W. S. Gilbert, never more precise in his demolition of Victorian hypocrisy (poetry division) and the D'Oyly Carte's stars – especially John Reed (Bunthorne) and Kenneth Sandford (Grosvenor).

Mr. Reed, as the cobwebby poet, and Mr. Sandford, as the open-air one, are delightful phonies, the only basic difference between them being that Mr. Reed knows he's a fake and Mr. Sandford, bowing under the weight of his own exquisite purity, doesn't.

The objection, and you've heard it before, is to the D'Oyly Carte's refusal to re-think the work in terms of today's stage.

Nobody wants to see a rock version of "Patience," but surely the company should do something about the utterly dull gowns of the chorus, the rigid blocking, the anticlimactic encores, and the "traditional" rigmarole that muffled last night's performance as 10 layers of varnish would muffle a wonderful old painting.

DAN SULLIVAN.

The New York Times 1st November 1968

'Mikado' Still a Crowd-Pleaser

BY WILLIAM LEONARD

IF one is to judge by the brevity and conservatism of the D'Oyly Carte Opera company's engagement at the Auditorium, Gilbert and Sullivan may not be the giants they once were.

But when their brilliant product, despite its age, is spun forth with style and spirit and skill, it possesses as much vitality and appeal as it did in good Queen Victoria's day.

"The Mikado," winding up the company's two-day, three-performance stand yesterday, was a glistening tribute not only to Gilbert and Sullivan, and to magnificent performers, but to the good taste of audiences that packed the big playhouse afternoon and evening. There were older customers harking back to yesteryear, and there were youngsters seeing their first Gilbert and Sullivan.

All ages seemed to enjoy the comedy as much as the melody. The D'Oyly Carte players know how to be respectful of tradition, and at the same time to inject lively touches that are fresh.

Chicago Tribune, 2nd December 1968

Great G & S Comes to Seattle

By WAYNE JOHNSON,
The Times' Arts and Entertainment Editor

THE brightest, bounciest musical company that has hit Seattle in some time breezed into the Opera House last night.

The most important thing to say at once about this group – the D'Oyly Carte Company of London – is that it will present its final Seattle performance ("Pinafore" is the work) tonight. If you like Gilbert and Sullivan or – to be less specific – if you like tuneful, rollicking theatrical entertainment, you should catch this show.

'THE MIKADO' is now 83 years old, but it seems newer and fresher than the recent batch of musicals which wear assertive newness and topicality as a badge of honor – and become dated within a month.

And you're not likely to enjoy it more than when it is offered by the D'Oyly Carte Company which has itself kept alive by keeping Gilbert and Sullivan alive for more than 90 years. It is not often possible to see definitive productions of anything, and although other top-flight companies occasionally stage good G & S productions, it is still the D'Oyly Carte Company which has the traditions, the talent and the continuing high standards to be able to provide the last word in G & S production.

The Seattle Times, 11th December 1968

D'Oyly Carte offers 'Mikado'

By JAY CARR

Detroit News Drama and Music Critic

THE sun may have set on the British Empire but, on the whole, it still shines benignly on Gilbert and Sullivan as maintained by those staunch guardians of the Savoyard tradition, Britain's D'Oyly Carte Opera Company.

The predictability that clings to the D'Oyly Carte evenings would be the undoing of many a troupe. Here it's an asset. Sitting through a D'Oyly Carte production is rather like settling into one of those over-stuffed, velvet-covered sofas. Your comfort is assured so long as you're not allergic to a little dust.

KENNETH SANDFORD'S Pooh-Bah is one of the D'Oyly Carte treasures. Last night his singing wasn't especially fresh, but his projection of disdainful corruptibility (wouldn't your corruptibility be disdainful if you could trace your ancestry to a string of protoplasmic globules, as Pooh-Bah can?) was the evening's most consistently expert piece of work.

The Detroit News, 27th November 1968

Bad case of mime in a good Mikado

By HERBERT WHIKTTAKER

Last night, I was favored by the company of two of the New Savoyards, Junior Division. They were in the happy state of loving The Mikado from recordings and were now seeing that remarkably happy creation in the flesh.

"It's too funny," was the surprising comment of one of them.

If Junior Savoyard No. 1 was referring to John Reed when he made his comment, I quite agree. Mr. Reed has a bad case of mime, as if he were used to playing largely to foreign audiences. I feel that a Ko-Ko has enough to do making the Gilbertian jokes funny by making them clear without setting up a side-circus.

And to crown all, Mr. Reed, who thinks that it is amusing to bring Gilbert and Sullivan up to date by introducing the Charleston, even stoops so low as to answer the Mikado's question about Nanki-Poo's whereabout with: 'Would you believe Forest Hill ?'

Kenneth Sandford's Pooh-Bah is blandness itself, of course, but there was a suggestion that the big balloon was not in full buoyancy last night.

Toronto Globe, 25th, 1968

Some Sparks Left in the Old 'Mikado'

By Hewell Tircuit

THE older one gets, the less one feels like Queen Victoria. Sitting through D'Oyly Carte's Tuesday opening of "The Mikado," I was definitely amused.

Julia Goss was a wonderfully scatter-brained Yurn-Yum, scoring a real flight of song with her first entrance, "Three Little Girls in School." She, Jane Metcalfe and Roberta Moreel managed to clown while remembering their ladylike poses. Even the occassional Cockney "slips" were achieved with grace.

Actually, from a purely vocal point, the show-stopper was Patricia Leonard's Katisha. She tore into her big rage songs as though they were from one of Verdi's Spanish melodramas.

So too, the masterful performance of Kenneth Sandford as Pooh-Bah ("The Lord High Everything Else") was most impressive. The sense of timing the little flick of scorn in the eye, even the fan business, were deftly tossed off. To be a comic and remain that subtle – there's something for you.

San Francisco Examiner, 1978

Gilbert and Sullivan and 'The Mikado'

By DONNA PERLMUTTER

Performing that bread-and-butter staple "The Mikado," night after night must severely tax the powers of imagination, even those of the most ardent Savoyards. So when the D'Oyly Carte Opera Company opened with Gilbert and Sullivan's best-seller at the Greek Theatre Tuesday it had clearly come up against one of those dutiful, perfunctory occasions that strike from time to time. At least throughout the first act.

Matters improved appreciably after that. And even at its lowest ebb the D'Oyly Carte can always safeguard the fortunes of G&S.

Otherwise all was as well as could be expected in the town of Titipu, The company's 103-year old tradition still can be relied upon to deliver a special brand of performance. Wit mingles with pathos, satire with sentiment – all in understated tones. The bombastic charade commonly made of G&S is gratefully absent here. D'Oyly Carte's most mediocre surpasses many another company's best.

One decided casting improvement, however, was the Katisha of Patricia Leonard. This so-called loathesome lady avoided comic exaggeration. She portrayed the character with intelligence and even managed grandeur in her scorn. What's more she commands a contralto of considerable quality and enunciates clearly.

The rest of the veteran cast went through its paces with accustomed finesse. John Reed pouted and puckered, sobbed and shuddered, tripped and skipped (even interpolated a mini-Charleston and a suggestion of disco). Mostly, though, his petite Ko-Ko vitalised the proceedings at every hilarious turn.

As his perfect complement Kenneth Sanford's immensely cultivated Pooh-Bah countered with a molasses like drollery both noble and wry. His wonderfully stylised lumbering made for a Lord High Everything Else of alluring inscrutability. Although Sanford has little voice left and no low notes, his performance is one to treasure.

Los Angeles Herald, 15th June 1978

'Iolanthe' of strength, beauty

By W. L. HORMANN

TRADITION can be a dull and deadening thing; but the English have been able to maintain so many of theirs as 'living' traditions, and the D'Oyly Carte Opera Company demonstrates very vividly that this can apply to musical traditions such as G & S as well.

On Monday night it opened its first Australian tour at the Canberra Theatre with a delightful production of 'Iolanthe', a production so different from what we usually see as G & S that some people may feel a little disappointed on seeing it. 'Iolanthe' is one of the more 'serious' Savoy operas, but if it is played too seriously it becomes dull, and if, as is more usually the case, it is played too lightly it becomes mere farce.

To me, this production gets closer to the real intent of the words and the music than any other I have seen: but those who like their G & S 'hammed-up' may think otherwise. The humour is there, but delightfully understated as in the playing of John Ayldon (Earl of Mountararat) and Meston Reid (Earl Tolloller), and in a most engaging performance by Kenneth Sandford as Private Willis.

And the ladies are not outdone, with an imposing yet quietly humorous Queen of the Fairies from Patricia Leonard, an Iolanthe in Lorraine Daniels who certainly looked much too young to be Strephon's mother, and excellent singing support from the rest of the fairies.

Canberra, 16th May 1979

TAKING THE MICKEY OUT OF 'MIKADO'

FOR the hundreds of ardent Savoyards who gathered at the shrine last night the D'Oyly Carte Company remained the true defender of the faith.

To them the company, in its long-awaited Melbourne debut, could do no wrong and every number, every joke, was tumultuously applauded.

Giving comic theatre last night they were superb. But giving an opera, even a light one, they were not.

UPSTAGED

The stars, so brilliant visually, exagerrated their roles as they wrung the most from every moment so that they continually upstaged each other, and worse, the music.

Musical opinion generally holds that Sullivan sacrificed his gifts to those of Gilbert. In turning "The Mikado" into high farce, the D'Oyly Carte almost did away with them.

An example. In the trio "Here's a Howe-de-do." Koko unfurls an Australian flag, which is funny. But the number becomes merely a vehicle for Koko as he stretches it interminably with fans, flowers, knitting, a trolley ride across the stage, etc., repeating the trio each time.

Gilbert's wit stands best alone: such extremes become intrusive.

That major reservation aside, the performance could barely be faulted.

John Reed made Koko, the Lord High Executioner, a beautifully abject buffoon, engaging and hilarious, while Kenneth Sandford was a magnificently pompous Pooh-Bah, the Lord High Everything Else who is one of the comic theatre's immortal creations.

The Melbourne Herald, 24th July 1979

IT'S NO GO FOR MIKADO

PERHAPS I went to the Princess Theatre last week expecting too much!

The D'Oyly Carte Opera Company's presentation of Gilbert and Sullivan's "The Mikado" was in many ways disappointing.

When a company is promoted as the best you expect to see the best.

The Melbourne audience did not get a 100 per cent performance from the D'Oyly Carte company at the opening night of The Mikado.

It appeared as though most of the performers in the production did not think much of the audience.

Consequently they did not seem to give of their all.

I may be wrong, but it wouldn't be the first time an international group of performers has treated an Australian audience with less than respect.

The audience seemed to laugh at anything and the performers appeared to react by giving them anything.

Several Australiansisms were sprinkled throughout the performance which in some cases were funny.

Apart from the disappointments the night was not a complete waste.

A few performances stood out including John Reed as Ko-Ko, the Lord High Executioner, who together with a good voice was able to capture the character.

I suppose he should have, he has been with the company for 25 years.

Melbourne didn't see the best performance of the sorry wandering minstrel, Nanki-Poo, falling in love with Yum-Yum the executioner's wife, but it was reasonable.

Melbourne Sunday Observer, 29th July 1979

DOWN UNDER WITH G & S

by JILL SYKES

AT THE musical run-through of Iolanthe, the darkened theatre was dotted with voices singing along. Gilbert and Sullivan gets to you that way.

The D'Oyly Carte is making its first visit to Australia since it was formed by Richard D'Oyly Carte more than 100 years ago to perform the works of W. S. Gilbert and Arthur Sullivan — "not only in London, but out on tour as far as steamship travel would allow."

By the time plane travel made an Australian tour a possibility, costs had made entrepreneurs unwilling to take on so many people, and the D'Oyly Carte will only travel as an ensemble. It is only through the determination of the English producer Derek Glynne, working with Michael Edgley that 57 performers and technical people are here in 1979. "It isn't an advertising gimmick any more to say it is a $2 million production – because it is." said Glynne.

Wandering around backstage in Canberra, it was great fun to do some role spotting. John Reed, who plays the string of tetchy, nimble-footed Gilbertian characters, such as Sir Joseph Porter, Ko-Ko and the Lord Chancellor, was easy to pick – distinguished, however, for lively charm rather than tetchiness.

So was Kenneth Sandford, whose very presence, upswept eyebrows downwards, announced him as Pooh-Bah, Lord High Everything Else. More than 2,000 appearances in the Mikado and 22 years on sentry-go as Private Willis in Iolanthe have made him the longest-serving principal in the company.

"People think it might be boring", said Sandford. "But it isn't. You are given a rare opportunity to develop and develop a role like no other actor can.

I think I would almost play without an audience. I find the characterisations fascinating anyway. The fact that there is an audience is a bonus."

Sandford says Gilbert's librettos are so good that there is always something more to be found in them.

Productions have relaxed over the years. too. In the latest D'Oyly Carte version of The Gondoliers. produced by Anthony Besch, Sandford's lascivious Grand Inquisitor is allowed far more licence than he was two decades ago. Where he used to play some lines straight-faced, he call now put a twinkle in his eye: "We have found the man underneath." Said with a twinkle in the eye, naturally.

The Sydney Morning Herald, 19th May 1979

He never gets tired of G and S

KENNETH SANDFORD relaxed and wrote letters home from his motel late yesterday, pleasantly aware that this is rest week, sandwiched between the "Mikado" shows in Brisbane and two weeks of performances (seven shows a week) from next Monday here and Wellington.

Twenty-two years a principal pleyer with D'Oyly Carte, Sandford begins to feel the pall of travel, and 30 years in show business.

In his mid-fifties, his family grown up and the need for financial security behind him, he hankers to move into grand opera while there is still time.

"I'd like to sing some of the music I've always wanted to sing," he says. "And I'd like to go back to my painting."

But now, as during 22 years, Gilbert and Sullivan has him hooked.

"I suppose I've stayed with G and S because I'm essentially a performer, I need a stage. I like character work . . ." he says.

One never gets tired of Gilbert and Sullivan, that's one of the great joys – and I've got some of the most interesting characters."

He ranges from a grand inquisitor to a Church of England clergyman, a jailer to a flamboyant despot. Most of all he likes being Dr Dayly in "The Sorcerer."

Sandford will say: "I've a feeling for G and S now. I think we play it as it should be played. Gilbert and Sullivan is something everyone knows how to play until they actually come to do it."

Auckland Star, 27th June 1979

New vitality sustained in 'Sorcerer'

WHY Gilbert & Sullivan's "The Sorcerer" is not performed more often, by amateur companies as well as by the pros, is something which has always puzzled me – it's so full of good fun, good tunes and good character roles.

That the D'Oyly Carte Opera Company who presents it so sparklingly, as they illustrated last night at the Theatre Royal Norwich, should now withdraw it altogether from their repertoire, is quite incomprehensible

When the company opened their two-week stay in Norwich last Monday, it was my pleasure to note the new vitality which had entered into them since they were publicly pilloried by the Arts Council. With just a few minor reservations, this splendidly enjoyable "Sorcerer" more than maintains that impression.

It is the perennial yet ever-fresh Kenneth Sandford – a phenomenon who never ceases to delight, and surprise – who provides the true centre piece, as the lovable and love-lorn Rev. Dr. Daley. His singing of "Time was when love and I were well acquainted" a Victorian drawing room gem by any measure – was given such felicity, and feeling by him that it achieved that rare unity of being both genuinely funny, and genuinely poignant.

The D'Oyly Carte are now fighting for their existence. On the strength of this last two weeks, they deserve to win. But were I to be devil's advocate for the Arts Council – which the gods forbid – I'd suggest that the exhilarating spring cleaning they've evidenced during this fortnight, though well advanced, if not yet wholly completed. May they finish the job – and live for many a year to come.

Eastern Daily Press, 6th June 1981

Chapter 7

THE CHARACTERS

IT has always been Ken's wish that the wealth of experience he has gained during his long association with the Savoy Operas should not be wasted. Too many performers make the mistake of thinking that Gilbert and Sullivan is easy, requiring only modest singing and acting skills. This common misconception irritates Ken who, after 42 years in the service of G & S, still loves to analyse and discuss dialogue and characterisation in the hope of gaining fresh insight into the words and music that he so admires. This constant search for the essence of a role may surprise the many admirers who consider his interpretations to be the benchmark by which all others are judged, but his desire for self-improvement is the secret of his success and he is anxious to share his approach and techniques with those who would follow in his footsteps. To that end, the following chapter is devoted to the eight characters for which he is best known, with the aim of encouraging the same in-depth application for which he is rightly acclaimed. He would stress that his methods are not the only methods; he simply hopes to open minds to the possibilities available to those who strive to do justice to the creations of Gilbert and Sullivan. If his thoughts and opinions serve to stimulate artistic imagination he will be a happy man, content in the knowledge that his life's work may help to perpetuate the Savoy Operas into the next millennium.

PRIVATE WILLIS

'I am generally admired'

'A poor look out for a soldier stout'

IT is often said that there is no such thing as a small part in a show; all parts are important because they make a vital contribution to the whole piece. Private Willis in *Iolanthe* provides an excellent example of a small, but significant, role without which the opera's plot could not reach its conclusion. It also illustrates Ken's point about falling into the trap of thinking that performing G&S is a breeze. In point of fact, Private Willis presents challenges unlike any others in the Savoy canon, demanding the sort of commitment, discipline and specific characterisation to tax any performer. It is by no means easy; on the contrary, it is easy to do badly. There is nothing more embarrassing than to watch a Willis with two left feet trying to march across the stage before fumbling his rifle and standing like a sack of potatoes in front of the sentry-box. It is a part which can only be made to look easy when in the hands of an expert performer.

First and foremost Willis is a Grenadier guardsman standing sentry outside The Houses of Parliament. The performer who forgets this immediately loses all credibility, regardless of how well he sings. This in itself presents a problem; the required military bearing, so essential to a convincing portrayal, calls for experience of parade-ground drill and the correct handling of a rifle. In this respect Ken was lucky. The years of drilling in the R.A.F. proved invaluable, but he was, understandably, concerned that the manoeuvres with which he was familiar would not be those used by Victorian soldiers. In his early days with the D'Oyly Carte it struck him as odd that a company which prided itself on its traditions was unable to reproduce the original staging of W. S. Gilbert, who must have known something about the drill of Victorian times. He wanted to present an accurate portrayal of a late 19th-century guardsman, but opted for what he knew, particularly as this seemed to be acceptable to the management. Over the years Ken has received many letters from elderly military types offering advice on the authentic moves, but these merely confused the issue. It seemed to him that if such advice resulted in the rifle being held in front of his face, he would lose his only means of communication with the audience – his eyes. Gestures were out of the question, as the demands of the character necessitated standing absolutely still whilst outside the sentry-box and with the bearskin and chin-strap covering his forehead and jaw, connecting with the audience was down to the way he used his voice and eyes.

Over the years he has concluded that it is more important to appear convincing as a soldier than to be strictly accurate in appropriate drill. Bearing in mind that contemporary audiences have little concept of how a Victorian guardsman would have marched or held a rifle, Ken feels sure that the somewhat less energetic moves of that time may appear unconvincing when compared with those to which we are accustomed nowadays. His advice to any prospective Private Willis on this thorny issue is to learn from a soldier or ex-serviceman how to march, come to attention, stand at ease and correctly move the rifle between shoulder and ground. As far as overseas performers are concerned, he thinks that achieving a credible military appearance is vital, be the drill American, Australian or from any other country. Provided that the use of the rifle does not resemble the twirling of a baton in a marching band (as he once witnessed to his horror in an American production), he is confident that a little military licence will not undermine the overall performance.

Having established the physical demeanour of Willis, the next consideration must be the interpretation of his song given the restriction of absolute stillness. Under usual theatrical circumstances a singer enjoys the luxury of movement, where appropriate, or the use of carefully considered gestures to help his portrayal. In the case of Private Willis, however, the performer may only rely on clear diction, word colouring and eye movement to involve the audience and this requires both concentration and self-discipline. In Ken's opinion, it is essential to invite the audience members to share the thoughts of Willis as opposed to singing directly to them. This subtle distinction can be achieved by using the imagination – the corner stone of acting technique. An ordinary soldier standing sentry throughout what might be a cold, wet night must find a way to take his mind away from the boredom and discomfort of such an onerous duty. His homespun philosophy and witticisms at the expense of politicians are the product of long hours of solitary contemplation. How else is he to while away the time and ignore the stiffness in his joints and muscles? The words of the song are merely thoughts set to music; the fact that they are a vehicle for Gilbert's satire should not be considered – if the singer sincerely believes he is that ordinary guardsman, the audience will quickly perceive the author's intentions. This spark of belief will automatically ignite the light in the eyes, bringing a glint of humour and fun which would not otherwise be conveyed across the footlights.

Another problem concerns the dialogue with The Queen of the Fairies. How far should Willis go in flirting with her and should he come out of character to do this? Ken believes that it is essential to remain a soldier throughout; any small movement or acknowledgement of her flattering comments almost involuntary and certainly against his better judgement. It is necessary to imagine the consequences for a sentry protecting the seat of government caught failing in his duty. However much he is tempted by the attentions of an attractive woman, he must try to keep cool and professional. Ken's handling of this situation was masterly; any reaction as a red-blooded male quickly followed by a recollection of his position, to hilarious effect. His response to the Queen's line:

> *'If I yielded to a natural impulse, I should fall down and worship that man'*

was to emit a prolonged and appreciative *'Ooh!'* which he quickly turned into an embarrassed clearing of the throat. The only time he allowed himself to come momentarily out of his military stance was during the exit music of the Fairy Queen's song. As the chorus of fairies drifted from the stage, The Queen looked longingly back at him, prompting him to briefly place his hand on his heart in acknowledgement of the obvious chemistry between them. During the song itself, he confined his reaction to the romance of her words to a slight turn of the head, which allowed their eyes to meet and mingle. The subtlety of this approach highlighted the seeming hopelessness of their affection, imbuing the scene with a humour and poignancy that less restrained reactions could never achieve.

Ken offers a final word of caution. Having advocated a strict adherence to the military characterisation of Private Willis, he feels that it would be a pity to undermine the good work by giving in to the temptation to go for a cheap laugh in Act II Finale. Following The Queen's announcement:

> *'You are a fairy from this moment'*

it is usual for Willis to flex his newly-acquired wings in a comic 'fairy' dance. Ken advises against taking the obvious opportunity to mince across the stage in camp, balletic fashion. He suggests that the humour comes from the astonished Willis appearing to be unable to control his actions, as if his dance steps are the handiwork of an unseen fairy choreographer. As ever, he is of the opinion that carefully-considered 'less' is far more effective than tasteless 'more'.

THE VOICE

Having endeavoured to look credible as a soldier, it is essential for the performer to find a voice to match the established military mien; one which complements the characterisation rather than spoils the image. Ken always replied to The Queen as if responding to the Sergeant Major on the parade ground; barking out his name and rank in a tone that suggested that he had recently swallowed gravel. Private Willis may have very few lines, but their delivery is important in the overall scheme of the character and Ken is certain that there is no point in cutting a fine military figure if you speak like a wimp!

MAKE-UP

Not very much. Between bearskin, moustache and chin-strap very little of the face will be visible. Ken always applied a medium base colour, using a mixture of 5 and 9 grease paint or an equivalent pancake. A sentry standing guard in rain or shine would have a weather-beaten complexion and certainly not look pale. He used lip colour such as crimson lake grease paint to emphasise the mouth and, most importantly, he drew a black line with either an eye pencil or liquid eye liner both above and below each eye. This helped draw the audience to his only line of communication with them.

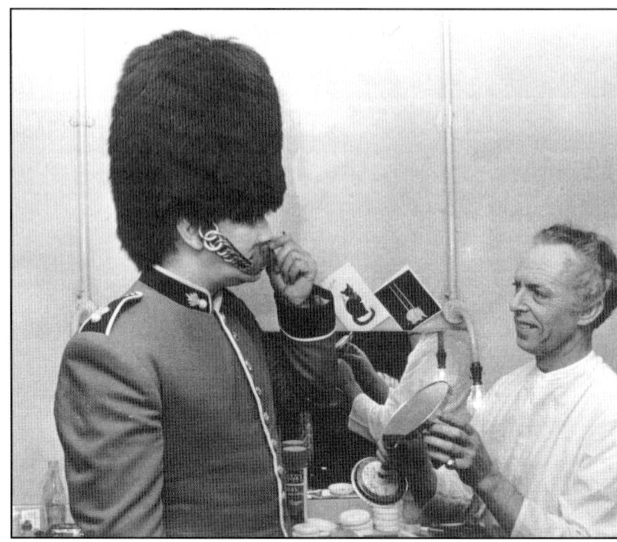

John Reed helps Ken with his moustache

HORROR MOMENTS

Ken was fortunate in that he suffered no memorable disasters in the guise of Private Willis, but he does recall his first appearance in the role at the Arie Crown Theatre in Chicago during the 1976 tour of North America. Marching across the biggest stage he had ever seen, he arrived outside his sentry-box to be picked up by an enormously powerful spotlight. Unable to see the musicians in the pit, let alone the front row of the vast auditorium, he was overcome by a feeling of total isolation and a claustrophobic sensation of standing on the edge of infinity in a black vacuum. Quite unsettled by this unpleasant experience, it required a real effort of concentration and courage to get him through his song.

He also remembers getting dressed for *Iolanthe* one evening when he noticed a smell of burning. Looking around his dressing room, he was shocked to discover that his bearskin was standing too close to one of the dressing table lights. The resulting singed patch left him wondering what he should do to avoid the wrath of the Wardrobe Mistress. With admirable presence of mind, he took a pair of sharp scissors and carefully trimmed the fur around the circumference so that the excised burnt section didn't appear as a gaping hole! Much to his relief, nobody remarked on his new, slim-line headwear.

HAPPY MOMENTS

During a performance at Hollywood's open-air Greek Theatre in 1978, Ken had just started his song at the opening of Act II, when he became aware of movement near his boots. Between the verses, he took the opportunity to slyly glance down and was astonished to find a racoon sitting at his feet looking up at him in quizzical fashion. The sight of this cuddly admirer almost threw him completely, but he somehow managed to get through the second verse and was rather disappointed when his companion trudged off into the darkness, leaving him to wonder what the racoon thought of his performance!

A FINAL THOUGHT

Ken warns against underestimating the artistic demands of a small role such as Private Willis. Small does not necessarily mean easy.

ARCHIBALD GROSVENOR

'Yes, Patience, I am very beautiful!'

'For what, we ask, is life without a touch of Poetry in it?

KEN is often asked which of the roles is his favourite. Although he loved something about all of them, if pushed to make a choice it would have to be Grosvenor in *Patience*. It is now 17 years since he last played that most rewarding of parts and he still misses the pleasure of performing a character which he describes as 'a gift' to any actor. He has often said that if he could be granted a wish, it would be to play the opening scene of Act II once more. In this unlikely event, he contents himself with performing a shortened version of it in concerts. Realising that he is nowadays a somewhat mature Grosvenor, he shamelessly delights in being surrounded by the 'Rapturous Maidens' of *The Magic Of Gilbert & Sullivan* chorus, most of whom are also not in the first flush of youth. Together they defy the clock, giving D'Oyly Carte devotees a tantalising glimpse back at one of Ken's finest characterisations.

On approaching the role for the first time, many performers may well feel intimidated by the florid dialogue and egocentric posing of such an unlikely man. Actors try to base a stage persona on the recognisable traits of others, but who has ever seen or met an Archibald Grosvenor? The delight of Gilbert's creation lies in the exaggeration of several human foibles within one larger than life man. When first preparing the role in 1957, Ken was faced with the problem of trying to convincingly portray the type of man who only existed in the fertile imagination of W. S. Gilbert. He had very little to go on and received no guidance from the company, so he embarked on a careful examination of every facet of the character in his search for the core of the 'idyllic poet'. At first sight Grosvenor is a complex personality, yet Ken believes that the key to the man is to be found, paradoxically, in his innate simplicity.

The physical appearance of Grosvenor was Ken's starting point and he soon came to the conclusion that elegance was going to be all-important. In this respect he was lucky; blessed with a tall, broad-shouldered figure and long, artistic hands he was able to develop an unhurried, gliding walk that was balletic, yet manly. The small book of poetry that he carried was a useful prop, enabling him to pose as if deep in creative thought, or turn over a page with studied grace. He decided that movements must be leisurely, but poised, as if giving a well-rehearsed act to please the ladies. Facial expression was going to be particularly important in conveying the underlying sadness and frustration of Grosvenor's life, so he adopted a permanent look of sorrow and world-weariness to highlight his unrequited love for the simple farm girl, Patience. This pained expression was also useful when overwhelmed by the cloying attentions of the lovesick maidens, when all Ken had to do was pause before replying to their demands for his attention. The resulting laughter made him realise that a look can be worth a thousand words if you have the courage to use the silence.

Ken's greatest difficulty was in coming to terms with the line:

'Yes, Patience, I am very beautiful'

Having a good physique was one thing, but his claim to beauty was quite another and he was concerned that he should not appear foppish or camp. Grosvenor is not a buffoon and it is important that his costume should be understated. Ken has seen productions in which he is dressed outrageously and it annoys him that directors cannot see that the humour lies in the man's conceit and not in his clothes. Ken's D'Oyly Carte costume struck the right balance, being neither flamboyant nor plain. He wore grey-green velvet breeches with matching jacket, a white frilled shirt with a large collar and floppy tie, green tights and plain black shoes. Admittedly, Ken felt anything but beautiful in the collar-length blonde wig and he was worried that he would not be able to present an image of masculine perfection when he felt rather ridiculous! That is where the simplicity came in. All he had to do was sincerely believe that every woman found him irresistible – the ultimate male fantasy. With this in mind it was easy to go on to the next stage of accepting Grosvenor's physical perfection as the driving force in his life. Grosvenor really believes that having women worship him is his reason for being and that the sacrifice of his own happiness is the price he must pay for sharing his beauty with a grateful world. Such martyrdom was bound to reflect in every aspect of his characterisation and Ken began to feel more comfortable with the part. As long as he kept sight of the fact that Grosvenor is, at heart, a simple man who requires nothing more from life than to live simply with his true love at his side, he could not go too far wrong.

It struck Ken that the other poet in the opera, Reginald Bunthorne, admits to being a con man. He uses his ability to write flowery, but meaningless, poetry as a ploy to attract women to him because it is the only way he can get their attention. Grosvenor, on the other hand, is a lousy poet who is sickened by all the female adulation but gets it anyway. He was beginning to get the point. The contrast in the motives of the rival poets made Ken all the more certain that he must play his part absolutely straight and with the utmost sincerity if he was to convey Gilbert's intentions of poking fun at male vanity, female fickleness and bad poetry. Having reasoned thus far, the Act II transformation of Grosvenor into an ordinary young man was not difficult for Ken. In physical appearance, mannerisms and speech he made the real personality everything his alter ego was not. Obviously, the change into short wig and loud check suit helped, but he replaced the elegant walk with a heavy-footed stride and the permanent sad expression with a happy grin. Again it was quite simple. Grosvenor's words in the preceding duet with Bunthorne gave him all the clues he needed. Ken is sure that elegance of figure and grace of movement are central to a successful portrayal, but recommends that the performer should not get bogged down in deep thought processes as he originally did. The character is uncomplicated, although the dialogue might initially suggest otherwise. Grosvenor sincerely believes that his handsome looks cause every woman to fall in love with him; if the actor can convincingly convey this to the audience, everything else will fall into place. There is no need to play for laughs; it is the very fact that that he takes himself so seriously that is funny - a conceited person is never aware of how ridiculous he, or she, is. The actor need only immerse himself in the fantasy and he will be well on the way to success.

THE VOICE

It is always important to give careful consideration to an appropriate speaking voice, which an actor hopes will reflect and enhance the physical appearance, personality and background of the character he is playing. Most people, at one time or another, have made the comment that an actor they do not like sounds the same in every part. Kenneth Sandford had a different voice for every role he played, but this was not a matter of luck. Having decided on how the character would look, move and think, he worked hard to find a voice to match. In the case of Grosvenor, he opted for a quiet, cultured speaking voice with a creamy tone which he hoped would add to the impression of unhappiness that he wanted to convey. Having decided on a softly spoken approach, it was necessary to look for dynamic contrast in the dialogue, lest his delivery become monotonous. Fortunately, Grosvenor presents many such opportunities, most obviously the *'Teasing Tom'* poem and the exchange with Bunthorne prior to their Act II duet. Ken stresses that variation of volume, tone, pace and colour in the speaking voice is a fundamental part of an actor's craft, yet this basic element is frequently neglected by inexperienced performers and the directors on whom they should be able to rely for guidance. He wishes that audio tape recorders had been freely available when he was first preparing his characterisations, as the benefits of listening to one's own voice as others hear it are obvious. It becomes clear that the voice that we hear in our head is very different to the voice that the audience hears. Archibald's transformation into a *'commonplace young man'* in Act II Finale calls for a dramatic change in speaking voice and, in the D'Oyly Carte production, Ken used a cockney accent, although he can see no reason why some other broad brogue would not be acceptable. The audience laughter at the change of voice is due to the fact that that it comes unexpectedly as much as to the accent used; it is the sudden change that is important and Ken happily espoused a working-class twang which never failed to bring the house down.

THE DIALOGUE

Grosvenor's dialogue always gave Ken enormous pleasure and by the time of the D'Oyly Carte's closure in 1982 he had learned to use his long experience to extract every last ounce of humour from his exchanges with the other characters. It was this role that taught him the perils of acting at acting and about the comedic rewards that a sincere delivery can bring.

The first scene with Patience is critical to the establishment of Grosvenor's personality and should be thoroughly prepared; however clever the words, the artist must never take them for granted or assume that they will interpret themselves. After the macho bluster of the Dragoon Guards, the arrival of the 'picturesque' Archibald, with his conceited posturing, should come as an unexpected contrast to surprise and delight the audience. Having registered his joy on seeing Patience, his expression must then convey the depth of his love for her even before he has spoken. He must allow sufficient time for her to look at him blankly before realising that she has not got a clue as to his identity. If his reactions to her failure to recognise him are hurried, he will miss the opportunity to show his mix of astonishment and injured feelings. This will provide an early chance to show his absurd pomposity on the line:

'Oh, Chronos, Chronos, this is too bad of you!'

The line should not be said with irritation, but with genuine surprise that anyone could possibly forget him. Ken's next piece of advice is given from painful experience. He recommends that time be allowed for audience reaction after the lines:

'Yes, Patience, I am very beautiful'
and
'Gifted as I am with a beauty which probably has not its rival on earth'

There was, invariably, someone in the audience who chose to laugh at him rather than at the character, so he always shared the fun with a subtle pause. Without taking his eyes from Patience, he used the silence to indicate his agreement with the sentiments expressed by the unkind giggler but never looked in their direction. These lines must not be said in such a way as to provoke the laughter, but should be delivered with complete sincerity as Gilbert intended. During the next few lines, Grosvenor should explain who he is and what he does in a quiet, but patronising, voice which only gains momentum to a rising climax on:

'I have loved you with a Florentine fourteenth-century frenzy for full fifteen years'

when the alliteration should be used to maximum effect. The declaration of their love and ensuing parting will benefit from a touch of melodrama, particularly if he intersperses his unhappy outbursts with a return to his usual bland conceit where the opportunity arises. It is important to say that the success of the scene is dependent on both performers. Patience must also say the dialogue with complete sincerity, unquestioningly accepting everything that Archibald tells her with innocence and wonder. There is no substitute for hard work and both should discuss and rehearse their characterisations until they are completely at home in this tricky scene. Ken's acclaimed Grosvenor was only as good as his Patience, the humour relying on both.

As mentioned earlier, the opening scene of Act II was always a favourite moment in Ken's working life, providing many opportunities to display his talent for the mysterious art of 'timing'. The first speech beginning:

'The old, old tale.
How rapturously these maidens love me'

needs to be said with quiet intensity, as if thinking aloud. Seeing Patience in his mind's eye, Ken imbued the lines with as much emotion as possible, but avoided the temptation to let his delivery become hammy. He feels that the ache in Archibald's heart is best expressed by restrained sorrow - once again, less is more. The dramatic intensity can be enhanced if Lady Angela has the courage to wait before disturbing this private moment on:

'Sir, will it please you read to us?'

This signals a return to reality for Grosvenor, who reluctantly moves into his well-oiled routine to please the ladies. Stung by the fact that Bunthorne can always be relied on to read them his poetry, Archibald should meet the challenge at his pompous best on:

'What am I but a trustee?'

The first poem needs to be recited with a measured, pedantic rhythm and Ken was careful to slightly emphasise the last word of each couplet to underline the childishness of the verse. His next line after Angela's sugary response to the poem provides an excellent example of how to time a line, as he allowed three to four seconds before saying:

'Here's another.'

This delay allowed him time to look at her with an expression of slight distaste before dutifully moving on to his next creation and it always made the audience laugh. A performer with less experience or vision may hurry on and miss the chance to share an amusing moment.

The underplayed recitation of the first poem is a spring-board into a complete change of style for the second and Ken took full advantage, declaiming the catalogue of Tom's misdemeanours with great animation of voice and gesture. It may be a statement of the obvious, but Ken advises against subtlety in the final couplet, preferring to stress the second syllable of *'totally'* to make a dreadful rhyme with *'corps de ballet'*. He would be the first to agree with any accusation of 'ham' acting in this section, justifying the over the top delivery as necessary dramatic contrast in a section which W. S. Gilbert designed as a ridiculous demonstration of the rewards of good over evil. Having discharged his self-imposed duty to read to the ladies, Grosvenor resumes his depressed air as he politely asks to be left alone, his offer to sing *'The Magnet and the Churn'* only made in an attempt to convince the ladies that their love for him is futile, as he is in love with the unattainable. With their departure, he is free to bemoan his fate and Ken thinks that Archibald should display a flash of anger on:

'A curse on my fatal beauty,
for I am sick of conquests!'

This is another glance at the real man behind the carefully-constructed façade and will help prevent the characterisation from becoming too bland, but it is important to remember that his outburst should not be said to the audience – he is merely thinking aloud, albeit in something of a temper.

With the unexpected arrival of Patience, his highly-charged emotions are still in full flight and the performer should seize the chance to revel in the passionate declarations of love, whilst she indulges in self-pity and moral rectitude. When played absolutely seriously by both actors, the humour of this unlikely conversation leaps out at the audience and the resulting laughter is the due reward of artistic integrity. Ken points out the importance of recognising one's place in a scene. Although both have wonderful lines, Patience's contribution should remain in the memory – it is her moment. An artist must realise when his character is dominant in a scene and when it is secondary to the action. There is nothing more amateurish than to steal a scene which is intended as a vehicle for another character; one must always know when to give and take on the stage.

The opening of the scene between Grosvenor and Bunthorne late in Act II was covered in chapter four, but Ken would add that Archibald needs to retain his smug composure until Bunthorne's threat to curse him. By so doing, his sudden collapse into quivering panic is all the funnier, particularly if played with great seriousness by both men. For those who never saw the D'Oyly Carte production, it is worth mentioning the addition of a few words not present in the libretto. After Bunthorne's line:

'You must cut your hair, and have a back parting'

Ken replied with:

'Beg pardon?'

said in such a way as to sound similar to *'back parting'*, which then required John Reed to repeat himself. Ken is unsure as to the origin of this subtle play on words, but it always caused some amusement. Grosvenor's final lines of the Act are straightforward, requiring only a much less refined tone and uncouth style to contrast with his earlier cultured turn of phrase.

In summing up his thoughts on Archibald Grosvenor, Ken can offer three important recommendations. Firstly, the character calls for such elegance and unhurried poise as to make him credible, despite his conceited posturing. Secondly, the performer must have courage, both to use the silence between lines to achieve comedic timing and to avoid the temptation of playing directly to the audience if they laugh at his supposed beauty. Finally, sincerity: keep this to keep the character.

'Oh, Mr. Bunthorne, reflect, reflect!'

MAKE-UP

Ken used a medium to pale base colour, which he thoroughly powdered down to give a matt finish. The 'alabaster' effect achieved by the use of baby powder proved useful in later years, when he recognised the need to fill in the cracks! He used more reddish-brown highlighting on his cheek bones than for other roles and also painted a full mouth with crimson lake grease paint in the hope of attaining a look of beauty. He shaped and defined his eyebrows and carefully drew a black line on the top eyelid and beneath the lower lid to emphasise his eyes. Ken never made up his hands, except as King Paramount in *Utopia Ltd.*

HORROR MOMENTS

Apart from the earlier-mentioned fiasco when Peggy Ann Jones likened him to a spaceman, his worst moments as Grosvenor were in connection with the quick change of costume prior to his entrance for Act II Finale. With just two minutes of dialogue in which to effect a complete change of clothes, shoes and wig, it was always a close call and, early in his career, he realised that the change needed to be planned with the precision of a military operation. With his dresser standing by in the wings and the help of the Ladies Angela, Ella and Saphir, who knew the exact order in which garments were discarded and assumed, he usually managed to get ready by the skin of his teeth, but there were many occasions when jacket buttons were fastened in the wrong holes and his wig on back-to-front. I can well remember watching the nerve-racking procedure whilst waiting to dance on after Ken, convinced that he would never be ready in time. Even after 25 years practice, that quick change represents the sort of theatrical nightmare that every performer experiences and he was always relieved to appear for the finale with his costume and dignity intact.

It is worth noting that the trousers of his checked suit were made several sizes too large, so that he could put them on over his velvet breeches. Such sensible practicalities are sometimes neglected by theatrical costumiers.

HAPPY MOMENTS

Having struggled through a performance with a very painful toe, Ken asked the advice of the St. John's ambulanceman on duty at Edinburgh's King's Theatre, who recommended that he should go to the local hospital at the end of the performance. Having found the hospital, he was uncertain as to which department he needed, so he limped through a dimly-lit area and hailed two passing interns. They informed him that non-emergency facilities had closed for the night but, after listening to Ken's story, offered to examine the inflamed digit. Leading him to a deserted operating theatre, they quickly diagnosed a septic toe and volunteered to deal with it immediately if he did not mind having it done without anaesthetic. Feeling quite sure that he would soon awaken from some horrible dream, Ken thanked them for their kindness and made a hasty exit, muttering about the alcohol intake of junior doctors. After enduring a night of considerable pain, he made an early-morning return to the hospital, where he was given a general anaesthetic whilst his toe was cauterised. In the recovery room, he was told not to drive his car for 24 hours, but nothing was said about taking time off from work. Ever the professional, he knew that the show must go on, so he caught the bus to the theatre and performed Grosvenor as never before. Drifting through the opera in a delightful haze, he felt that he had never sung or acted the role better and injected total sincerity into the line:

'I am called Archibald the Allright –
for I am infallible'

By the end of the show he could remember nothing about his performance, except that it was magnificent and that if any of his colleagues had been there, they would have agreed with him! Looking back on that surreal experience, Ken has often thought that if he could have bottled and sold the anaesthetic to insecure performers, he would have been a millionaire by now.

A FINAL THOUGHT

Grosvenor is not a vehicle for cheap laughs; the temptation to play to the audience can be avoided by a sincere interpretation of Gilbert's words – the audience will find the humour from an artist who has the courage and imagination to trust in a pause.

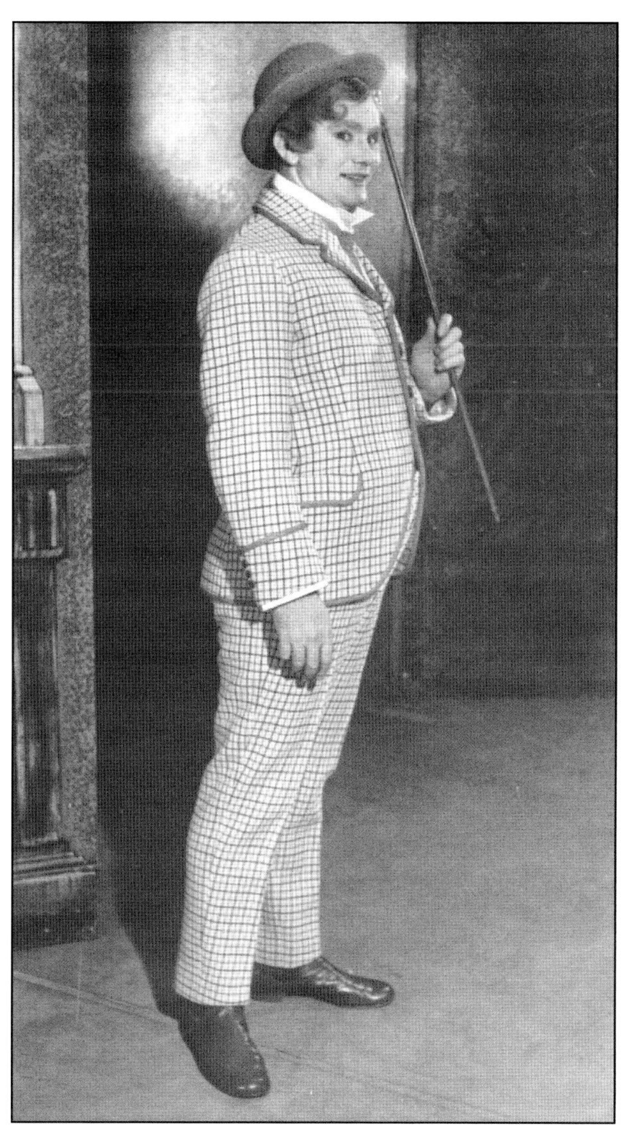

'A common place young man'

SIR DESPARD MURGATROYD

'Me whose hands are certainly steeped in infamy'

'You very wicked Peer'

THIS part, which ranks highly in Ken's affections, has been a source of enormous pleasure and artistic satisfaction, his only regret being that *Ruddigore* was performed less frequently than he would have liked. If he was lucky, it was played once in every two weeks and, occasionally, for a whole week during a London season, when he welcomed the chance to consolidate his characterisation over several consecutive performances. Sometimes, *Ruddigore* was left out of the repertory for a tour, allowing one of the other 'less popular' operas such as *Princess Ida* to receive a provincial airing. Ken was always saddened by this, particularly as his role in the latter show was nowhere near as rewarding. Seldom successful at the Box Office, it remains a mystery to him as to why so-called lovers of Gilbert and Sullivan who rush to see *The Mikado* or *The Pirates of Penzance* are so reluctant to embrace *Ruddigore*. Such people readily voice the opinion that it is inferior to the best-loved operas, yet make little effort to get to know a show which, in Ken's opinion, boasts a glorious score and a libretto packed with witty dialogue and colourful characters. He would like to see more people make the effort to become familiar with the lesser-known Savoy operas and is sure that the rewards for the initiate will be well worthwhile.

When first getting to grips with Sir Despard Murgatroyd, Ken was immediately struck by the dramatic possibilities of playing two distinct roles in one, but he would have to prepare the character twice over and that was going to mean a great deal of hard work. He had little experience of Victorian melodrama, but knew that he would be required to work in a broad, stylised way and certainly enjoyed the challenge of developing his Act I Despard with licence to overstate every aspect of his characterisation. It was obvious that he would need to move around the stage in a way which added to the effect of brooding villainy that he wished to create and this required careful thought. A normal walk was out of the question – nothing about Despard could be described as normal and, as exaggeration seemed to be the order of the day, he decided on a powerful stride. By elongating his usual step, he generated an aggressive energy that helped him to imagine himself as a feared criminal, something that was outside his previous theatrical experience. This intimidating style of movement worked well with his costume, which consisted of a caped, emerald green riding coat, tight grey breeches, knee-length black boots and a feathered hat. Feeling that he was on the right track, he turned his attention to the gestures he might use as Despard which, he realised, must match his strong, striding movements and in this respect he was helped by the horsewhip which he carried as a prop. Whilst reinforcing the image of malevolence, it proved invaluable for stressing an individual word or pointing at other characters. Used with a flourish, it was a great way to achieve exaggerated gesture. In fact, Ken soon came to realise that, due to the unique demands of melodrama, gesture was going to be more important in this role than any other of his parts in the Savoy Operas.

Having rushed onstage forcefully for his first entrance, he used the eight crashing orchestral chords to stamp his feet and simultaneously brandish his riding crop at the terrified chorus, before driving them to the sides of the stage using the two triplets prior to him singing. These synchronised gestures helped to establish the nature of the character before he had uttered a note, leaving the audience in no doubt that the 'baddy' had arrived. Throughout the section:

'Oh, why am I moody and sad?'

Ken struck dramatic poses and illustrated his dilemmas with grimaces, lunging movements and strong gestures, pointing sharply to his face on such appropriate lines as:

'You'll see it at once in my face'
and
'It's the workings of conscience, of course'

He had never before acted in this 'over the top' style and was, at first, concerned that he might be overdoing things, but audience reaction and a lack of adverse comment from the D'Oyly Carte management suggested that he had found the right level. From experience, his advice on Sir Despard in Act I is that if you think you are going too far, you are getting it just right.

The following scene should continue in the same vein and Ken used every opportunity to make unexpected movements and gestures on a grand scale, most notably when listing his early-morning crimes and subsequent acts of philanthropy. He would mime plucking a child from its mother's arms, or holding up a bank, using the horse-whip as a 'gun', before waving it wildly in the direction of Rose Maybud's cottage and finishing with arms raised aloft exultantly at the prospect of atoning by building a cathedral. The audience loved it. The more he sensed them entering into the spirit of the melodrama, the more he strutted, flailed and raged around the stage. It is every actor's dream to be able to ignore the usual conventions of stage technique and let down one's artistic hair in such outrageous fashion and Ken came to love every moment of the scene. It was such a refreshing change to the usual discipline of D'Oyly Carte productions, presenting him with the chance to be totally uninhibited. However, he warns, as always, against directing the stage business to the front; every movement, gesture and facial expression must be prompted by the words, music and dramatic situation rather than the laughter of the audience.

In the dialogue with Richard Dauntless, Ken played down his movements lest they become distracting, confining himself to eccentric, yet hilarious, backward paces of shock on:

'He (step) *did not?'*
and
'Can this (step) *be possible?'*

He points out that it is, after all, Richard's moment to shine and another good example of when to take second place in an exchange. However, at the end of the scene, when the emphasis shifted back to him, his understandable gestures of exultation led easily into the duet, in which he kicked up his heels with glee.

In Act I Finale, Ken again used a dramatic segment of orchestral music to electrifying effect. After:

'I claim young Robin as my elder brother'

he advanced menacingly on Robin Oakapple with one powerful stride to each bar, which Robin mirrored as he retreated in horror, ending by prodding the riding crop into Robin's chest on the sforzando horn chord. Although these moves were choreographed, they worked well because of Ken's feel for melodrama, but it is always important to be aware of moments in the score which give the performer time to utilise the music to artistic advantage. Having played the whole of Act I in such an exaggerated manner, it was fitting that he joined in the final dance, the jig, with wild abandon. Always an athletic dancer, Ken left the audience in little doubt as to his delight in being released from the toils of evil doing!

Considering the characterisation of Sir Despard in Act II presented him with less difficulty, as it seemed to require a complete reversal of everything he had done in Act I. The aggressive striding was replaced with a dignified, soft-footed step and the expansive gestures with the minimum of restrained hand movement, which helped to indicate his transformation from villain to pillar of the community. Ken feels that there is no great mystery to this change, it is common sense. He never cared for his costume which, he felt, made him look like a Music Hall comedian. In a black tail-coat, drain-pipe black leggings and white socks he felt like a Victorian Max Wall, a famous English comedian who dressed in similar fashion. The strange entrance which required he and Mad Margaret to walk on behind each other at half speed bothered him. However amusing it may have looked to the audience, he could not but feel that it was inappropriate, coming as it did before either of them had said a word about their astonishing change of appearance. He would have preferred a simple arrival, which would have allowed the humour of their situation to become apparent from the words of the duet, rather than from the D'Oyly Carte department of silly walks. In his opinion, it removed the element of surprise from their quaint *'blameless dances'* at the end of each verse, but that was the way it was always done and he regrets never having had the chance to develop the theatrical possibilities that a less contrived approach might have offered. Throughout the following scene with Margaret and Sir Ruthven, his movements were deliberately unhurried and calm, his expression impassive and his gestures few and far between, with only an occasional warning wag of the finger when Margaret allowed her newly-acquired restrained demeanour to slip. In fact, he was as quiet and composed as he had been frantic in Act I and the contrast worked wonderfully. As a prop, he carried a rolled umbrella, which was helpful in that his gestures were restricted, only hooking it over his arm for the dances in the duet. Ken's Act II Sir Despard was a study in underplaying which, after his carefully-judged histrionics of Act I, was an object lesson in acting technique.

Having reaped the rewards of such detailed preparation for Sir Despard's physical appearance and mannerisms, Ken is in a good position to maintain that the real joy of this glorious character may only be gained by performers who have discipline on the stage. The broadness of style required for melodrama is not a licence to deliberately play to the gallery and it can only be truly successful when approached as seriously as any other theatrical genre.

THE VOICE

As previously mentioned, Ken always gave careful consideration to the voice he was going to use for a role, endeavouring to find an individual quality of speech for each of the diverse characters he was required to play. Hitting on the right voice for Sir Despard Murgatroyd was no easy task, but everything else about him was larger than life, so Ken reasoned that his speech must also reflect the idiosyncrasies of the big, bad baronet if his portrayal was to be successful. The title of 'Sir' gave him his first lead; however wicked the man's deeds, he was an aristocrat and would, presumably, speak in a cultured and educated manner. That was the easy bit. He found another and more obvious clue in his opening song:

'Oh, why am I husky and hoarse?'

Given the nature of the dialogue, he thought that the likely cause was too much shouting, so he made a mental note to avoid such excess. He would need to find a voice that achieved his artistic purpose, but which could be easily sustained; the demands of as many as eight performances every week made it imperative to conserve vocal stamina. Eventually, he was satisfied that he could produce a voice that would not only reflect Despard's background, but also have the slight huskiness indicated by Gilbert and, despite the fact that he made his voice project more loudly than usual, he suffered no throat problems. Ken felt that it was important to try to convey in his voice a feeling for the dark despair of the reluctant villain driven to crime by fear of the terrible threats of his unearthly ancestors. Although at heart a good man, he is racked by guilt, but incapable of facing the prospect of an agonising death and Ken wanted this to be apparent from the way he coloured his words. The line:

'Aye, but he died. Oh, Ruthven!'

might well be interpreted with justifiable resentment, but Ken preferred to imbue the words with a quiet poignancy that was a wonderful contrast to his earlier tirades and provides an excellent example of how to use dynamic light and shade in dialogue. It is almost impossible to instruct a performer in how to achieve voice colouring; Ken can only say that imagination is the key. If you truly believe you are the character, feel his emotions and think with his mind, the desired effect will be achieved. The husky voice was much easier to produce, requiring a physical, rather than cerebral, process.

Ken found Act II to be much less complicated. Sir Despard is a reformed character. Knowing that it was important for the audience to immediately recognise that Despard and Margaret have mended their ways, he made his speaking voice quiet and gentle, with a warmth that was completely removed from the huskiness of his Act I character. Achieving such contrast is, once again, a matter of common sense; the character goes from one extreme to the other and the performer must do likewise.

When playing a character part, Ken reiterates the importance of producing a voice that can be maintained without discomfort throughout a performance or, if necessary, for a year-long run. There is no point in creating an effective voice if laryngitis is the result.

THE DIALOGUE

Having given so much thought to Sir Despard's voices, Ken was rather sorry that he had so little dialogue in which to use them. Unlike most of his other roles, his lines were confined to one sequence in each act, so he was determined to make the most of them. Admittedly, these scenes were challenging enough for any actor, but he loved the character and would have enjoyed more of the same. Working without guidance in an unfamiliar style was not easy and he was concerned about finding the right level, but he was guided by audience reaction. By experimenting with the timing of lines or using a different emphasis on a word, he was able to gauge his successes or failures by how much the audience laughed. On this trial and error basis, he gradually developed a characterisation which delighted D'Oyly Carte audiences for a quarter of a century and his transition from guilt-racked criminal to abstemious village school teacher was both funny and poignant. His great facility for timing lines was evident in both facets of Despard's personality and his use of variation in his speaking voice masterly.

Ken was grateful that Despard's long first speech gave him something substantial on which to work and establish the character. The melodramatic dialogue was outside anything in his previous experience, so he needed to think long and hard as to how he should approach it. His first thought was that the speech needed contrast; if he set his level too high he would leave himself nowhere to go dramatically. He found a problem with the first line:

'Poor children, how they loathe me'

which could be interpreted in two ways, both quite valid. His initial reactions were of sympathy for the young people he had terrorised and self-pity. However, he realised that the same words could be said with explosive bitterness which, when immediately followed by a much quieter:

'me whose hands are certainly steeped in infamy,
but whose heart is as the heart of a little child'

allowed the man's dual personality to become immediately apparent. He decided to take the second option and realised that he could bring in the element of self-pity straight after, in the section beginning:

'But what is a poor baronet to do'

With three distinct changes of emotion in just a few lines, he felt that he had made a good start and continued to look for every possible opportunity for contrast.

It did not take Ken long to come to the conclusion that the over the top nature of Despard's dialogue would benefit from a slower and more marked delivery than he would use for his other parts. It would also give him the time to colour individual words to either humorous or dramatic effect. A good example of this was his use of the word '*loathe*', which he elongated and rolled round his mouth with great relish. He used the same technique with '*excruciating*', which allowed time for appropriate facial contortions. Building up to full melodramatic speed in the second half of the speech, he was, again, conscious of the need for contrast, using each of the three repetitions of '*I do good*' differently. Rising in volume and pitch during the first two, he cleverly took the audience by surprise by whispering the third with an angelic look on his face. Ken warns of the perils of long lists or repetition of the same word. There must be variation and shape within the list, or the delivery will be amateurish, flat and boring. He cites as an example Pooh-Bah's list of titles in *The Mikado*, when he varied the emphasis of his voice and speed of speech to avoid becoming monotonous.

Despard's description of his recent crimes had to be handled carefully and Ken used each of them to illustrate the two sides of his nature, belligerently announcing each evil deed before suddenly dropping the image of a wicked man and assuming the piety of a do-gooder. Starting at a vocal and dramatic level which left room for enlargement, he gained momentum to an almost hysterical level on:

> *'and atone with a cathedral!'*

After this, he reduced the intensity and slowed the lines so that he could again build up dramatic energy for the climax of the speech:

> *'and nobody shall ever look upon their faces again!'*

Although Ken was aware that in the following scene with Richard Dauntless he must play second fiddle, his contribution must, nevertheless, add to the humour and so he looked for ways to vary his portrayal. Keeping his speech slower than normal, he was able to spread out individual words for comedic effect and found that putting an 'h' in the middle of certain words kept up the melodrama without stealing his colleague's thunder. There were two particular points where he used this ploy. Firstly, during:

> *'a complete apparatus for conducting the circulation of the blood through the veins and arteries of the human body'*

he added an 'h' to '*blood*' so that the word had two syllables, as in 'bloo-hod' and did the same with '*bo-hody*'. Secondly, in:

> *'Then you really feel yourself at liberty to tell me that my elder brother lives – that I may charge him with his cruel deceit'*

he repeated this ploy with '*li-hives*' and also separated the two syllables of '*cruel*', with a strong emphasis on the second of them. These may seem to be small points, but such attention to detail was the hallmark of Ken's work and an illustration of how meticulous an artist must be when preparing a role. The audience always enjoyed these eccentricities and he concluded the scene in a spirit of wild delight as he celebrated his release from the curse of the Murgatroyds.

Sir Despard's dialogue in Act II was certainly much easier to prepare; with the melodramatic style of Act I behind him, Ken was able to concentrate on developing the contrast between the two sides of the character. Several key words came to mind; quiet, calm, sober, gentle, patient and ordinary amongst them. None of these adjectives could be applied to Despard in Act I, so with such qualities firing his imagination, he set about his task.

With two exceptions, Ken never let the dialogue become emotional. By keeping the volume down and the pace measured, it was easy enough to suggest a man of reformed character. In his first exchange with Margaret:

'We have been married a week'

he gave the impression that he had been coaching her in what to say in the hope of keeping her outbursts under control. Whenever she reverted to type, he remained stoically unmoved, his face impassive as he quietly reminded her of her new life and its responsibilities. He was patient with her, never allowing any irritation into his words and explaining why she should keep her composure as if addressing a child. Ken loved Gilbert's irony in the line:

'but a district visitor should learn to eschew melodrama'

and gave the last two words a little more emphasis without disturbing the flow of the scene. He always made a pause before his line:

'Because it's too jumpy for a sick-room'

as if so astonished by her inability to comprehend why she should not have hysterics in the presence of sick people, that he had to resist the urge to tell her not to be so stupid, before calmly telling her the reason.

In traditional productions it is usual for an extremely loud clattering to be effected offstage prior to the line:

'But soft – someone comes'

and Ken showed his wonderful sense of timing by pausing for 3-4 seconds before quietly stating the obvious. Margaret's wild reaction to the noise prompted one of the two occasions in the scene when he became more animated, as he momentarily raised his voice in frustration; the fear of being found in possession of a loopy wife sufficient to make him momentarily lose his patience with her. The second time Ken deliberately moved away from his restrained delivery came in the section beginning:

'Remember how you trifled with this poor child's affections'

during which he gradually built up dramatic momentum and speed peaking at:

'when they were at the very zenith of their fullness'

before winding down in intensity on:

'Oh fie, Sir, fie – she trusted you'

The last of Sir Despard's dialogue to be given the unique Sandford treatment was the simple phrase:

'Oh, I've married her'

given in response to Robin's enquiry as to which of the two brothers has tied the knot with Margaret. After another of those magical pauses, the look of forbearance on his face and long-suffering tone in his voice as he quietly claimed the dubious honour, invariably reduced the audience to fits of laughter.

Ken's imaginative acting skills, flexible speaking voice and capacity for hard work combined in every part that he played, but his brilliant portrayal of Sir Despard Murgatroyd remains a firm favourite with his admirers, with one notable exception. The first page was very complimentary indeed and Ken was flattered. The second page of the lady's letter mentioned her son's school performance of *Ruddigore*. Pages 3-12 left him feeling deflated and completely inadequate as she tore every detail of his characterisation to shreds and extolled the brilliant interpretation of his teenage counterpart, which she explained in great depth and urged him to adopt forthwith. The breathtaking arrogance of such people is an occupational hazard, but Ken still has that faded letter as a reminder of the perils of complacency. For everyone else, his performances may never be surpassed.

MAKE UP

Every aspect of Sir Despard had to be prepared twice over and this also applied to make up. Ken was used to having to change his costume during the course of a show, but *Ruddigore* was the only one of the Savoy operas in which he had to change his make up. It has often been said about Ken that his eyes twinkle when he is on the stage, but he is also blessed with unusually mobile eyebrows, which he used to expressive effect. He was sure that they would be particularly useful during the emotional excesses of Act I, when he wanted his make up to reflect the dark, brooding nature of a man who is, quite literally, haunted by fear. Having applied a medium foundation by mixing his trusty numbers 5 and 9 greasepaint, he used a black pencil (or black pancake) to make his eyebrows large and bushy, before drawing lines above and below his eyes. Feeling that he would probably be baggy-eyed and hollow-cheeked in Despard's situation, he mixed together dark brown and crimson lake grease sticks to produce a murky colour which was ideal to give him a haggard look. He applied this concoction with his fingers or a brush, above his eyes, below them to form bags and in a triangular shape under his cheekbones. With his long sideburns, the latter gave him a gaunt appearance which, along with the bags, gave the impression of many sleepless nights. By getting to know the bone structure of one's face, it is easy for even a young person to follow the natural contours and apply a convincing character make up – it is always possible, by smiling or frowning, to see where lines and wrinkles will, inevitably, appear and draw them in accordingly. More mature performers will have no need for the facial gymnastics, having only to emphasise what is already there.

Ken used a number 5 stick or an equivalent ivory colour to highlight the dark areas he had painted onto his face, which made the bags and hollows look more natural, as if casting shadows across his face. Using a small brush, he applied the number 5 above the darkened areas of his eyes and cheeks and to the bags under the eyes. With the mixture of dark brown and lake he outlined the bags and also the lines leading down from the side of the nose. Finally, using crimson lake, he drew in slightly twisted and down-turned lips to make his mouth look cruel, with a little of the murky mixture under the mouth for extra emphasis. He always powdered the make up, because it helped set the grease paint into the face and gave a matt, as opposed to shiny, finish.

Having taken such care with Sir Despard's Act I make up, Ken had to start all over again at the interval. Fortunately, he had plenty of time before he appeared in the second act, so he was able to remove his villain's mask and create a much gentler appearance in keeping with the character's change of life-style. He began with a paler base, because this looked better against his predominantly black costume and neat, dark brown wig. He then added the usual lines above and below his eyes, but made his eyebrows much less fierce. The new crime-free Despard would probably sleep soundly, so there was no need for the bags and dark shadows under his eyes or hollow cheeks. Having removed his whiskers, Ken used a little reddish colour to highlight his cheekbones and replaced the cruel lips with a little crimson lake to define his mouth. He purposely made the Act II make up simple; the contrast in facial detail being equally as important as the contrast in the other facets of his characterisation. Every detail mattered if his change from Public Enemy Number 1 to paragon of virtue was to be credible and he took great care with his make up plan to achieve this end.

HORROR MOMENTS

Towards the end of their long D'Oyly Carte careers, both Ken and John Reed were conscious of the fact that they were getting a little long in the tooth for some of their roles and often shared a joke about it. They had no problem playing their various character parts, but Grosvenor, Jack Point and Robin Oakapple were another matter, requiring every resource in the make up box to help them counteract the ravages of time. During a performance of *Ruddigore*, John returned to their dressing room after giving an encore of his song

> *'My boy, you may take it from me'*

somewhat out of breath, giving Ken the opportunity to pass a sarcastic remark about him getting too old for the job. He continued to take the mickey out of John by adding that, at his age, it was rather ridiculous to be called *'young Robin'*. Pleased with his point scoring over John, he hurried to the stage for the Act I Finale, still chuckling at his own humour. In a rare instance of lack of concentration and focus on the job in hand, Ken rushed onto the stage and declaimed:

> *'Hold , bride and bridegroom, ere you wed each other, I claim young Strephon as my elder brother'.*

Needless to say, the audience was either horribly confused or in fits of laughter, as was every person on the stage; John, quite literally, had the last laugh and sufficient ammunition to last for some time. Naturally, our hero was mortified.

HAPPY MOMENTS

During a performance of *Ruddigore* in New York, Ken made his first entrance to a barrage of hissing and booing from the audience that took him completely by surprise. He was astonished that the theatre-going public of The Big Apple joined him in the spirit of the melodrama and presumed that they would soon get tired of heckling the villain. He was wrong. The chorus of disapproval continued throughout Act I and, once he had made the necessary adjustments to his timing to accommodate the noisy reactions, he revelled in their participation, giving one of his hammiest performances ever. Having thoroughly enjoyed this experience, he felt that it was a pity that reserved British audiences were too inhibited to react in such a way and resolved to encourage the hissing and booing at the first opportunity. After all, the same staid people automatically hissed and booed during a pantomime. Before the company's first *Ruddigore* on returning to England, he had a word with the string section of the orchestra and asked them to hiss and boo on his first entrance. This, he was sure, would encourage the audience to join in the fun. Sadly, his scheme went awry. The orchestra, game for a laugh, duly hissed and booed when Ken appeared, but he was very disappointed when the audience rounded on the musicians and told them to shut up! The management was not amused and automatically blamed the orchestra, never considering for a moment that its distinguished principal baritone could be behind such an unprofessional scheme.

A FINAL THOUGHT

It is not often that a performer has the chance to play two roles in one. Sir Despard Murgatroyd offers the artist a platform on which to display his versatile acting and singing skills. The character calls for extreme contrast in every aspect of presentation; it is physically and mentally demanding, requiring a great deal of preparation and detailed thought. Ken advises that melodrama is not a form of slapstick comedy, but a style of playing which requires a broad delivery and imaginative use of words and movement. It must be taken seriously and not used as an excuse to play to the audience. It is funny because it is serious.

'Poor children, how they loathe me'

DON ALHAMBRA DEL BOLERO

'And a very nice little lady, too.'

'Oh, beware of his anger provoking'

THE role of the Grand Inquisitor in *The Gondoliers* is another of Ken's particular favourites and one which, owing to the popularity of the opera, he was lucky enough to perform on a regular basis. It holds a unique place in his affections because Anthony Besch's ground-breaking 1968 production liberated him from the artistic straight-jacket of the D'Oyly Carte's 'traditional' style, allowing him to create a dynamic new characterisation that was to have a profound effect on the way he approached his other roles. After 11 artistically frustrating years, he experienced a renewal of enthusiasm for his work, convinced that Besch's naturalistic treatment of the stage business and interaction of characters was the way forward.

For some time, Ken has been of the opinion that Gilbert's original stagings of the Savoy Operas, which must have reflected the theatrical conventions of his day, need now to be replaced by productions which make sense to modern audiences. He has no wish, however, for the Victorian style to be forgotten or ridiculed; it is an important part of British theatre history and the D'Oyly Carte productions of the late 19th and early 20th

centuries should not be completely lost. He is firmly convinced that both Gilbert and Sullivan would acknowledge the importance of making their masterpieces accessible to the theatre-going public of today – after all, it is possible that they did not envisage their work still being popular in the year 2000. Ken has no wish to see cheap gimmickry pass for a production of G & S, but does long for all of the wonderful characters to be treated with theatrical integrity by directors who remain true to the spirit of the original, but whose presentations embrace present day theatrical styles.

Ken played the part of The Don in three D'Oyly Carte productions of *The Gondoliers*, but it was the last of them on which he bases his observations. George Foa's re-staging in the early 1960s was a huge disappointment for Ken, who was hoping that the director would offer him fresh insight into his portrayal of the Grand Inquisitor. Sadly, the Venetian-born television director had not much to offer and, despite his heritage, added little to the existing production, leaving Ken with almost identical moves and dialogue still delivered out front. All that was to change with the appointment of Anthony Besch for yet another production. Having worked with Besch at the Opera School, Ken was optimistic that this time things really might change for the better and he eagerly awaited the rehearsal period.

He was not disappointed. Besch broke down the rigid, synchronised blocking for the chorus and introduced natural movement and gesture, immediately creating a realism previously unknown to the company. Principals, too, found that they were expected to be real people and Ken was, at last, encouraged to relate to the other performers on the stage. Anthony Besch re-enforced his own ideas and gave Ken the freedom to act in the way he had always believed to be right.

With the production updated to the Edwardian era, Ken's costume was very different from the classical braided coat and knee breeches that he had previously worn and this meant a complete rethink in terms of movement, gesture and manners. His new Act I costume consisted of a black cassock trimmed with purple edging, purple cummerbund, black cloak and a broad-brimmed clerical hat. With his tall figure, he looked every inch a man whose absolute authority is never questioned and this had to be reflected in the way he moved. He walked with an unhurried, but purposeful step and was always aware that his very presence must be intimidating. Knowing that his reputation makes him a man to be feared, Ken wanted The Don to show a human side which, he felt, would add to the depth of his characterisation and Besch's relaxed restaging gave him the perfect opportunity. To contrast his powerful position as the Grand Inquisitor, Ken assumed an appearance of charm and suave sophistication. He created a Don Alhambra who not only had a sense of humour, but also an eye for the ladies and this radical approach was very well-received by audiences and the press alike. Of course, it did not meet with the approval of Snookie Fancourt. After the first performance she remarked to Ken:

> *'He's no longer a 'grand' Inquisitor, Kenneth'*

Nevertheless, for the first time in his D'Oyly Carte career, he felt he was really able to do justice to the character and continued to add the touches for which his interpretation became famous. Ken was sure that not hurrying his movements and gestures was of the essence. In fact, he moved as little as possible, with only an occasional gesture to emphasise a point, preferring to keep his hands loosely clasped at his waist for much of the time, making sure that the large ring on his right hand was always visible. One of the few gestures that he did use was quite brilliant in its understatement. At the end of his Act II exchange with the two gondoliers and their wives, he moved upstage in a leisurely manner towards his exit, before turning back to Tessa and Gianetta to say: *'Good evening'* in such an oily way as to make the girls feel quite disgusted. Before disappearing, he gave them the smallest of waves, barely moving his fingers. It was suggestive, but not cheap and had the effect of making every woman in the audience feel grossly uncomfortable. This was no cardboard cut-out Grand Inquisitor, but a very real man with the usual human foibles and, once again, Ken achieved his purpose by underplaying.

He also realised that by moving around the stage as little as possible, he was able to emphasise the Don's complete control of every situation. Having informed Marco and Giuseppe that one of them is the King of Barataria, Ken let them do the rushing around as they clumsily tried to explain why a Republican would make a good king. He stood quietly amused as they frantically tried to convince him of their suitability for the demands of royalty. His authoritarian position again benefited from stillness at the end of the Cachuca in Act II. Having entered unobserved at the back of the stage, he stood motionless until everyone realised he was there. Instead of indicating the revellers to leave, he allowed his towering presence to do this for him and the effect was chilling. He sat throughout his song, *'There lived a King'* and used the minimum of gesture, finding that a gentle shrug of the shoulders or raising of a hand was all that he needed to convey his point to the eager young kings. Even in the reprise of the Cachuca at the end of Act II Finale he remained in character. Resisting the temptation to dance energetically, he indulged in a reserved, but beautifully stylish fandango with Inez, maintaining his dignity to the end.

His change into purple cassock and biretta for Act II made no difference to his characterisation, it was merely a change of clothes which accentuated his status. A man in the position of the Grand Inquisitor has no need to hurry, he is always in control. In Ken's view, economy of gesture and movement can help to highlight the authority that sets him aside from everyone else.

Ken in Act II of Besch's production

THE VOICE

Finding a suitable voice for his Don did not present Ken with too much of a problem. Given that he wanted him to be, on the surface of things, a real old charmer, the speaking voice would need to be as smooth, suave and unhurried as his behaviour. Ken felt that just as the Grand Inquisitor had no need to move with urgency, he had no need to hurry his speech or raise his voice. What need has such a powerful man to speak loudly or threateningly? The threat is there anyway and Ken made Don Alhambra seem much more sinister by using a quiet, faintly mocking tone, as if amused by the situations developing around him. He never raised his voice or spoke angrily – again, there was no need, he always had the upper hand.

When slapped on the back by Giuseppe, Ken showed his displeasure by hardening his tone; he certainly did not show anger. The sudden iciness in his voice was sufficient to show that the Don is not a person with whom to take liberties. Having witnessed servants dancing alongside court dignitaries, his remonstration with the two kings for allowing such unseemly behaviour was achieved without annoyance or irritation. Instead, he used a touch of sarcasm that was wasted on the not too-bright Marco and Giuseppe, but much appreciated by the audience. In short, Ken's Don Alhambra del Bolero spoke quietly, in the same unhurried way that he moved. By using his imagination to create subtle variations of tone, he could make his voice humorous, mocking, charming, lecherous or sinister without the need for dramatic changes of volume or pace.

THE DIALOGUE

Ken had always loved Don Alhambra's dialogue, but Anthony Besch's production made it possible for him to use it as never before. With the performers expected to play the scenes to each other rather than to the audience, he was able to bring to the words the subtlety which he had always believed to be missing. His first entrance, in which he is introduced to Casilda, presented him with an ideal platform from which to launch his remodelled characterisation and establish a very human Grand Inquisitor. Walking across the stage to meet her gave him time to take in her beauty, so that his first line:

> *'So this is the little lady who is so unexpectedly called upon to assume the functions of Royalty!'*

was said in such a way as to make it quite clear that he found her extremely attractive. By lingering on *'this'* and pointing *'little lady'* he immediately conveyed his fascination with women. Before continuing the line, Ken had to wait until Casilda had knelt to kiss the ring on his right hand, giving him the opportunity to look down at her cleavage. This piece of business gave a new meaning to:

> *'And a very nice little lady, too!'*

As she hurriedly covered her bosom, he helped her to her feet and she flounced back to her mother in some annoyance. In the sanitised world of the D'Oyly Carte, where physical contact between the sexes was deemed undesirable and unnecessary to the plot, such stage business was revolutionary and somewhat controversial. It must be stressed that Ken was careful to avoid overplaying this moment. His desire to convey a man whose eye for the ladies belies his calling and thus makes him appear more sinister, was artistically valid, but his actions were subtle and never lewd. His reaction to her show of spirit was to say:

> *'Naughty temper'*

as if this further enhanced her delights. With the Duchess' intervention, Ken brilliantly defused the situation by at once giving his attention to her, turning on the charm so fluently that her frostiness melted within a few seconds to the obvious astonishment of The Duke, who could never provoke such a softening of her heart. It is interesting that the way Ken chose to deliver his speech beginning:

> *'He is here, in Venice, plying the modest but picturesque calling of a gondolier.'*

gave scope to the other performers. A less accomplished actor might speak the lines as if merely passing on information, but he directed them at the Duchess with a charm that bordered on flirting and this was not lost on the others involved in the scene. Instead of just standing and listening to an explanation of the King's whereabouts, The Duke was able to register a little jealousy at the Don's success with his formidable wife, the Duchess reacted coyly to the flattery, whilst Luiz and Casilda exchanged glances of amusement at the Don's smooth tactics. As if by magic, a simple statement became a vehicle for five characters to make their various points and this provides a good example of the reward for an actor whose imaginative use of dialogue gives his fellow characters an opportunity for reaction.

For the first time in his D'Oyly Carte career, Ken was allowed to sing his song, *'I stole the Prince'* directly to the others involved in the scene. Seated around a café table whilst The Duke and his family ate a meal, he was able to tell the story within a credible situation and he found that the following dialogue followed on more naturally as a result. The Don's reply to Casilda's question regarding the identity of her husband might well be delivered quite seriously, but Ken said:

'Without any doubt of any kind whatever'

with humour. This prompted a look of impatience from her that wiped the self-satisfied smile from his face and brought him back to the point. Thereafter he became serious and business-like, his control of the situation in complete contrast to his unctious flattery of the ladies a few minutes earlier. Ken used the final sentence of the scene to demonstrate the horrifying power of the Grand Inquisitor, again illustrating the effectiveness of a pause. Without changing the matter-of-fact tone of his voice on the line:

'The persuasive influence of the torture chamber will jog her memory.'

he slightly emphasised *'persuasive'*, but stopped abruptly and paused before leaning on *'jog'*. This clever piece of timing left nobody in doubt as to the gruesome nature of the work of this charming elderly man and it made the flesh crawl. Instead of taking the less subtle option of making his voice sound blood-thirsty, or pointing *'torture chamber'*, he showed, once again, the benefit of imagination coupled with understatement.

Ken thoroughly enjoyed Don Alhambra's next scene with the two gondoliers and their new wives. His mockery of their attempts to regroup after Giuseppe's declaration of their Republican ideals and subsequent discovery that one of them is a king, was extremely amusing, both for his character and the audience. At the start of the scene, The Don is curious as to the cause of the celebration and Ken adopted an attitude of good humour to disguise his attempt to discover the reason for their high spirits. By pleasantly joining in their youthful banter, he was soon able to find out what he wanted to know. Ken used the news of the gondoliers' nuptials to present a side of the Grand Inquisitor that he felt would not often be seen – a momentary crack in the composed façade. He wanted the all-knowing Don to appear temporarily flummoxed by an event outside of his control, to the point of seeming incredulous at the news of the unforeseen weddings. As Tessa and Gianetta poked fun at him, Ken chose not to appear annoyed or embarrassed but, instead, subsided into deep thought as if trying to quickly plan his next move. His reply:

'No, no, I wasn't! I wasn't!'

was said rather absently, as if he had hardly noticed their disrespectful teasing. He used Giuseppe's slap on the back to bring him back to the moment and the lengthy political speech to regain his usual composure. During the course of the Republican diatribe, Ken liked to appear as if barely able to conceal his amusement at the irony of the situation. This was carried over into his line:

'Bless my heart, how unfortunate!'

which he said with a wicked sense of fun, before becoming more serious as he delivered the bombshell about one of them being the King Of Barataria. A moment for contrast follows immediately and Ken made full use of :

'And I trust - I trust it was that one who slapped me on the shoulder'

as he put an icy tone into his voice to become the frighteningly powerful Grand Inquisitor once more. The following sequence, in which the gondoliers endeavour to regain the initiative, is an example of Ken's contention that the Don has to do very little but watch everyone else working hard. His occasional interjections were delivered with a mixture of amusement, sarcasm and mockery that went unnoticed by the frenetic gondoliers, but which gave him great pleasure. His reply to Giuseppe's ridiculous statement about only detesting bad kings:

'I see. It's a delicate distinction'

was loaded with ironical humour, but that humour was for his own benefit. If the audience cared to join him in the fun, that was fine. Ken assumed a business-like tone as he detailed the arrangements made for them to rule jointly and this was only interrupted by the girls' announcement that they were off to pack.

'Stop, stop – that wont do at all – ladies are not admitted.'

was said without the need to raise his voice. Ken feels that at this point, The Don is completely in control of the situation and has no need to break his smooth flow; he knows that he cannot be opposed, so why shout at them? His final line of this fascinating scene presented an opportunity for Ken's Don Alhambra to show a rare flash of sympathy. Ever susceptible to the ladies, he allowed himself a moment to feel genuinely sorry for Tessa and Gianetta on:

'This is very awkward! Only for a time – a few months.'

His voice suggested genuine compassion for the predicament of the two girls as he tried to make them believe that separation from their new husbands was not the end of the world. It is likely that he also felt sorry for Marco and Giuseppe, but for a very different reason!

Each of the Don's three dialogue scenes is substantial enough to allow the performer time in which to build the various facets of his characterisation. Ken found that the last of these sections in Act II gave him the scope for detail on which he thrived as an actor, adding depth and variety to the personality of his Grand Inquisitor. It also provided him with the best exit in any of the operas, which he exploited to the full.

On first entering after the Cachuca, Ken maintained his quiet authority, despite his astonishment on finding servants and court officials dancing side-by-side. His tone to Marco and Giuseppe on:

'But I saw a groom dancing, and a footman'

was that of a school teacher disappointed by the poor performance of his pupils, but not of annoyance. He did not become impatient with them, choosing to gently coax them into seeing the error of their ways rather than reprimanding them. Given the context of the line:

'But surely, surely the servants' hall is the place for these gentry?

it would seem natural to be irritated by the stupidity of the two kings, but Ken preferred a less aggressive approach, his gentle rebuke being accompanied by a fatherly smile. Again, it would be reasonable to exclaim angrily on learning that the gondolier-monarchs have applied their Republican political ideals to the Kingdom of Barataria. Ken, however, chose to say:

'What!'

with amused disbelief rather than the more obvious anger. Another example of his ability to apply original thinking to dialogue is evidenced by the way he answered Giuseppe's query about his health on the line:

'Yes – gout.'

He said this in a rather distant way, as if still preoccupied with trying to find a way to get through to his dense protogees. Otherwise, in Ken's opinion, it is difficult to link these two words with the following:

'You see, in every Court there are distinctions that must be observed.'

If, however, they are treated as an extension of his previous line when he vaguely declines any refreshments with:

'No, no – nothing – nothing,'

it is then easy to move on as if the Don has suddenly thought of a way to make Marco and Giuseppe understand what he means about court protocol. Thereafter, Ken treated the two kings as naïve children, explaining what they must and must not do with patience and humour. Even :

'No, no, it wont do'

was said more with amusement than despair as he struggled to make his point.

The dialogue following Don Alhambra's song *'There lived a King'* provided Ken with one of his favourite moments on the stage. He was in his acting element as he poked fun at the numskull gondoliers, briefly lost his composure as their wives unexpectedly turned up and regained the upper hand with a display of oily flattery that was tastefully lecherous.

At the beginning of the scene, Ken used the references to Casilda's beauty to make himself seem like one of the boys, his 'all men of the world' attitude particularly evident on:

> *'But the daughter – the beautiful daughter! Aha! Oh, you're a lucky dog, one of you!'*

when his innuendo was anything but subtle. Stung by being referred to as *'incomprehensible'*, he reverted to his normal glib style, using the repeated phrase:

> *'Whichever you are'*

to mock the young men without them realising that he was having fun at their expense. Shaken out of his smug amusement by the sudden appearance of Tessa and Gianetta, he was briefly unable to hide his concern. That his control of matters was suddenly in doubt was evident in his unguarded:

> *'Oh dear, this complicates matters! Dear, dear, what will Her Majesty say?'*

but he regained his composure by cleverly using the girls' verbal attack on their husbands to be obviously thinking up a new strategy. The sickly charm with which he then described them as:

> *'two such extremely fascinating and utterly irresistible little ladies'*

was such that they immediately melted at his suave flattery. By standing very close to them and making his speaking voice as sensual as possible within the bounds of good taste, he not only smoothed the ruffled feathers of the ladies but also convinced the audience that he meant every word of it!

Ever the master of the pause, Ken demonstrated the usefulness of this underestimated tool to great effect in his line:

> *'the old lady who nursed the Royal child is at present in the torture chamber, waiting for me to interview her.'*

By pausing for a second between *'to'* and *'interview'* he made his meaning doubly clear, leaving the audience to work out what sort of interview he had in mind.

As mentioned earlier, he rounded off the scene, in which he dominated the stage, with the wonderful exit which featured the meaningful gleam in his eye and that memorable little wave to the girls.

Ken owes a great deal to Anthony Besch's production of *The Gondoliers*. For too many frustrating years he had craved the freedom to develop as an actor within the Savoy Operas. His new interpretation of Don Alhambra del Bolero broke the mould and showed him the way forward, giving him the determination to fulfil the potential of all of his roles.

MAKE UP

Ken's make up for Don Alhambra was designed around the fact that the Grand Inquisitor is Spanish and elderly. Despite the hours spent in the unwholesome gloom of the torture chamber, his complexion should be dark and his skin lined.

With this in mind, Ken applied a dark base colour to his face and neck. He, as always, used grease paint, but performers who prefer pancake need only take into account that their skin colour must not be too pale. Ken had grizzled, grey sideburns and used his crimson lake and dark brown mixture to make a triangular hollow underneath them. He then put the same colour under his eyes to form bags, on his eyelids to create a hooded effect and along the sides of his nose. He made his eyebrows grey by using a black pencil overlaid with a little white greasepaint rubbed roughly over the top. With a fine brush he then drew age lines on his face, paying particular attention to the forehead and crow's feet at the side of his eyes, as well as those lines running down from either side of the nose and mouth. Wherever on his face he put shading and lines, he used number 5 above to highlight them and prevent the facial contours from appearing flat. He then added the all-important black lines above and below each eye and a dab of lake to emphasise his mouth. He finished by thoroughly powdering the make up. It is important to remember that a young performer needs to use shade and highlight on his neck. In the latter part of his career Ken only needed to use a base on his neck, the natural jowls needing no assistance! However, in more youthful times, the shading started under either side of the chin and descended in a line of approximately half an inch in width, ending near the collar. Another reminder for the young; age lines on the face can be temporarily formed by frowning or smiling.

HORROR MOMENTS

The eating of spaghetti during the Don's first act song *'I stole the Prince'* was considered controversial by many observers. It is an unwritten law of the theatre that stage business must not be allowed to take attention away from the development of the plot. On this occasion, however, Ken did not mind at all. It was such a relief to be able to sing the number to the other characters, that he happily accepted it. Besides, with a consummate artist like John Reed doing the eating, he knew that the amusing sucking up of a single strand of spaghetti would be cleverly timed to avoid compromising the words. Having become used to singing as John munched his way through a pile of steaming pasta, he was ill-prepared for the shock occasioned by one of the company's best-loved characters, Jon Ellison. A company stalwart of more than 20 years, Jon was a much-admired performer who gave of his all in everything that he did for the D'Oyly Carte. In Besch's *Gondoliers* he was the obsequious and fussy little waiter responsible for serving the tureen of spaghetti to the Duke's table. A notorious practical joker, he hurried on one evening and, with a wicked gleam in his eye, removed the lid of the dish with a flourish that suggested mischief. Bowing himself off, he hid behind a flat in the wings to witness the upshot of his handiwork. With the first verse of his song well under way, Ken watched John Reed help himself to a plateful of pasta and was horrified to see an eyeball nestling amongst the strands. For the rest of the song he struggled to maintain his concentration as the Duchess and Casilda audibly reacted with revulsion, whilst the Duke tried to cover up the offending orb. It was, of course, only a glass eye, but Mr. Ellison was conspicuous by his absence when the nauseous Ducal party left the stage! After such an unpleasant experience Ken was always wary of looking at the dish of spaghetti and although various unlikely objects appeared in it over the years, the impact was never quite as bad.

HAPPY MOMENTS

The news that Sir Winston Churchill had decided to celebrate his birthday by attending a performance of *The Gondoliers* was received with interest by the members of the company. Accompanied by his friend, Field Marshal Montgomery, he was introduced to the cast during the interval. Before returning to the auditorium for the second act, Montgomery asked if anyone knew the score of a football match involving his favourite team. An obliging journalist volunteered to find out the result and the two distinguished visitors returned to their seats in the middle of the front row of the stalls. As Ken started his song *'There lived a King'*, an usher moved down to the front row, pointed at the Field Marshal and handed over a piece of paper which was duly passed along the row. Unfortunately, the note stopped at Sir Winston who, without reading it, assumed it to be a summons to return to the House for an important division. Whispering to Montgomery, the elderly statesman struggled to his feet and, along with his companion, made his way out of the theatre. With every eye, including those of Don Alhambra, Marco and Giuseppe, following his painfully slow progress, Ken had never felt quite so *'de trop'*. By the end of the song, Sir Winston was still making his getaway and Ken was very tempted to ask if he needed an encore!

A FINAL THOUGHT

An actor should learn to look beyond the obvious. There may be several equally valid ways to say a line and this is the crux of interpretation, but looking past the first reaction can bring great artistic rewards. Ken's portrayal of the Grand Inquisitor was an object lesson in subtlety. Without being overtly authoritarian or sinister he was able to be precisely that by assuming the guise of a wolf in sheep's clothing.

An example of the 1950s postcards available to D'Oyly Carte fans

WILFRED SHADBOLT

Ken's early Shadbolt

'No, no, no, not intelligent'

ONE of the great pleasures of Ken's D'Oyly Carte career was that the Savoy repertoire offered him a wonderful variety of characters to play. Their diversity kept him constantly fresh and the individual demands of the roles challenged him as much in 1982 as they did on first acquaintance in 1957. After a five-month American tour playing mainly Pooh-Bah and Private Willis, he would suddenly find himself as Grosvenor or King Hildebrand and needing to do some hard work to re-establish the parts he had last played many months previously. But he loved picking up the threads and moving overnight from the sublime to the ridiculous; the cultured joys of Archibald Grosvenor followed within a few hours by the coarseness of the stubble-chinned Wilfred Shadbolt in *The Yeomen Of The Guard*. There was certainly no room for complacency or boredom; the audience expected and he delivered.

Shadbolt was always great fun for Ken, giving him the chance to show his versatility as an actor who could move effortlessly between the sophisticated and the crass. In his early days with the company he enjoyed working on Wilfred's physical appearance and mannerisms. He had never before played such a brutish character and it was a welcome addition to his experience. One thing was patently clear; graceful movement and elegant gestures were, for once, not going to be required. His costume was decidedly dowdy in comparison with his splendid outfits in the other operas. It consisted of a rough, dark green jerkin, matching breeches, plain black shirt, black stockings and ankle-length suede boots. He had a long, straggly dark wig surmounted by a close-fitting black cap, although these were replaced in the 1960s by a close-cropped wig in the style of a crew cut. This pleased him, because he no longer inhaled a mouthful of hair every time he sang. He also wore a broad leather belt from which hung his dungeon keys and a thumbscrew. In such unattractive attire he felt well on the way to finding the character.

Ken was aware that his height and broad shoulders gave him a naturally good bearing, but that was the last thing he wanted for Shadbolt, whom he perceived as a lumbering oaf. He soon discovered that by hooking his thumbs into the front of the belt and hunching his shoulders, he lost his good deportment. Next, he experimented with a leaden-footed plod which, along with the slouch, made him look decidedly uncouth. Realising that he was heading in the right direction, he was struck by the fact that it is much easier to learn how to look like an inelegant hulk than a sophisticated gentleman and he enjoyed the change of image. Ken wanted Shadbolt to be a slow-witted man and felt that this would not be easy to convey if his movements were hurried. With the exception of his arrest in the Finale of Act I and the 'Shot' scene in Act II, in which he rushed on and excitedly claimed to have shot the fugitive prisoner, he spent much of the opera shambling around the stage with the urgency of an arthritic tortoise.

Ken discovered that gesture mattered less to his characterisation of Shadbolt than to any other of his roles, but facial expression was more important. When he did break out of his sullen thumbs-in-belt stance, it was to express strong emotion; be it anger, jealousy, delight or cowardice. His humiliation by Phoebe at the end of the opening scene of the opera leaves Wilfred in a jealous rage, but Ken did not gesture angrily towards her retreating figure. Instead, his bitter tirade was accompanied only by a look of utter frustration mixed with indigestion. On the line:

'And disorders his digestion'

he ruefully rubbed his stomach, but preferred the pained expression on his face and colouring of his words to create the effect that he wanted. His clumsy attempts to woo Phoebe also relied heavily on facial acting rather that gesture. During her song *'Were I thy bride',* the range of emotions passing across his face always provoked audience laughter. From astonishment at her sudden change of heart to healthy lust and all points in between were clearly indicated in his mobile face. He had no need for superfluous gesture when his body language said it all. In the dialogue prior to the song, he restricted himself to moving closer to her and his only strong gesture came during his line beginning:

'nay! Suppose it for the nonce'

when his hands came up suddenly, palms towards Phoebe, as if partly in apology for his presumption and partly in self-defence. He did, however, allow himself a joyous little shimmy of anticipation on:

'cheery, joyous, bright, frolicsome husband'

but even then, it was more body language than definite gesture.

In Act I Finale, Shadbolt is informed by the Lieutenant of the Tower that he will be killed instead of the escaped prisoner. Ken cleverly used this to show the cowardice of every bully, his pleasure at the imminent execution of his rival quickly giving way to grovelling fear. Having fallen to his knees to beg for mercy, he clutched at the legs of the Lieutenant before being dragged, kicking and protesting, to the dungeons.

In the Act II sequence with Jack Point, Ken reverted to his sullen, round-shouldered plod which, along with his look of self pity, expressed Wilfred's depression on losing his job. Point's promise to teach him how to be a jester sparks an instant change of mood and Ken, once again, found that it was body language rather than big, happy gestures which best illustrated Shadbolt's delight. His only definite gesture came on:

'And thou wilt qualify me as a jester?'

when his amazement seemed to warrant him pointing to himself as if to make sure he had not misunderstood. Ken believes that, in most cases, gestures should be sparingly used and never left to chance. Due consideration as to their placing, as in the above instance, helps to make a very definite point. For most of the scene, Ken relied on subtle body movements and facial expression to show Shadbolt's transition from misery to joy. A careless shrug of the shoulders demonstrated the Head Jailer's willingness to lie and his unhappiness was enhanced by a slight rocking movement of his upper body as he talked. During Point's long speech regarding the need for a jester to keep the gags flowing however unhappy he may feel, Ken needed to stand and listen so as not to disturb the flow of this important passage of dialogue. Nevertheless, it is necessary for Wilfred to react to the bitterness of Point's words, most of which he does not understand. Ken's face did this for him. Whilst keeping perfectly still, he was able to let the audience see his puzzlement turn to a look which suggested that he was in the presence of a complete nut case. The ever-popular *'cock and bull'* duet gives the performer a wonderful comedic opportunity and Ken knew exactly how far to go without resorting to slapstick. Although he ineptly copied the jester's display of nimble footwork, he avoided playing for laughs and, as ever, kept within the character. It is the jailer trying to be a jester that is funny, not the dance itself.

Ken views the 'Shot' scene as giving Shadbolt the chance to get back into favour with the Lieutenant and improve his street credibility with the inhabitants of the Tower of London, whom he has deprived of the spectacle of an execution.

He injected more energy and enthusiasm into the character in this scene than any other in the opera. Instead of entering with a dull plod, he ran onstage with great purpose, although he was careful to maintain Shadbolt's lack of grace. Despite the demanding and confusing nature of the words in the duet with Jack Point, he was forceful in his explanation to the Lieutenant and impatient with the constant interruptions from Point, repeatedly pushing him aside with some vigour. Ken made Wilfred revel in the congratulations of the people; the back-slapping and hand-shaking accompanied by a huge grin of triumph. The contrast between his doleful appearance at the start of the act and the gloating of this scene typified Ken's ability to bring out every aspect of a character's complex personality.

The dialogue with Phoebe prior to the Finale of Act II is another of Ken's favourite moments and one in which he ran the gamut of emotional extremes. Every possible feeling was visible in his face; from the realisation that Phoebe is in love with Fairfax, to the violent reaction at her perceived flirting with her brother and the childish sulkiness of the wronged fiancee playing hard to get. Throughout this section Ken used very few gestures but, when he did so, they were very strong. Whilst trying to get Phoebe to disclose the identity of her lover, he grabbed her arm and shook her violently, his usual lethargy replaced by jealous rage. Having been soothed by her promise of marriage, his temper erupted again as he advanced threateningly on her brother, Leonard, his arms held as if ready to pounce. It was at this point that Ken displayed his comic genius with wonderful timing. As Leonard unexpectedly pulled a knife on him, Ken stopped dead; his threats subsiding into pitiful embarrassment as the coward in him sent him scurrying to Phoebe's side for protection. After Leonard's departure, he adopted the look of a sulky little boy. As she wheedled her way around him, he stuck out his bottom lip and petulantly shrugged off her advances, pretending to be no longer interested in her. In a few brief moments, his mastery of the art of facial acting and knowledge of how and when to use a gesture, resulted in comedy of such quality that the audience took the dim-witted Head Jailer to their hearts.

THE VOICE

Finding a suitable voice for Shadbolt was not too difficult for Ken, but finding one that did not ruin his singing voice was much harder. He thought it unlikely that a Head Jailer and Assistant Tormentor would be a cultured man, so Ken had to search for a voice that reflected his uneducated background and sadistic enjoyment of his work. He toyed with the possibility of being a cockney, but he would need to be convincing and, as he had not been blessed with a gift for regional accents, he thought better of it. Bearing in mind the slowness of Shadbolt's mind and his shambling gait, Ken decided on using a dull, lifeless tone which would suggest that the jailer's I.Q. leaves a great deal to be desired. However, as with all character voices, it is necessary to make sure that clear diction is not sacrificed for colourful effect and Ken made sure that his consonants were crisp. The other disadvantage of using a strong regional accent becomes obvious when trying to sustain it in the singing voice. Distorted vowels can ruin the vocal line and muddy the diction; there is no benefit from having an authentic accent if the audience cannot understand the words. Ken is aware that the speaking voice he used for Shadbolt became rougher over the years as he found a level which he could sustain without upsetting his singing voice. He warns, however, of the perils of too much shouting – there is always the next performance to consider.

Having found a voice which he felt to be right for Shadbolt, Ken looked for the moments when he could vary the tone to match the character's changes of mood. When trying to woo Phoebe, Ken made his speaking voice much gentler, with a warmth that suggested genuine affection. This gave him room for vocal manoeuvre when she rejected his overtures, allowing anger and frustration to replace his attempt to sound romantic. He never allowed his tone to her to be suggestive; when painting the image of an evening alone with Phoebe, the very thought of his attentions should be enough to revolt her without the need for cheap innuendo. Ken found that by picturing the scene in his mind, he achieved a quality of longing that was totally sincere and it gave Phoebe the chance to react her horror.

Wilfred's delight at the prospect of becoming a jester calls for a brighter tone to contrast with his dreary self-pity, so that he actually laughs. Ken feels that there is no great mystery to achieving such changes of vocal tone and colour. Once settled into the character's voice, the imagination does the rest. The act of smiling immediately changes the energy level in the voice and the tone will brighten automatically. If anger is felt, the reason for such a strong emotion will give a hard edge to the tone without the need for the actor to create it. Thus, Ken's many changes of voice in his final scene with Phoebe were the result of the rapidly-changing situation in which he found himself. He reacted with spite in his first remarks about her always weeping, nonchalance in his denial of a relationship with a servant of the Lieutenant, horror on realising that he has encouraged Pheobe to canoodle with Fairfax and on to uncomprehending fury, violent threats, childish sulking and finally, the winning of her hand. Every change in his voice was achieved by being completely involved in the unfolding drama and he is convinced that an actor thinking the right thoughts will achieve the appropriate vocal quality. He believes that by concentrating on the meaning of the words in a scene, the correct volume, colour and tone of the speaking voice will happen without conscious effort.

THE DIALOGUE

Ken never tired of performing in *The Yeomen of the Guard*. Wilfred Shadbolt may not be the greatest role for a singer, but it has dialogue to delight an actor and Ken loved playing the part of an uncouth clod. Most of his other parts required him to be cultured and well bred, so it was always an exhilarating change to play the part of a man whose unpleasant occupation and rough manners made him an unpopular figure. His interpretation was strongly influenced by his appearance as Shadbolt in a production staged at the Tower of London in 1962. Walking around the Tower precincts in the darkness and passing the ravens on his way to change gave him a powerful impression of the significance of the place in English history. He found it possible to see the stirring and sometimes horrific events in his mind's eye, giving him a feel for his role as the D'Oyly Carte production could never do. In fact, he longed for a director who had the vision to populate the Tower with people who would add colour, flavour and atmosphere to the company's pristine staging. He disliked the appearance of the clone-like lady choristers in

John Cameron and Ken in the 1962 production at The Tower of London

their spotless aprons and the smartly-dressed male citizens. He wanted to see the rough and dirty side, too, but it was never to be.

Ken's portrayal of Shadbolt was based on the belief that the Head Jailer and Assistant Tormentor is as thick as two short planks and that only two things matter to him; his love for Phoebe and his love for his gruesome work, which he believes gives him status. Ken's interpretation of the dialogue was anchored in these three traits and, in his opinion, everything that Wilfred says can be directly linked to his slow wits, unrequited love and pride in his work. Ken approached the opening scene as if Shadbolt is fully aware of the fact that Phoebe finds him repulsive, his tentative greeting:

'Mistress Meryll!'

given in the expectation of another rebuff; his love for her driving him to take that chance in the hope that she might, miraculously, change her feelings about him. This, of course, does not happen and his pathetic:

'Haven't you anything to say to me?'

was sulky and self-pitying. Phoebe's reference to him as a '*brute*' must sting him into self-defence and Ken's feels that Wilfred's statement that he does not do his job because he likes it should be a deliberate untruth. After all, she would never fancy him if he admitted to enjoying torturing people. The thinly-veiled allusion to Colonel Fairfax as a sorcerer sparks a sequence in which they bandy childish comments to see who can goad the other the most. During this exchange, Phoebe's admiration for

Faifax becomes increasingly clear to the frustrated Shadbolt. His response is to spitefully remind her of the Colonel's fast-approaching fate. At the end of the line:

> *'Ah! I'm content to chance that. This evening at half-past seven – ah!'*

Ken transformed the *'ah!'* into a gutteral sound meant to represent the descent of the axe blade onto the neck of the unfortunate victim. Phoebe's horrified reaction causes her to let it slip that she has noticed Fairfax's good looks and Ken used this as the fuse to ignite his jealousy. On:

> *'How do you know he's young and handsome?'*

he shouted at her angrily. By imagining what he would like to do to his rival, Ken produced a harshness in his voice that made his jealousy frightening, barking out the line much faster than any of his previous lines. This, in turn, gave Phoebe the chance to make a complete fool of him by smartly announcing that she has been watching the Colonel take his daily exercise. At this point Ken stopped abruptly, realising that he has jumped the gun and that she has not been secretly meeting Fairfax. His anger suddenly abated, he chose not to shout:

> *'Curse him!'*

but said it almost to himself, with such quiet bitterness that he immediately gave Phoebe the opening to taunt him about his unworthy jealousy of a man about to be executed. Deflated by her attack on him and aware of the futility of his love, Ken avoided the more obvious option of reacting with aggression, preferring to say the speech beginning:

> *'I am! I'm jealous of everybody and everything'*

in the sulky, self-pitying tone that he used at the top of the scene, his hang-dog expression evoking sympathy from the audience. He maintained this for:

> *'You used to like 'em.'*

Ken did not say this with any hope, or as a recrimination, but more with a feeling of dull resignation as he endured another humiliating rejection. Her parting shot at him, in which she implies that she is always polite to people whom she barely knows, is more than Wilfred can bear and his temper erupts as she leaves. In the final speech of the scene, Ken always addressed his lines in the direction of her exit and never to the front. He gave Shadbolt's hurt feelings full reign with a discharge of venom in which he carefully coloured several key words for maximum effect. To illustrate the man's suffering in the line:

> *'I don't believe you know how it eats into a man's heart and disorders his digestion.'*

he hit the word *'eats'* with some force and a hardness of tone that told of real pain. Ken loved saying the word '*disorders*', in which he rolled the second syllable around his mouth making it sound like a gurgling stomach. In the last part of this wonderful line:

> *'and turns his interior into boiling lead.'*

he used the same tactic to make '*boiling*' sound as if his insides were doing precisely that. To end the speech he reverted to anger, bellowing in her direction with the howling of a wounded animal, before limping off to lick his wounds.

In this first scene, which sets up Shadbolt's character and his relationship with Phoebe, Ken stresses the need for contrasting levels in the dialogue. It is easy enough to rant and rave from start to finish, but W. S. Gilbert provides opportunities for a variety of emotions and reactions. Wallowing self-pity can be portrayed by slowing down, anger or frustration by quickening the de-livery. If the performer delves beneath the surface of the words, he will discover the many facets which make up the Head Jailer's personality and the means to express them.

The second of Shadbolt's three scenes with Phoebe has always been a great favourite with performers and audiences alike, it's high comedy never concealing the dramatic situation which forces her make up to the man she loathes. Ken revelled in a section which allowed him to demonstrate the three key elements in his interpretation of Wilfred's character. He began the scene looking as though his efforts to work out why the Lieutenant is interested in a minstrel girl were making his dull brain hurt. With the arrival of Phoebe, Wilfred immediately assumes that normal service is about to be resumed and goes onto the offensive before she can start berating him. He is so stupid that it doesn't strike him as odd that she is suddenly being friendly towards him. Until she calls him '*dear Wilfred*', he is too busy feeling sorry for himself to notice her change of attitude. Ken's reaction to being addressed by this unexpected term of affection was hilarious. Having done a double take as if not convinced that he had heard her correctly, he assumed an expression of bliss that lasted for all of three seconds. Her unfortunate choice of words about the comparison between live asses and dead lions, soon wiped the happy smirk from his face, convincing him that she had found a new way to plague him. Having reacted angrily on:

'Oh, they say that, do they?'

Ken pushed Shadbolt back into his defensive shell for the next line:

'Oh yes, as an assistant tormentor.'

which he said with a mixture of sarcasm and the usual self-pity. Phoebe then cleverly recovers her lost ground with display of outrageous flattery that only an idiot would believe, given her record for insulting him. But, of course, Wilfred happens to agree with her assessment of his professional attributes and this is the key to his next speech beginning:

'Truly, I have seen great resolution give way under my persuasive methods.'

Ken's delivery of this speech turned around his demonstration of the skill required to work a thumbscrew, which he gave with enthusiasm in the belief that Phoebe is genuinely interested. He made a slight pause before drawing out the word '*persuasive*', which he said with a sadistic smile on his lips prior to starting the thumbscrew lesson. Ken took the next line very slowly and quietly, taking plenty of time to demonstrate Shabolt's technique. As he said:

'In the hundredth part of a single revolution.'

he made minute adjustments to the screw over 6-7

seconds, taking the same length of time to say the line and making pauses between the words to accommodate each small turn. The fact that he spoke so slowly had nothing to do with giving Phoebe and Sergeant Meryll plenty of time to steal his keys. Ken wanted Shadbolt to be so absorbed by the demonstration that his failure to notice the theft would look entirely plausible. Having spoken so slowly, he increased both tempo and volume during:

> *'and a torrent of impulsive unbosoming that the pen can scarcely follow.'*

rising to a climax by laughing at his own wit. Between the laughter and:

> *'I am a mad wag.'*

Ken pretended to have inadvertently turned the screw so that he squashed his own thumb, his laughter turning into a yell of pain. This enabled him to say the line with embarrassment, as if conscious of making a fool of himself instead of impressing her. Phoebe's forced amusement at his drollery should renew Wilfred's confidence, so that he begins to relax in her company. Confident that his luck has at last changed and that she is there for the taking, he said:

> *'Ah, we might be passing happy together –'*

with a dreamy quality in his voice that suggested a foregone conclusion and not as though trying to encourage her to accept him. Ken played the line as though it never enters Shadbolt's thick skull that she might now turn him down and this also applied to the way he said the next line:

> *'For thou wouldst make a most tender and loving wife.'*

This can be interpreted as a further attempt to cajole her into agreeing to marry him, but Ken preferred to say it as though he was conjuring up a beautiful mental picture of delights to come. During Phoebe's teasing speech in which she speculates on the identity of her future husband, Ken reacted with wonderful facial expressions to indicate his suitability for the vacancy. After:

> *'Now say that it is I – nay!'*

Phoebe's reaction of mock outrage made him become more circumspect, as if aware that he has been too presumptuous, the *'nay!'* and the following:

> *'suppose it for the nonce. Say that we are wed – suppose it only –'*

said as an attempt to placate her. With '*suppose*' being said twice, Ken was careful to use each of them differently. He emphasised the first one, but moved quickly over the second to make '*only*' more important. His treatment of the next section of the speech:

> *'and I thy cheery, joyous, bright, frolicsome husband.'*

was one of the funniest moments in the scene. He managed to make the list of pleasant-sounding adjectives sound anything but pleasant and with facial expressions to match, this unlikely description of himself left Phoebe looking shell-shocked. The last section of the line offers an opportunity for imaginative timing and word colouring. By using

Wilfred's imagination rather than his own, Ken painted a nauseating picture of married life chez Shadbolt; his use of three key words creating a nightmarish scenario for his prospective wife. In the line:

'thou and I are alone together – with a long, long evening before us!'

he paused between '*alone*' and '*together*' as if Shadbolt is unaware that he is stating the obvious, but determined to stress the implication of such privacy. Moving close to Phoebe, he made the second '*long*' precisely that, dropping the level of his voice and breathing heavily through the word to horrifying effect. This is a classic example of Ken's skill in making the most of word repetition, a skill which he believes may be acquired by any performer who is made aware of the technique and its rewards. He read the final line:

'Aye! – wert thou my bride – ?'

as Wilfred taking it for granted that Phoebe has agreed to marry him. Raising his voice by half an octave, he said the words with great excitement, his sudden vivacity in complete contrast with the earlier sullenness.

Ken thinks that the final speech of the scene is difficult in that Shadbolt is alone on the stage. Many performers of the role use the lines detailing Wilfred's sexual conquests as an excuse for slapstick comedy but he, as always, recommends a more subtle approach. He said the first line:

'No, thou'rt not – not yet!'

in the direction of Phoebe's exit, making it quite obvious that he believes it to be only a matter of time. Thereafter, the dim-witted jailer is really thinking aloud, convinced that his latest success is hardly surprising in view of his proven track record with the ladies. Knowing himself to be alone, he indulges his inflated ego by reminiscing about the different women who have thrown themselves at him, getting so carried away by vanity that he mimics their methods of seduction. The section beginning:

'I have been woo'd boldly, timidly, tearfully, shyly – by direct assault,'

needs careful attention to detail in order to avoid a repetetive delivery. Ken allowed himself time to illustrate each example, changing his tone, pace and pitch according to which type of woman or mode of attack he wanted to convey. He avoided cheap gestures, preferring to let his voice and appropriate facial expressions make the comedic impact. He feels strongly that there is no place for vulgarity in this speech, or anywhere else in Gilbert and Sullivan for that matter. It is easy to get a cheap laugh by giving in to the temptation to be crude, but it is much more rewarding to provoke laughter with genuine acting skills.

To conclude this wonderful scene, Ken said:

'But this wooing is not of the common order:'

with a mixture of astonishment and admiration, making it plain that Shadbolt has never before encountered such a woman. Beginning the line fairly quietly, he increased volume and momentum through:

'who must needs woo me,'

stressing the word '*needs*' and rising to a climax on:

'if she die for it!'

which he repeated with some force as he strode triumphantly from the stage.

Shadbolt's dialogue with Jack Point in the early part of Act II includes moments of great humour and moments of great pathos. Although the scene belongs to the heart-broken jester, Wilfred's contribution to the drama is vital, his stupidity bringing comic relief at a time when Point's quick-witted, but cynical description of life as a professional comedian threatens to overwhelm both himself and the audience with depression. Ken's flair for timing lines was much in evidence during this scene and he provoked laughter without detracting from the poignancy of Jack Point's terrible unhappiness.

Conscious of the fact that Wilfred has lost his job and narrowly escaped execution, Ken started the scene in morose mood, irritated by Jack Point's spiteful allusions to his professional incompetence. His response to being goaded:

> *'Aye, it's well for thee to laugh. Thou hast a good post, and hast cause to be merry.'*

came after a pause of approximately 3 seconds. This delay allowed the audience to recognise the misery that Point is feeling despite his display of forced merriment. Ken used the pause to feel sorry for himself before saying the line with self-pity. By thinking as Wilfred, he appeared to be worrying about himself, rather than just waiting for the three seconds to elapse. Throughout Point's lengthy speech about the sorry lot of an unhappy man paid to make people laugh, Ken used sufficient facial expression to indicate that he didn't understand a word of it, but not enough to take the attention from the jester. During the painfully sad final section of the speech, Ken appeared to be so wrapped up in Wilfred's thoughts as to be not listening at all and this was the key to the timing of his next line:

> *'Yet I have often thought that a jester's calling would suit me to a hair.'*

This always got a huge laugh, but only because he allowed a five-second gap before saying it. Such a time lag gave the audience time to become emotionally involved, their pity for the plight of the jester usually making them feel uncomfortable. Shadbolt's ridiculous assertion that he would make a good jester broke the tension and enabled them to lighten up. Ken started his next speech:

> *'Aye, I have a pretty wit'*

very indignantly, as if put out by Point's dismissal of his suitability as a jester. He went on to enthusiastically explain the merits of torture chamber humour, giving Point the opportunity for appropriately appalled facial reaction. Another moment for good timing and word colour comes in the line:

> *'I have tried it on many a prisoner, and there have been some who smiled.'*

Ken paused for a second between *'who'* and *'smiled'*, using the time to picture the poor prisoner trying to laugh at his jokes. He drew out *'smiled'* by smiling himself, the cruel twist of his lips elongating the word and making it sound very creepy. He ended the speech by getting a little of his own back on Jack Point, sarcastically implying that he didn't rate him as a jester, saying:

'Seeing that thou art one.'

with a large dose of spite.

Ken thinks that after the song *'A private buffoon'*, Wilfred is somewhat befuddled by all the details of a jester's responsibilities. Rather than being inspired by them, he should go back into his shell, saying:

'She did well.' and *'Thou art a very dull dog indeed.'*

with heavy sarcasm. As he listened to Point telling him how easy it would be to come up with a story about having shot Fairfax, Ken brought out Shadbolt's pragmatic side by using facial expressions which clearly indicated his reluctance to get involved in such a scheme. Nevertheless, tempted by the prospect of learning how to be a jester, Ken made a pause before saying:

'I am to lie?'

as if such a thought would never cross a decent man's mind. As Point promises to back up the story, Shadbolt should obviously be giving the scheme serious consideration, so that on:

'And thou wilt qualify me as a jester?'

his resolve is clearly weakening, needing only the promise of a glimpse at the ultimate prize, *'The Merrie Jestes of Hugh Ambrose'*, to close the deal.

A performer playing Shadbolt has many opportunities for comedy during his three scenes with Phoebe, but the last one offers the discerning actor the most possibilities for creating laughter. The humour must stem from Wilfred's confusion at the situation developing around him rather than being sought by a deliberate display of buffoonery.

Wilfred enters feeling very pleased with himself following his return to favour with the Lieutenant and Ken made the first line:

'In tears, eh? What a plague art thou grizzling for now?'

very unsympathetic, as if unable to fathom why she is always crying. He is so cock-sure of her devotion to him that he assumes her admission of jealousy is, naturally, about him. After a pause indicating Wilfred's slow thought processes, Ken said:

'But I have never given thee cause for jealousy.'

with such a look of bemused innocence that the audience roared with laughter. He then went onto the defensive again, reassuring Phoebe that her suspicions are unfounded. Frustrated by his crass stupidity, she carelessly reveals the identity of her lover and Ken used her tirade against him to slowly, but surely, indicate that something she has said makes no sense. As if thinking aloud, he took his time in saying:

'The man thou lovest is to marry Elsie Maynard?'

before the truth hit him like a bolt of lightning. With the sudden realisation of her deception, he became aggressive, grabbing her arm on:

'Speak! Who is this man'

shouting in a rough voice to get the truth from her. He stopped abruptly after:

'with my connivance, too!'

as though struck by another bolt from the blue in realising the implication of his own involvement. Ken believes that this is the one moment when Shadbolt would think quickly, his anger causing him to put two and two together and get the right answer for once. Ken's response to Phoebe pointing out the gaping hole in Wilfred's story was very funny. With his mouth opening and shutting like a fish out of water, he stuttered his way through:

'A - I - I may have been mistaken.'

before recovering his composure and becoming aggressively determined in a desperate attempt to cover his tracks. His reaction to her resigned promise to marry him:

'Is that sure?'

held an element of warning against messing him about again, but mostly conveyed his disbelieving delight.

With the appearance of Leonard Meryll and Pheobe's ecstatic reaction to the news of Fairfax's reprieve, Shadbolt immediately jumps to the wrong conclusion and assumes that Leonard is a rival. His jealousy explodes into rage as he watches her kissing another man. Ken used a very harsh tone for:

'Ods bobs, death o' my life! Art thou mad? Am I mad? Are we all mad?'

stamping around with uncomprehending fury, before advancing menacingly towards Leonard on:

'As for thee, sir, devil take thee, I'll rip thee like a herring for this!'

Using the same gravel tone, he spoke quietly, but rasped out the consonants of '*devil*' and '*rip*' to sound very threatening. After slowly building to a terrifying level, he stopped dead as Leonard drew his knife. Having looked at the knife and then at the unflinching expression on the face of his rival, he slunk away to hide behind Phoebe's skirts in a cowardly about-face. In the line:

'I'll – oh! Phoebe! Phoebe! Who is this man?'

he substituted the '*oh!*', which followed him seeing the knife, with an embarrassed clearing of the throat as he ran back to Phoebe. Not satisfied by her explanation that Leonard is her brother, he reacted with biting sarcasm on:

'How do I know this? Has he 'brother' writ large on his brow?'

Ken made the unjustified display of jealousy gradually subside into sulking and he petulantly shrugged off Phoebe's attempts to placate him. It is interesting that he added four words in the middle of her efforts to win him round. As she said:

'Come – I am thy Phoebe – thy very own –'

she tickled his neck, to which Ken responded, despite trying to maintain his sulk, with a giggling:

'Do not do it!'

He cannot now recall how this came about, but remembers that the audience always laughed. He also added a teasing '*No!*' after her question:

'Is not that enough for thee?'

before sweeping her into his arms. As Phoebe explained to her father the reason for their canoodling, Ken stood grinning like a love-struck teenager; his final line of the scene:

'It's the same thing!'

delivered with slushy sentimentality as he chased her from the stage.

Ken's later Shadbolt

MAKE UP

Ken always had in mind the fact that Shadbolt's appearance should be repulsive to Phoebe, so he decided that his make up needed to be quite extreme. He never pictured him as being any older than mid-thirties, so age lines were not necessary. A Head Jailer and Assistant Tormentor would have spent a great deal of time in the fetid atmosphere of the dungeons, so he probably had a pasty complexion. Ken started his make up with a pale base, using more of the lighter number 5 colour in his greasepaint mixture. Next, he roughly applied black pancake over his chin and cheeks to give the impression of heavy stubble. Again using the black, he enlarged his eyebrows so that they almost met over the bridge of his nose, giving him a stupid expression. With his usual mix of dark brown and lake, he applied dark shadows under his eyes and then, using number 5, drew a broad, twisted line down the length of his nose to make it look broken. In his early days with the D'Oyly Carte, he also painted a twisted mouth to make himself look cruel. However, in later years, he toned this down considerably, feeling that it was unnecessary to make Shadbolt look disfigured. Instead, with crimson lake, he made his mouth more pronounced than usual with a heavy lower lip. He applied his murky mix along either side of his nose as shadowing to emphasise the break, added the all-important black eye lines and finished off by powdering down as usual.

HORROR MOMENTS

When running from the stage in pursuit of Phoebe after their final scene together, Ken worked up quite a pace. In order to stop his momentum in the confined space of the wings, he always put his hands forward and braced himself against the wing wall. The first time he appeared in *The Yeomen of the Guard* at the Theatre Royal in Norwich, he set off after Phoebe as usual, stretched out his hands to stop himself, only to discover, too late, that the wall was actually the emergency exit. Unable to control his forward momentum once through the door, he landed face-down in a large rain puddle feeling somewhat dazed. With his entrance for Act II Finale following almost immediately, he had no time to dry off and so, having been hauled to his feet by Phoebe, he escorted her onto the stage in a very bedraggled state. As if trying to clear his mind for the difficult vocal ensembles ahead was not enough, he had to contend with the incredulous stares of his colleagues, who had no idea why Shadbolt was dripping wet. Needless to say, the curiosity and amusement created by his soggy appearance did little to enhance the tragic conclusion of the opera.

HAPPY MOMENTS

Ken's appearance as Wilfred Shadbolt in the 1962 production of *Yeomen* at The Tower of London was a memorable experience. The effect on his characterisation of performing in the real place, as opposed to on a painted set, was profound. The brooding atmosphere engendered by the night shadows on the massive stonework inspired him and made it easy to believe that he was the Head Jailer in those cruel times. However, Tower Green has no washing facilities. Forced to drive home to West London in his grotesque make up, he remembers with great glee the startled look on the faces of the drivers pulled up next to him at the traffic lights and their obvious impatience for a green light!

Ken considered that the enormous explosion engendered by the bomb tank placed at the back of the stage, to represent the shot in the 'Shot' scene, was somewhat extravagant given the size of the arquebus that was supposed to have produced it. Until the dangerous practice of smoking in the wings was banned, he used to light a cigarette, inhale a mouthful of smoke and blow it down the barrel of the gun, which was still 'smoking' as he ran on stage. He has never denied having a juvenile sense of humour.

A FINAL THOUGHT

W. S. Gilbert created a stupid man in Wilfred Shadbolt, but he did not create a clown. There is no need for cheap comedy; the many funny moments between Shadbolt and Phoebe arise from their previous history and the circumstances leading to their betrothal. Physical comedy has its place, but humour stemming from imagination and good timing is more important.

DR. DALY

Ken as the lonely Vicar of Ploverleigh

'He's a clean old gentleman.'

PEOPLE are invariably surprised by Ken's assertion that, in a D'Oyly Carte career spanning nearly a quarter of a century, he never became bored by his roles. It is something of a cliché to say that every performance is different, but Ken found that to be exactly the case if he looked for every opportunity to bring something fresh to a characterisation. There were times when he wished that there might be more performances of *Ruddigore*, *Patience* or *Princess Ida*, but he happily climbed into whatever costume was hanging in his dressing room and enjoyed the challenge of the evening. He was, however, excited to find out that *The Sorcerer* was to be re-introduced into the repertoire for the 1971 tour and that he was to play Dr Daly. Gilbert and Sullivan's first full-length collaboration had not been performed by the company since 1939, when costumes and sets were destroyed in an air raid. Ken knew little about the opera except that it boasted some good songs for Dr Daly and he never imagined that the part of the lonely vicar would bring him so much joy. It had been many years since he had accepted the challenge of learning a new role and he set about the task with much enthusiasm. Before very long, he realised that Daly's music lay perfectly for his high baritone voice and the lyrical style of the songs called for the legato singing that he so enjoyed. Added to that, the delightful and witty dialogue gave him the material with which to create a character completely removed from any of his other parts. It is fair to say that the inclusion of *The Sorcerer* in the company's touring schedule was a great creative tonic for Ken and he welcomed the refreshing change of artistic fare.

It has always been accepted that Dr. Daly is an elderly man. Indeed, he describes himself as *'an old fogy'* in the first scene with Constance and Mrs. Partlet. Ken, however, was concerned that he must not make the parson too decrepit if his attractiveness to the teenaged Constance was to be credible. He thought that Dr. Daly would be in his sixties, of good bearing and with distinguished features that echoed his earlier handsome looks, making Constances's love for a much older man seem plausible. When giving thought to how Daly might move, Ken was faced with the same problem; getting on a bit he certainly might be, but arthritic and gammy, not necessarily. To indicate the parson's advancing years, he made his broad shoulders a little stooped, but he came down firmly against any suggestion of a slow gait. On the contrary, he made the vicar purposeful of step and quietly energetic. He wanted to create the image of a parish priest busy about his pastoral duties and in this, he was helped by the costume. He wore a knee-length black coat, black trousers, black waistcoat, white clerical collar and a wide-brimmed black hat. In a collar-length white wig with a centre parting, matching sideburns and sporting pince-nez spectacles, he looked every inch an English country parson. Presuming Dr. Daly's eyesight to be not as good as it was, he developed the rather endearing mannerism of leaning slightly towards the person he was addressing, as if, subconsciously, trying to see them more clearly. He was certainly glad that he had created a vicar in robust health, because the D'Oyly Carte production required Dr. Daly to lift Aline from the ground and swing her around in an outpouring of newly-found love. If Ken had decided to make Daly very frail and elderly, such stage business would have been nonsensical. The characters and their behaviour frequently stretch the imagination without the performer adding to the incongruity of already unlikely situations. The challenge for the actor is to bring a sense of reality to the sometimes improbable and exaggerated creations of W. S. Gilbert – and in this Ken excelled.

Whilst preparing his interpretation, Ken found himself very aware of vicars, his search for little details or foibles of behaviour making him observe them closely whenever possible. He wanted his Dr. Daly to be a gentle and rather melancholy soul, so his use of gesture and facial expression would need to reflect these traits. He was also struck by the romantic streak in the lonely bachelor and this, too, must be seen in his face. The first song gave Ken an early opportunity to bring out all of these characteristics, enabling him to show the sad, private side of a man used to putting on a cheerful professional front. During the recitative *'The air is charged with amatory numbers'*, he used the plaintive trilling of the clarinet to suggest birdsong, looking up into imaginary trees for a glimpse of the songster and smiling delightedly at the beauty of such an idyllic moment. With his hand momentarily cupped close to his ear as if to further enhance the glorious sound, he looked a picture of cherubic innocence, his face radiating the joy of life. He made it seem as if nature's music is timed especially to celebrate the imminent betrothal of Aline and Alexis, their happiness highlighting the emptiness of his own life as his expression of joy gave way to one of sadness. During the following song, *'Time was when love and I were well acquainted'*, he remained very still, allowing his face and the words to do the work as he reminisced about his younger days.

Throughout the opera Ken used gestures very sparingly, but they were always prompted by the words or his calling; from the gentle brushing away of a tear to a protracted and hearty handshake of congratulation, he let the words dictate his actions in a completely logical way. For the most part, he preferred to let his facial expressions emphasise his emotions and avoided using his hands too much, with the exception of clasping them in front of his chest whenever he wished to express delight and turning his hat in his hands when upset. In the Act II song, *'Oh, my voice is sad and low'*, Dr.Daly is frustrated to discover that every eligible female in the village has just become engaged. To reflect this, Ken replaced his usual brisk walk with a leaden step of despair and with his shoulders slumped, he looked the picture of misery. Apart from the distracted turning of his hat by running the brim through his fingers, he used no gestures at all in the song. Once again, his body language said everything for him. Even when becoming angry on:

'What a rogue young hearts to pillage'

he refrained from angry gestures. Instead, he paced agitatedly to and fro, with the turning of his hat becoming more frenetic.

Ken avoided playing the flageolet in the introduction to the song because he hated the idea that he would obviously be pretending to play it. Despite a tongue-in-cheek letter sent by the company's General Manager, Frederic Lloyd, he conveniently managed to forget about Miss Carte's instruction that he must put in the appropriate business for the next London season. Some eight years later he was still flageoletless!

A delightful conclusion to the hat-twirling came as, under the influence of the love potion, he saw and fell in love with Aline. Flinging it upstage as if symbolically dispatching his previous loneliness, he lifted her high into the air before sweeping her into his arms in grand romantic style.

Ken believes that many performers feel obliged to use lots of gestures simply because they are on the stage. If an actor is totally confident of the interpretation of the words, it should become clear where an appropriate gesture may be used to maximum effect without the need for vacuous arm waving. He also believes that Dr. Daly should not be played as a doddering old man. Too often, amateur performers make him so fossilised that the idea of a young girl being attracted to him is quite ridiculous.

BRIDGET D'OYLY CARTE LIMITED

P.O.Box 189 1 SAVOY HILL LONDON WC2R OBP

Cables : Savoyard London *Telephone : 01-836 1533*

9th July, 1974.

Dear Mr. Sandford,

Miss D'Oyly Carte has for a long time felt rather concerned that you do not play the flageolet on your entrance as Dr. Daly in "The Sorcerer".

We all know the very understandable reason that, at the time of the production, you felt that if you could not give a genuine performance on this instrument yourself, you would not wish to mime it but, by the time we open at Sadler's Wells Theatre, Miss D'Oyly Carte would like to see this piece of business back in the Opera.

Would you now be prepared to mime it or, if you still feel as strongly as you did, would you consider learning it so that you could play it on stage ? If you would like to do the latter, naturally we could discuss this and I could arrange for you to have the necessary instruction to master this very difficult instrument !

I am sure you will appreciate the position.

Yours sincerely,

General Manager.

Kenneth Sandford, Esq.,
Alexandra Theatre,
Birmingham.

P.S This will of course mean that I have to propose you for the M.U!
B

DIRECTORS: BRIDGET D'OYLY CARTE · MARTIN B. RADCLIFFE · F. C. SAWFORD · SIR HUGH WONTNER, C.V.O

THE VOICE

Finding the right voice for Dr. Daly presented Ken with some difficulty. In the D'Oyly Carte production of *The Gondoliers* he played Don Alhambra as a sophisticated, high-ranking Catholic priest, but he wanted Daly to be a very different kind of clergyman, with a completely different way of speaking. A simple country parson of the Victorian era was, usually, a well-loved and respected figure, around whom much of village life was focused. Ken was keen to portray the type of vicar who was all things to all people – pastor, friend, teacher or social worker; a permanent fixture who baptised babies, nurtured their spiritual development and took joy in marrying them some 20 years later. With these characteristics in mind, he made rather more visits to his parish church in Ealing than usual, with the view of concentrating on the vicar's style of preaching and also used his recollections of the many hours spent listening to sermons when singing in church choirs. Although aware of the need to avoid stereotyping, he was still struck by the undulating cadences and clipped diction that seem to typify everyone's perception of a preacher and made a mental note to do likewise.

Several key words came to Ken's mind when fixing on a voice for Dr. Daly; sincerity, warmth, projection, wistfulness and vagueness amongst them. By believing that Daly is always sincerely delighted to meet any member of his flock, he was able to imbue his voice with a warm tone that suggested real gladness whenever in the company of the villagers, be they humble or aristocratic. Nevertheless, Ken thought that, after a lifetime in the pulpit projecting his voice to the back of the church, the vicar would never quite lose the habit of making a small separation between his words and so, whenever in conversation, his slightly-exaggerated delivery would make him sound like a mobile sermon. Ken found this idea particularly useful when Daly offers Alexis his congratulations and blessing for his future happiness with Aline. The need for contrast never far from his mind, Ken used the moments when Daly is thinking aloud to bring out the loneliness of the parson who feels that love has passed him by. By dropping his pulpit enunciation and speaking more quietly, he brought the other side of the man to the fore. Imagining that Dr. Daly is remembering the innocent romance of the days when young ladies at village fetes and parish meetings practically threw themselves at him, Ken easily produced a dreamy and wistful quality of voice that was completely different from the vicar's professional tone, his sadness causing the audience to feel great sympathy towards him. Another facet of the character that Ken recognised is Dr. Daly's ability to be rather vague, as if he is not always on the same wavelength as everyone else. During the first scene, Mrs. Partlet dramatically announces that she may soon lose her daughter, Constance. Dr. Daly, never considering that she means marriage, replies with:

> *'Dear me, you pain me very much. Is she delicate?'*

Ken used a completely different tone of voice for this line. Having assumed the worst, he drew Mrs.

Partlet to one side and dropped his voice almost to a whisper, his shock tempered by the need for professional discretion. Whenever the opportunity arose for Daly to seem vague, Ken's imagination as to what might be going on in the vicar's mind induced a blank tone which perfectly illustrated his occasional slowness in grasping a situation.

Although the key to voice colouring lies in the imagination, Ken's portrayal of Dr. Daly benefited from his observations of the real thing, but he advises that studying other people in the cause of characterisation must not lead to caricature.

THE DIALOGUE

Having so looked forward to adding another character to his repertoire after 14 years with the D'Oyly Carte, Ken was disappointed when he realised that Dr. Daly has very little dialogue. As a singer, he loved the music, but the actor in him would have liked more than Gilbert had penned and this made him determined to make the most of every one of his wonderful lines. So successful was he at finding humour and pathos where others might search in vain, that his colleagues paid him the ultimate compliment of standing in the wings to listen to his hauntingly beautiful singing of *'Time was'* and the very amusing dialogue that followed it.

Ken began the scene with Mrs. Partlet and Constance as if disturbed from a reverie, his reply to Mrs. Partlet's greeting given after a slight start which brought him back to the present. Having expressed his pleasure on seeing her with great warmth and sincerity, he made a brief pause before:

'And your little daughter, Constance!'

as if it had taken him a moment to recognise the much-improved young lady. It is interesting to note that, in his early portrayal of Dr. Daly, he remembered her name without difficulty, but in this author's 1995 production he struggled to recall the name without a whispered prompt from Mrs. Partlet. Ken feels that this helps to establish the vicar's vagueness at an early opportunity and also gives Constance a chance to look upset by his forgetfulness. Using another short pause to lean forward and peer at Constance through his pince-nez, he said:

'Why, she is quite a little woman, I declare!'

as if suddenly seeing her in a completely different light from the child he still considers her to be, the surprise in his voice suggesting that the grown-up version rather takes his fancy. Having reacted with shock to Mrs. Partlet's imminent loss of her daughter, Ken took 3-4 seconds to lead her away from Constance before tactfully asking after her health on:

'Is she delicate?'

when his obvious confusion always got a laugh. He then allowed himself about 4 seconds before saying:

'Oh, I take you. To be sure,'

which gave time to allow for the puzzlement in his face to give way to the realisation of her meaning that her daughter might soon get married. This offers a great chance to demonstrate Daly's tendency to be slow on the uptake if the actor allows plenty of time for the penny to drop. Ken was very enthusiastic in Daly's assertion that Constance need not be considering marriage for several years, his inability to see through the plot to marry him off to Constance adding much to the humour of the scene. Ken believes that the audience should be given time to register a line before the next one is spoken, but there are occasions when the quick pick up of a cue can be dramatically effective and the line:

> *'To some strapping young fellow in her own rank of life.'*

is a good example. It is a continuation of the previous line:

> *'I shall have much pleasure in marrying her myself – '*

and should be hurried through as if the vicar is suddenly struck by the embarrassing thought that his words might be misinterpreted. The fact that Constance exclaims in delight between the two parts of the line is irrelevant to his thought process. Ken's ability to wring out every drop of humour from a line was evidenced by his treatment of:

> *'Be still my fluttering heart!'*

This is such a wonderful line that the most inexperienced performer should expect to get a laugh, but he did not say it before audibly gasping for breath as Mrs. Partlet's painful words caused him to suffer palpitations. This was not overplayed; the suggestion of physical distress caused by strong emotion being sufficient to bring gales of laughter, leaving Mrs. Partlet and Constance to react together until the hilarity subsided. After Mrs. Partlet's non-too-subtle assertion that a vicar needs a wife, Ken agreed heartily and then sank into reflection, pausing briefly before saying the line:

> *'Time was when it might have been; but I have left it too long – '*

as if suddenly unaware of their presence, hastily recollecting himself and making a joke about his age on:

> *'I am an old fogy now, am I not, my dear? - a very old fogy , indeed!'*

He used the repetition of *'old fogy'* to great effect, assuming the wavering tone of a 90-year old to make Constance laugh, oblivious of the fact that she is distracted by his assertion that he will never get married. As Mrs. Partlet led Constance from the stage, Ken watched them with an expression of puzzlement, as if Dr. Daly has not got a clue as to the cause of his young parishoner's distress. His blank look on:

> *'Poor little girl! I'm afraid she has something on her mind.'*

shows Dr. Daly at his vague worst and he always had to wait for the laughter to die down before continuing with:

> *'She is rather comely.'*

which he said with innocent admiration, rather than any suggestion that there might be life in the old boy yet. Having admonished himself on:

> *'But tush! I am puling!'*

he resumed his usual heartiness on the line:

> *'Here comes the young Alexis with his proud and happy father.'*

which he said with genuine delight for the happiness of his old friends and with a brightness of tone that dispelled his sadness of a moment earlier.

The passage of dialogue beginning:

> *'May fortune bless you!'*

in which Dr. Daly gives Alexis his best wishes for future happiness, is an ideal moment for the vicar to be at his pulpit best and Ken played it accordingly. The florid words are, of course, spoken above an elegant minuet – Sullivan's contribution to the atmosphere of old-fashioned etiquette which Gilbert was aiming to lampoon. Ken turned the need to be audible above the music to advantage, delivering the 11-syllable lines with the clipped articulation and increase of volume that Dr. Daly might use when addressing his congregation. He made Daly revel in the sentimental poetry, gradually increasing in intensity to finish with a rousing climax on:

> *'Into a new and glorious horizon!'*

when the emotion of the occasion provoked a few tears of joy. He continued in the same vein for the final lines of the scene:

> *'Ere Sol has sunk into his western slumbers!'*

pointing the unusual use of *'Sol'* with a chuckle at his own poetic wit.

Ken began the Act II dialogue:

> *'It is singular – it is very singular.'*

as if Dr. Daly is thinking aloud, his bemusement at the bizarre matrimonial plans springing up all around him making him unaware of the presence of Alexis and Aline. By emphasising *'very'*, he made a distinction between the double use of *'singular'*. As the speech progresses, Daly should become animated as he explains that every single person in the village wants to get married as quickly as possible. Ken found that by pitching certain words higher than others, he not only made a point, but also gave the confused vicar an air of pleasant eccentricity. For example, in the line:

> *'Hitherto the youths of this village have not been enterprising'*

he said *'yoooouths'* in a way that captivated the audience, his imaginative word-colouring adding even more humour to his portrayal. He built up volume and pace from:

> *'Judge then of my surprise'*

and ignored the full stop between:

> *'with as little delay as possible.'* and
> *'Even your excellent father'*

so that his astonishment was obvious, ending the section in a state of shock with the announcement to Alexis that his father has found a prospective wife. He was careful, however, to maintain the slight separation of the words that characterised the vicar's style of speaking even when he was excited. The next speech, in which Dr. Daly realises that he will be the only one left without a wife, gave Ken great possibilities to time lines for maximum comedic effect. Sinking rapidly into depression on:

'This universal marrying recalls the happy days – now, alas, gone forever – when I myself might have –'

Dr. Daly is guilty of self-pity and admonishes himself for this. He is, of course, unaware that he, too, is under the influence of the love potion and Ken said the line:

'And yet, within the last half hour, I have greatly yearned for companionship.'

as if it is the unexpected spate of engagements that makes him aware of his loneliness. Leaning on the word *'yearned'*, the romantic innocence with which he bemoaned the vicar's fate was in keeping with Gilbert's intention of tasteful understatement; the naïvety of his longing a wonderful contrast to the somewhat bawdier antics of the villagers at the opening of Act II. However, Ken found a typically subtle way of implying that Dr. Daly has rather more in mind than sharing the church flower arranging. He said:

'I never remarked it before, but the young maidens of this village are very comely.'

with simple admiration, but his timing of the following lines left the audience in no doubt as to his train of thought. Pausing before saying:

'So likewise are the middle-aged.'

he picked out *'aged'* as if surprised by this realisation and then allowed 3 seconds before following on with:

'Also the elderly.'

when he lifted *'elderly'* even more, as if to indicate his amazement that he could have looked at them in such a way. The prolonged laughter occasioned by this clever use of words and timing left Ken with no option but to pause before adding:

'All are comely – and all are engaged!'

His shock on discovering that he has been looking longingly at every female in the village was evident as he exclaimed *'All'* in a horrified tone, before accepting his fate with sad resignation.

In the last speech of this delightful scene, Ken showed that the imaginative use of one word can delight an audience. Extolling the virtues of personal hygiene, Dr. Daly says:

'for it can be renewed whenever it discovers symptoms of decay.'

and Ken showed the eccentric side of the vicar by stretching the word *'renewed'* for no apparent reason. Raising the pitch of his voice, he said *'reneeooooowed'* in undulating tones and always got a big laugh as a reward for his ingenuity. It is almost impossible to teach performers how and when to employ this kind of technique. The inspiration for word-colouring comes with experience and the knowledge that one is completely comfortable with the dialogue and interpretation of the character; when the freedom to be creative sometimes yields unexpected results. In his experience, many performers take so much time over the music, that they leave the dialogue to take care of itself. The spoken words deserve equal consideration if the artist is to be anything more than ordinary.

Dr. Daly's final speech of the opera, in which he explains to Alexis how he comes to be kissing his fiance, Aline, is straightforward. Alexis' unreasonable refusal to accept the explanation gives the gentle vicar an opportunity to show a rare flash of annoyance, which Ken followed with a tone of resigned martyrdom on:

'and bury my sorrow in the congenial gloom of a Colonial Bishopric.'

If the discerning actor accepts the challenge of finding both the humour and pathos in Dr. Daly's small amount of dialogue, he will send the audience home happy in the knowledge that the lonely Vicar of Ploverleigh eventually gets his girl.

MAKE UP

Ken's make up for Dr. Daly was largely dictated by the white wig and sideburns that he wore which instantly made him look elderly. He was in his late 40s when he played the role for the first time and already developing facial lines, so he decided, in this instance, not to add any more, preferring to concentrate on the complexion of the vicar. He used a pale base colour similar to the one that he used for Wilfred Shadbolt, mixing 5 and 9 sticks with the emphasis on the paler number 5. A darker base would not have worked with his white hair, but he decided that a lifetime spent in the healthy air of the country would give the vicar a rosy glow. Using a carmine red grease stick, he dotted it onto his cheekbones and then blended it into the base colour so that the flush appeared quite natural, this giving him a look of well-being that was positively angelic. He then powdered the make up thoroughly, before using a white grease stick on his black eyebrows so that they toned in with the wig and facial hair. When whitening his brows in this way, he outlined their shape with a black or brown pencil, so that they stood out against the pale base. Finally, he added eye lines and a little lip colour. He advises that younger performers playing the part of Dr. Daly will need to draw in age lines using shading and highlighting as described for Don Alhambra, but advocates the use of white or grey sideburns which give the appearance of ageing as painted lines can never do.

HORROR MOMENTS

Ken can recall only one embarrassing moment as Dr. Daly. Having played the role without disaster for several years, he went on one evening for Act II unaware that he was about to make a classic *faux pas.* Whilst bemoaning his single status to Aline and Alexis, he was supposed to say:

'I never remarked it before, but the young maidens of this village are very comely.'

Inexplicably, he substituted the word *'youths'* for *'young maidens'*, leaving Julia Goss and Meston Reid trying to contain their laughter and the audience in no doubt as to why Dr. Daly never got married! His bloopers may have been few and far between, but they were well worth the wait.

HAPPY MOMENTS

Frequently described as a professional's professional, Kenneth Sandford occasionally indulged his boyish sense of humour in a surprising way. During the Act I duet between Lady Sangazure and Sir Marmaduke, the D'Oyly Carte production required groups of choristers to be in 'frozen' action for its duration – a direction demanding great discipline and concentration. Whilst waiting in the wings for his next entrance, it has been known for Ken to make funny faces at the chorus members trying desperately to ignore his efforts to distract them. He now vigorously denies this accusation, but I know – I was there.

In 1995, some 13 years after he had last played the role, Ken was asked to be Dr. Daly in the International Gilbert & Sullivan Festival production at the Buxton Opera House. He was absolutely delighted, having never imagined that he would have another opportunity to play one of his favourite parts. It was as if time had stood still as he revelled in the beautiful songs and once more heard the audience laughing at his dialogue. To add to his pleasure, he again found himself on stage with Peggy Ann Jones, a delightfully wacky Mrs. Partlet, as well as many other of his former D'Oyly Carte colleagues. Happy moments, indeed!

A FINAL THOUGHT

Dr. Daly is a gentle and kindly man, whose purity of thought and affection for his parishioners should not prevent the actor from looking for ways to make him an interesting character. His words and music give numerous chances for both comedy and sadness and although W.S.Gilbert intended to poke a little fun at the clergy, the performer should avoid obvious stereotyping if his efforts to convincingly portray the elderly country parson are to be truly successful.

Osbert Lancaster's original sketch of Dr. Daly

KING HILDEBRAND

Ken's King Hildebrand

'A King of autocratic power we'

KEN had a love-hate relationship with *Princess Ida*. He relished King Hildebrand's beautifully-crafted dialogue, which made him feel like a Shakespearian actor, but was not so happy about the singing, the vocal line being too low for his high baritone voice. *Princess Ida* was always a welcome change in a repertoire that included so many Pooh-Bahs and Private Willises and, on balance, he derived more pleasure than pain from his performance.

Ken found no difficulty in deciding on how King Hildebrand might move around the stage. Having reflected that he might be a fairy tale King in a time when monarchs were all-powerful and their subjects subservient, Ken strode the stage majestically. His long, powerful paces on his first entrance immediately suggested the authority of a King who is in absolute control and who commands attention. Even when standing still he adopted an autocratic pose, with his arms folded or feet apart with hands on hips, but he never lost the look of a man who knows himself to be the most important person in the room. He moved with energy and purpose, but not aggression, his height and broad shoulders helping him to cut an imposing figure. Not every performer playing the part will be as tall as Ken, but he believes that imagination is more important than height. If the actor truly believes himself to be a King of absolute power and moves with the confidence of a man who is both loved and feared, the audience will also believe in that King. Such conviction can be promoted by an appropriate costume and Ken felt very much the part in his splendid robes. Above white hose and tights he wore a full-length red velvet tunic which had a detachable black velvet stole around the shoulders, white sleeves that flared out into dark fur cuffs and a wide gilt belt decorated with an ornate lion's head. With a long black beard and a head-dress that resembled a decorative battle helmet, he looked impressive indeed.

Ken used very few gestures in this role. King Hildebrand's will being law and with courtiers hanging onto his every word, he had no need to emphasise anything he said. For much of the time Ken carried a short sceptre which restricted hand movements and his only strong gesture came with the line:

'Come, bustle there!'

when he waved an arm imperiously to provoke a flurry of activity in the court. As always, once confident of his characterisation, Ken preferred to let his body language and facial reactions make his point. Anger, wry humour and impatience were clearly transmitted from his eyes without the need for anything but the occasional planned gesture. The art of acting without constantly using one's hands is not learned overnight, but it is a skill which all performers should endeavour to acquire.

THE VOICE

Although Hildebrand has very few lines, Ken made the most of them by varying the colour of his speaking voice according to the dramatic situations in which the King is involved. Whenever in the presence of the full court, he spoke out with the clarity of someone who is used to issuing orders and making proclamations. He did not achieve this merely by speaking loudly, but by taking the words at a steady pace and making the consonants crisp. By contrast, he used a quieter and much warmer tone when in conversation with Hilarion, Cyril or Florian, the intimacy of their exchanges allowing the audience to see a more relaxed side to the King's character. This is particularly important if he is not to appear cold and inhuman. Ken gave Hildebrand a dry sense of humour which was evident on several occasions. By enjoying a joke himself, Ken was able to convey amusement in his voice whilst keeping a straight face.

In the first act scene with King Gama, Ken's responses to the acid comments of his adversary were delivered in the even tone of a diplomat determined to remain unflustered. However, when Hildebrand's intelligence is insulted, he reacted with sudden fury, barking out his words with a harshness of tone that was genuinely frightening. His constant search for contrast in the voice and, hence, in the personality of the character he was portraying was the hallmark of Ken's work and his King Hildebrand was a lesson in how to achieve a great deal with very little material.

THE DIALOGUE

Ken never got used to the idea that most of his evening's work was finished within half an hour of the curtain going up, but such was the case with King Hildebrand. With the end of Act I came a lengthy wait in the dressing room until his appearance to sing in the second act finale, followed by another interval and then just 33 words to say in Act III. Despite these intermittent appearances, he thoroughly enjoyed the challenge of dialogue that gave him the chance to think as a classical actor. He remains fascinated by Gilbert's skill as a wordsmith and marvels at the creativity of a mind capable of producing such incisive and imaginative poetry within the self-imposed restraints of blank verse.

Hildebrand's first line:

'See you no sign of Gama?'

enabled Ken to immediately establish the King's authority. It was not a polite enquiry, but an impatient demand delivered in stentorian tone. During the following speech, Ken had to be aware of his responsibility in explaining to the audience the significance of the eagerly-anticipated arrival of King Gama and his daughter, Princess Ida. This had to be done in character, so Ken treated it as a reminder to the assembled court of the reason for the coming of the Royal visitors and the consequences of their failure to appear. He did not hurry the lines, his clipped consonants and strong tone making it easy for the audience to pick up the first part of the plot. Ken used the chorus' reactions to his angry and bellicose threat:

'There's war between King Gama and ourselves!'

to effect a complete change of mood. Drawing the trusted Cyril to one side, Ken lowered his voice for:

'Oh, Cyril, how I dread this interview'

giving the audience a glimpse of the King in less confident mood. His style whilst addressing Cyril was more relaxed and his tone less forceful, the edge on his voice replaced by a warmer quality. He made sure that the awkward word *'awry'* was clear by pausing briefly before emphasising it and then coloured *'crumpled'* by hitting the first consonant hard and rolling the *'r'*. It is worth mentioning that the D'Oyly Carte cut the line:

'His sting is present, though his stung is past.'

presumably because audiences seldom understood Gilbert's play on the previous line:

'his sting lay in his tongue'

Ken was glad of this, because he found it very difficult to convey the intention without labouring the joke.

Hildebrand's final speech of the scene beginning with:

'One never knows.'

is wonderful for an actor, its alternating lines laying out the rewards and punishments to be prepared for Gama giving a chance to vary the pace, volume and colour of the words. Ken addressed the opening of the speech to Cyril, his quiet tone showing a touch of sardonic humour in:

'One never knows. She's a strange girl, I've heard, and does odd things!'

Having shared this with Cyril, he suddenly reverted to being the formidable King during the lines beginning with:

Come, bustle there!'

giving his instructions in a voice that none dare question. During each of the three orders to prepare lavish hospitality Ken became expansive, taking his time to paint a picture of luxurious clothing, exquisite furniture and fine food. With a warm and enthusiastic tone he paid particular attention to the superlatives in:

'richest robes', 'best spare bed' and *'costliest banquet'*

By lowering his voice and quickening the pace, he then made the contrast between life in the palace and life in a dungeon sound sinister indeed. In a menacing tone he used the same tactic of emphasising the superlatives:

'coarsest' and *'deepest'*

before rattling out:

'cold water and dry bread!'

He started the final speech:

'so shall King Gama have much more than everything –'

in the earlier expansive style, making *'everything'* the climax of the phrase, before dropping his voice and pausing before:

'much less than nothing!'

when he spat out *'nothing!'* with such venom that he made it easy to believe that King Hildebrand is not a man to cross.

In the short scene with Hilarion, Ken went back to the intimate tone that he used when speaking to Cyril in the previous scene. Here, the King is in informal conversation with his son and Ken made his voice as sympathetic as possible in the line:

'King Gama is in sight, but much I fear with no Princess!'

He could not, however, resist the temptation to add a little wry humour to his sympathy on:

'Then I should say the loss of such a wife is one to which a reasonable man would easily be reconciled.'

which he said with a distinct twinkle in his eye. Ken believes that it is important to have such moments of quiet humour if the character of the King is to be credible and the brief scene with Hilarion is an ideal time to contrast his tyrannic bluster with ordinary human warmth.

The sequence of dialogue between Gama, Hilarion, Cyril, Florian and Hildebrand was Ken's favourite moment in the opera. He loved the sparkling exchanges and, despite his few lines, became completely involved in what is, arguably, some of W.S. Gilbert's most brilliant writing. For much of the time he was confined to facial acting, but this was very enjoyable given the quality of insults flying around the stage and he was happy to listen to the other characters scoring points against each other.

Having been taken in by Gama's smooth flattery, Ken said his first line:

'Oh, really, King!'

with a mixture of delight and modesty, his face expressing surprise at the unexpected change in Gama's character. His pleasure quickly turned to shock as the viciousness of Gama's insults struck home. Believing that Hildebrand would not want Gama to see his annoyance, Ken put on an impassive expression which briefly cracked into a smile when Cyril's quick-witted riposte throws Gama into a rage. However, wishing to take the heat out of an ugly situation, Ken began:

'We are in doubt whether to treat you as an honoured guest, or as a Traitor knave who plights his word and breaks it.'

with restraint and diplomacy, as if anxious to get to matter of the Princess' whereabouts, before adopting a more threatening tone in the second part of the line. He ignored Gama's quick retort and calmly continued to bring him back to the point. His question:

'Why is she not with you?'

was asked sternly. Ken maintained this cool approach throughout Gama's next two speeches, his stony expression giving no hint of Hildebrand's true feelings until he is likened to a pauper unfit to be in the presence of the Princess. Ken exploded into:

'Stop that tongue, or you shall lose the monkey head that holds it!'

his rapid-fire delivery in sharp contrast to the expansiveness of earlier scenes. When this is met with another smart reply, Hildebrand should realise that he must not be drawn into Gama's verbal web. Ken visibly made a supreme effort to control his temper on:

'Where is she now?'

separating the words through gritted teeth in an effort to regain his composure. For the rest of the scene, Ken kept King Hildebrand's rage hidden behind an impassive expression, aware that he should not lose his dignity in front of the court.

This scene shows how important it is for actors to involve themselves in dialogue which does not actively include them. Ken thinks that if the actor listens to every line, rather than waiting to say the next one, the right reactions will be obvious.

In the Finale of Act III, Ken had little to do but stand around looking imposing and being amused by the inept fighting of King Gama's sons. His line:

'A noble aim!'

reflected his amusement at the whole situation, his mock-serious tone showing that Hildebrand considers Ida's philosophy to be nonsense. He retained the mockery in his voice for his final speech beginning:

'But pray reflect –'

and his final line:

'How is this posterity to be provided?'

was said after a pause and with the smugness shown by men in response to like-minded women of generations past, present and to come.

MAKE UP

Because Ken's face was dominated by a long black beard, he needed only to pay attention to his eyes. He applied a pale greasepaint base and then, using black pancake, he made his eyebrows heavy to give him the appearance of being fierce. When he first played the role he was in his early 30s and felt that he needed to add age lines to make himself look at least 55 – the age he imagined Hildebrand to be. Using his murky mixture of dark brown and crimson lake, he drew lines at the side of and just beneath the outside corner of each eye. With the same colour, he painted shadows under his eyes and then used a number 5 ivory stick above the lines and shadowing to make them stand out on his face. As he got older, nature gave him a helping hand and he did not bother with the crow's feet. Once he had added the black lines above and below his eyes, he powdered the make up and put on the beard. As this had no moustache to it, he finished off by colouring his lips with a little crimson lake to give definition to his mouth.

HORROR MOMENTS

When he first played King Hidebrand, Ken was given the beard worn by the renowned D'Oyly Carte baritone, Fisher Morgan. It was a long, black, straggly affair and although it may have been a snug fit on Morgan's ample jowls, it swamped Ken's modest chin, with embarrassing consequences. Before every performance he secured it as best he could but, as soon as he strode imposingly onto the stage and spoke his first line, it shot up and covered his mouth, making intelligible speech impossible. He could not help but feel that removing strands of hair from his mouth and surreptitiously yanking down the offending hirsutism did little for his royal dignity and soon decided that it had to go. On voicing his complaint to the management, he received no sympathy and was told that a new beard would cost far too much money; he must continue to wear the one provided. Numerous attempts to glue, snip and trim proving futile, Ken was left with no alternative but to make his own. Having bought a length of crepe hair, he painstakingly copied the ill-fitting beard and enjoyed its comfort for many years without the management being any the wiser.

HAPPY MOMENTS

The second act of *Princess Ida* may be entertaining for the audience, but it is tedious for Kings Hildebrand and Gama; the former not appearing in it until the finale and the latter not at all. With over an hour to kill after Act I, Ken and John Reed had to find ways of relaxing in the dressing room until their next entrances. If he had finished The Daily Telegraph crossword and was feeling in skittish mood, John would entertain himself and Ken by doctoring the wart on his large false nose. Using special putty, John cleverly made a deformed nose for King Gama and always added a wart as a final flourish. During his long break, he sometimes removed the uncomfortable nose and stuck it to the mirror ready for later use. Over the years, Ken watched with amusement as John, always game for a laugh, carefully sculpted the wart into the shape of a lighthouse, castle or other edifice, whilst Ken marvelled at the intricacy of his work. The real joy of the exercise came in John's Act III entrance, when the wart appeared to be just that to the distant audience, but clearly resembled a building to his colleagues on the stage. Having shared the fun in the dressing room, Ken was able to enjoy the suppressed giggles around him whilst maintaining Hildebrand's stern façade.

In the late 1970s, West End theatres were the target of numerous bomb hoaxes and Ken can remember two occasions when Sadlers Wells Theatre was evacuated mid-performance. The performers, well-drilled for such events, were instructed to gather in the street outside the Stage Door to await the all-clear. Having received a warning during a performance of *Princess Ida*, it took the police some time to declare the theatre safe, leaving the chilly performers to huddle in the street or seek sanctuary in the Stage Door pub. Ken was lucky enough to have grabbed his wallet before leaving the theatre, but forgot his cigarettes. In full King Hildebrand regalia – sword, helmet and all – he strolled into the nearby small shop and was greeted with:

'Twenty of your usual cigarettes, Mr. Sandford?'

Once the theatre had been given the all-clear from the police, the performance continued where it had stopped, with Hilarion, Cyril and Florian singing:

'Gently, gently, evidently we are safe so far'.

A FINAL THOUGHT

Ken, who was used to playing such major roles as Pooh-Bah, Don Alhambra and Archibald Grosvenor, never considered the minor parts of King Hildebrand or Private Willis to be beneath him. On the contrary, he prepared them as meticulously as the more demanding characters and strove to extract as much as possible from such words and music as Gilbert and Sullivan had furnished. By so doing, he derived great satisfaction from his efforts and remembers King Hildebrand as the part which made him feel like a serious actor. Quality is not dependent on quantity and Ken advises that there is much to be learned and achieved from every role, regardless of its size.

POOH-BAH

'This haughty youth'

'What name have you for such an one?'

AND finally, there was Pooh-Bah – arguably Kenneth Sandford's most famous role and yet, paradoxically, the one which gave him the least satisfaction because he felt that he never did justice to the character. To the many Pooh-Bahs who, over the past forty years, have tried in vain to reproduce his inimitable interpretation, the idea that **the** Pooh-Bah has doubts about the way he played the part may seem like heresy. Nevertheless, the perfectionist in Ken is certain that he could have done much more with a role which, to this day, perplexes him. It is probably true to say that he never quite broke free from the restrictions of the traditional D'Oyly Carte Pooh-Bah as taught to him by Snookie Fancourt in 1957. He has always felt that something was missing, but has never been able to pinpoint the problem. It is ironical that he has recently come up with some fresh ideas when Old Father Time dictates that it is too late to try them out on the stage. For that reason, he welcomes the chance to share his thoughts on what he did and what he might have done with this most difficult of characters.

Any early ideas that Ken may have had as to how Pooh-Bah would move were forgotten on the day when he was fitted for the costume. As the heavy trousers, tunic and train were added over the layers of thick padding, he realised that he would be lucky to do anything more than lumber around the stage and this feeling was confirmed when he tried to keep upright on the boots with the narrow platform soles. He knew, of course, that the characters in *The Mikado* would be in Japanese costume, but he had not anticipated that his outfit would be so restrictive – not to mention hot. Seemingly, the D'Oyly Carte's Pooh-Bah had always been played as a fat man and yet Ken could find no reference to this in the libretto. True, Ko-Ko refers to him as *'a tremendous swell'*, but the dictionary defines this as a 'smartly-dressed person', or 'someone of substance' and he could see no reason why Ko-Ko had to say it with a gesture that indicated the size of Pooh-Bah's girth. Whether or not this *double entendre* was Gilbert's original intention he would never know, but he was stuck with the fact that he must play the part as a heavyweight and set to work accordingly.

Ken's yellow-green costume had decorative fan motifs and circular shapes embroidered onto the tunic and a distinctive pattern of white circles on a dark green background on the flared trousers. In his 'bald' pigtail wig with long sideburns and a 15-inch tall black hat, he felt very much the part of a Japanese nobleman and this proved helpful in establishing how he would play the part. He maintains that if you look and feel right in a costume, you are well on the way to a successful characterisation. He certainly found it difficult to do anything but move slowly in such a heavy costume, but this was not a disadvantage given Pooh-Bah's pompous personality. In the first act, he had nowhere to go in a hurry, so he walked sedately with his shoulders pulled back, the padding allowing his stomach to go first. By lifting his chin and assuming an expression of distaste, he created an air of superiority and arrogance that set him aside from the other characters. In Act II, the circumstances surrounding the arrival of The Mikado throw the normally imperturbable Pooh-Bah into something of a panic and Ken used his bulk to indulge in the sort of physical humour that he usually preferred to avoid. When entering in a hurry to announce that The Mikado is approaching the city, his portly attempt to run and the accompanying puffing and panting were comical indeed. The need to prostrate himself before The Mikado provided him with another chance to play on his size; getting up and down from his knees with great difficulty as Ko-Ko and Pitti-Sing managed this effortlessly. Whilst in this prone position, the D'Oyly Carte production required Ko-Ko to shove Pooh-Bah with his foot so that he rolled over onto his side. Ken's protracted and painful efforts to right himself showed masterly timing as he lay precariously balanced, before eventually dropping back down onto his front with a dull thud. When having to dance in *'The flowers that bloom in the spring'*, he never forgot that he was supposed to be a fat man and made his steps suitably cumbersome. In short, his movements as Pooh-Bah were decided by the restraints placed upon him by his costume and the need to play the part as an overweight man. Whether walking ponderously or struggling to move quickly, he succeeded in making the upper-class snob amusing by playing on his large size in a way that is considered unacceptable in today's politically correct world.

Ken's use of gestures as Pooh-Bah was restricted by the large, red fan which he carried. Unlike some of the other characters, he wore no belt or sash in which to put the fan when it was not required and so, it became an integral part of his performance. In such a heavy costume, there were times when he was very grateful for its cooling properties but, on the whole, he used it for effect, its size when unfolded matching the stature of its owner, making him look like a galleon in full sail. Ken feels that it is important for Pooh-Bah not to use the fan vigorously, a gentle fanning action being more in keeping with his laboured walk. His most famous gesture was, undoubtedly, the opening of a hand to indicate his willingness to take a bribe. It was distinctive because, instead of extending the arm away from his body, he kept the elbow close to his side and turned his hand palm up. The subtlety of this gesture gave the impression that it was clandestine and strictly between the briber and the bribed. For much of the time, Ken kept his fan closed, resting it along with his other hand on top of his large stomach. Pooh-Bah is too concerned with being dignified to indulge in superfluous gestures and Ken found that his pompous stillness made a wonderful contrast with Ko-Ko, whose nimbleness and fluttering fan movements made him appear permanently busy. The exception to this came when he was in the presence of The Mikado. Ken made numerous bobbing attempts to bow as low as his tummy would allow, his obsequiousness towards the Emperor both funny and embarrassing.

Pooh-Bah is described in Act II as a *'haughty youth'* and this must be taken into account when considering facial expressions. Lifting his chin certainly helped Ken to maintain a disdainful expression as he, quite literally, looked down on other people. But Pooh-Bah can also be described as a greedy, self-serving and devious social climber; characteristics which must be made obvious from the look on his face as well as in the words that he speaks. The idea of making a fast buck motivates Pooh-Bah more than anything else. Whenever taking a bribe, Ken replaced the usual look of superiority with a gleam in his eye and just a hint of a self-satisfied smirk, which he also used to indicate his appreciation of his own cleverness on acquiring so many well-paid jobs. This change of expression was not overplayed but, when accompanied by an equivalent change of tone in his speaking voice, it was enough to suggest what really makes Pooh-Bah tick. In the first act Ken never smiled broadly, confining his sense of humour to the occasional trace of a smile on his lips and a wicked glint in the eye – most notably at the prospect of The Lord High Executioner trying to cut off his own head, when he was quietly amused by Ko-Ko's inability to recognise sarcasm. In the second act, however, he used the presence of The Mikado to show Pooh-Bah's desire to ingratiate himself with anyone he perceives as being useful to him. When The Mikado laughed heartily he laughed heartily, although he never seemed to notice that his sickly smiles when trying to impress the Emperor had the opposite effect, or that his obvious fawning made everyone cringe. Ken's use of body language and facial expressions to convey the complexities of the larger-than-life Pooh-Bah were more effective than any number of gestures. He advises those performers who use a gesture to make a point because they do not know what else to do, to consider the dialogue carefully – the answer can always be found in the words.

Although he had to play Pooh-Bah as a fat man, Ken believes that a convincing interpretation of this complex character has nothing to do with being overweight. We have become so conditioned to seeing Pooh-Bah played in this way, that it is hard to picture him as, possibly, a small, slim man. Yet insufferable arrogance, pomposity and self-aggrandisement are failings to be found in many human beings, regardless of their shape or size. Ken would have loved the opportunity to play the Lord High Everything Else without the padding. He has always wanted to explore the possibilities offered by the dialogue without the 'heavy' humour and although he understands why audiences find visual humour amusing, he is sure that just as much amusement is to be found in the absurdity of the developing situations of Act II and the interaction of the characters in response to them.

THE VOICE

Pooh-Bah is a nobleman. He is also pompous, condescending and arrogant. These traits gave Ken plenty to work on in his early days with the D'Oyly Carte. Once he had dismissed the direction to purse up his lips in order to produce the company's idea of a refined way of speaking, he soon found a suitably upper-class voice. He felt that Pooh-Bah should be a crashing bore, always happy to reel off his long list of official functions whether or not people want to listen. He settled on a flat tone for the first act, but realised that he would need to vary his pace and colouring if the many repetitions of his numerous titles were not to become monotonous. In his scene with Nanki-Poo, he made his voice patronising and boastful, which was not difficult given W. S. Gilbert's delightful description of Pooh-Bah's lineage. The Act II scenes allowed him to drop the condescension from his voice in favour of a shamelessly smarmy tone designed to impress The Mikado and Katisha. Along with the fear in his voice when faced with execution and his return to pomposity when blamed by Ko-Ko for their plight, he was able to bring a variety of emotions into his voice and even managed a genuine guffaw of laughter at the prospect of Ko-Ko having to marry Katisha. As far as audiences and the press are concerned, he made the part his own, his portrayal of Pooh-Bah becoming famous across the Gilbert and Sullivan world. But Ken was never satisfied with his characterisation and the voice he used in Act I was part of the problem.

The D'Oyly Carte of the 1950s and 1960s was not the sort of company in which performers discussed the interpretation of their roles or made significant changes to their characterisations. Ken was concerned that his fears about his delivery becoming monotonous were well founded, but he was not sure what to do about it. He knew that the production staff had nothing to offer him and so, against his instinct, he continued in the same vein, unable to dig himself out of the artistic hole into which he had fallen. With experience, he did manage to bring variety and humour to the long lists of titles, but it was the scene in which Ko-Ko asks for Pooh-Bah's advice that gave Ken most concern. He had to list no less than 13 of his jobs and did so using the same tone of voice for each, with the exception of Archbishop of Titipu when he intoned:

'It would be my duty to denounce my dishonesty'

in the manner of a priest. He pondered on the possibility of using a different voice for each of the officials; such a ploy would work well enough for the first two or three, but would soon become predictable. It might be fun to mimic the present day Leader of the Opposition, but he was not very good at impersonations. The use of props appropriate to some of the offices might be helpful, but that, too, would become predictable – not to say impractical. It was possible that whatever he tried might be frowned upon by a management reluctant to embrace new ideas and so, however hard he tried to find a solution, he found himself stuck in the same repetitive rut.

He remains convinced that there must be a way to bring more variety and colour to Pooh-Bah's voice and words than ever he achieved in his time with the D'Oyly Carte and now believes that the key to this may lie in the reactions of the other characters. But more of this anon.

THE DIALOGUE

Pooh-Bah's first entrance is critical to the early establishment of his overbearing personality and Ken found it problematical. In the D'Oyly Carte production, he had to enter at the back of the stage, stand listening to Nanki-Poo and Pish-Tush and then walk downstage between them in time for his first line. It didn't take him long to realise that the difficulty lay in the fact that he was making an entrance for no apparent reason – he was just there. He found that by imagining Pooh-Bah is on his way somewhere for a specific purpose, it was easy enter, notice the other people talking and be obviously eavesdropping on a private conversation. This made his first line beginning:

'It is. Our logical Mikado, seeing no moral difference between the dignified judge'

sound like the rudeness of an arrogant man who sees nothing wrong in butting in on matters which are not his concern, an attitude which Ken feels sets out the character at the earliest moment. He believes that it is important for a director to realise that Pooh-Bah needs to be purposeful when making his first entrance and not left standing around merely waiting to say his first line. After Nanki-Poo has thanked him for the unsolicited information, Pooh-Bah becomes condescending, seizing the opportunity to impress a stranger with his importance. Ken treated the words of this speech with great care, taking his time over the first part in which Pooh-Bah boasts about his heritage. This not only gave the impression that Pooh-Bah is revelling in self-importance, but it also gave the audience time to digest the unusual phrases :

'Pre-Adamite ancestral descent'

and:

'protoplasmal primordial atomic globule'

Although the performers may be used to hearing and understanding such colourful words, it is always worth remembering that some members of the audience may be seeing a show for the first time and that they are entitled to the chance to register the meaning of unfamiliar language. Ken had great fun with *'globule'*, using the word in onomatopoeic fashion to the delight of the audience. He did the same with '*sneering*' in the line:

'I can't help it. I was born sneering.'

He picked up the pace from:

'But I struggle hard to overcome this defect.'

when his explanation as to how he came to hold so many important positions sounded anything but apologetic.

In the following speech, the first of several lists of Pooh-Bah's titles needs to be considered and Ken was well aware of the dangers involved. It begins with:

'It is consequently my degrading duty to serve this upstart'

After a short pause he said '*upstart*' as if this description of The Lord High Executioner was the rudest word he could use in public. Once into the list of jobs Ken varied his pace, sometimes allowing equal space between the titles and sometimes moving on quickly so that the delivery did not become metronomic. He hurried through:

'Groom of the Back Stairs'

because this less important function was beneath his dignity, before lingering proudly over:

'Archbishop of Titipu and Lord Mayor, both acting and elect'

which titles he thought more suited to a man of such distinction. He continued the speech as though shocked to find himself in paid employment, the ignominy of working for an ex-tailor being an insult to his family name. Ken became much more animated during this sequence, with :

'And at a salary!'

increasing in volume and pace until:

'I a salaried minion!'

which he said with mock self-loathing certain to impress Nanki-Poo. Pausing for a second before:

'But I do it! It revolts me, but I do it!'

he abruptly reduced the intensity to give the impression that Pooh-Bah is a selfless martyr in the service of his city, although the gleam in his eye clearly suggested more mercenary motives.

Ken feels that Pooh-Bah's section of dialogue before his song should be said as if Nanki-Poo has heard enough and is trying to make a polite escape. Most people have been in the company of the type of bore who ignores the fact that the person whom they are addressing is trying to move away from the one-sided conversation. He said:

'But I don't stop at that.'

to make it difficult for Nanki-Poo to leave and continued to describe his virtues in a pompous tone. Ken used:

'I accept refreshments at any hands, however lowly'

as a direct insult to Nanki-Poo. By looking at him pointedly and leaning on the last two words, he made his meaning clear. He then effected a complete change of approach after Nanki-Poo's failure to take the hint about the sale of State secrets. Dropping the patronising tone from his voice, he spoke quietly and confidentially on:

'For instance, any further information about Yum-Yum would come under the head of a State Secret.'

Ken split the last line of this speech by saying:

'Another insult,'

in the expectation of a large bribe, before judging the weight of the coins in his hand and adding:

'and I think a light one!'

with considerable disappointment.

The dialogue between Pooh-Bah and Ko-Ko after the *'Little list'* song gave Ken considerable difficulty. It starts with another list of titles and was not easy to remember because, like the previous one, it begins with:

'As First Lord of the Treasury'

Thereafter, the titles are different and Ken found that it was easy to go into the wrong list. Even after some 2000 performances, he had to concentrate to make sure that the many jobs were in the correct order. When asking Ko-Ko which official he wishes to consult, Ken made his way through the titles taking care to vary the delivery, but he felt that this was not enough – it was predictable and dull. Unable to come up with a way to solve this problem and with nobody on the production staff with whom he could have a fruitful discussion, he left well alone. No complaints were made, so he assumed that it must sound better than he thought. He has now realised that more involvement with Ko-Ko offers one way to make Pooh-Bah's list more imaginative. If a pause is made after each capacity is listed and Ko-Ko uses the space to look puzzled or confused by the titles he doesn't understand, this will allow Pooh-Bah time to suggest another official. As each suggestion is rejected, he can become irritated by such ignorance until he offers:

'or Private Secretary?'

as a last resort, knowing that Ko-Ko will at least know what that is. Given Ken's aforementioned concerns about using a different voice to illustrate the different dignitaries, he contented himself with trying to convey each of them with appropriate style and body language. For example, on:

'Speaking as your Private Secretary'

he moved closer to Ko-Ko and adopted a confidential tone, which quickly gave way to grandness as he moved on to:

'Of course you will understand that as Chancellor of the Exchequer'

Similarly, he used a dry and matter-of-fact tone for:

'Oh, as your Solicitor'

and followed with self-righteousness on:

'as Lord Chief Justice, I am bound to see that the law isn't violated.'

During the speech beginning:

'Of course, as First Lord of the Treasury'

Ken believes that Pooh-Bah is enjoying his intellectual superiority over Ko-Ko to such an extent that he inadvertently ties himself up in verbal knots as he realises that fiddling the books will lead to him having to arrest himself. He varied the pace by emphasising important words such as:

'special vote' and *'cook'*

and ended the speech:

'and give myself into my own custody as First commissioner of Police.'

with an expression on his face suggesting that the holding of so many high offices might lead to unwelcome complications. During the final section of this challenging scene, Pooh-Bah quickly regains the initiative with:

'I don't say that all these distinguished people couldn't be squared;'

After a brief pause, Ken pulled out the word *'squared'* to make it obvious to Ko-Ko that he expects a large bribe in return for ignoring any misappropriation of city funds. He completed the scene by continuing the tradition of putting in the unscripted comment of his predecessor, Rutland Barrington:

'No money, no grovel.'

in a tone that suggested no compromise.

Despite feeling that he would have liked to do have done much more with this scene, Ken's performance was never less than entertaining. It saddens him to think that semi-retirement allows the time to think about what he might have done, but no opportunity to give his ideas an airing. He would certainly like to hear from any Pooh-Bah who might be able to throw more light on what is, in his experience, a most difficult role.

Pooh-Bah's first contact with the Three Little Maids gave Ken plenty of time to indulge his disdainful expression before he had to address them. When he did so with:

'Go away, little girls. Can't talk to little girls like you. Go away, there's dears.'

his tone suggested embarrassment at being seen with such flighty and ill-behaved young ladies, their irritating presence undermining his all-important dignity. He was not quite rude, but very nearly. When Ko-Ko offers to introduce him to his wards, Pooh-Bah shows no desire to respond and Ken said:

'What do you want me to do to them? Mind, I will not kiss them.'

as though Pooh-Bah doesn't have the faintest idea as to what to do with a pretty girl. Ken finds it fascinating that the character shows no interest in women; his Act II flattery of Katisha is merely a ploy to ingratiate himself with the Royal party. In most productions, Pooh-Bah ends the opera romantically linked with Pitti-Sing, but in the D'Oyly Carte *Mikado* this happened by default, because each needed a partner with whom to take a bow at the end of the opera. There was no development in their relationship to suggest such an outcome and Ken feels that it would have added another dimension to his characterisation if he had been encouraged to show the reluctant attraction prompted by their squabbling in Act II.

Still trying to avoid having to speak to the Maids, Pooh-Bah makes the remark that:

'They are not young ladies, they are young persons.'

and Ken paused before saying '*persons*', making the word sound as insulting as possible. His eventual half-hearted acknowledgement of them:

'How de do, little girls, how de do? Oh, my protoplasmal ancestor!'

was accompanied by an uncomfortable little wave and followed by a plea for forgiveness from his illustrious forbear. Stung by their mocking laughter, Ken used the lines beginning with:

'I see nothing to laugh at.'

to demonstrate Pooh-Bah at his pompous best, his repetitions of the greeting becoming angrier as the girls struggled to suppress their laughter. Ken said the final line before the quartet:

'We know how delicate it is, don't we?'

as if taking revenge for being humiliated by the Three Little Maids, indicating that only more money will prevent him from disclosing Ko-Ko's plan to plunder the city coffers in order to finance an expensive wedding.

Ken often wished that some of his roles had more dialogue, but Pooh-Bah certainly kept him busy with four scenes in the first act. The last of these gave Ken scope to smugly enjoy watching Ko-Ko try to extricate himself from a dilemma of his own making. His first line beginning:

'Well, it seems unkind to say so'

was said with a smile in his voice, if not on his lips. He believes that Pooh-Bah is contemptuous of the working-class Ko-Ko, whom he sees as a petty criminal, but he cleverly conceals this contempt because it is in his financial interest to keep him happy. Nevertheless, Pooh-Bah cannot resist the temptation to suggest that Ko-Ko should execute himself, his amusement at Ko-Ko's horrified reaction kept behind a straight face. By the time the bemused Lord High Executioner declares that cutting off his own head might prove somewhat tricky, Pooh-Bah should be hardly able to contain his mirth and Ken said:

'A man might try.'

with subtle black humour, fully aware that Ko-Ko is treating the matter seriously. Encouraged by the equally contemptuous Pish-Tush, he suggests that The Mikado will be impressed if an attempt at self-decapitation is made and Ken spoke the line:

> *'It would be taken as an earnest of your desire to comply with the imperial will.'*

with great seriousness, showing no sign of the humour that he is sharing with Pish-Tush.

During his next line:

> *'This professional conscientiousness is highly creditable to you, but it places us in a very awkward position.'*

Ken played on his large size. Struggling to get to his feet with as much difficulty as he had shown when trying to sit on the floor at the start of the scene, he gasped out *'awkward position'* just as he managed to stand up. He advises that if an actor is going to indulge in a visual gag of this kind, he must time it carefully and not overdo the slapstick.

Having been offered the chance to become Lord High Substitute for the execution, Pooh-Bah continues to have fun at Ko-Ko's expense. Ken replied with a smile:

> *'I should be delighted. Such an appointment would realise my fondest dreams.'*

as if Pooh-Bah has every intention of getting Ko-Ko off the hook by accepting the dubious honour. He then dropped the bombshell:

> *'But no, at any sacrifice. I must set bounds to my insatiable ambition!'*

in a tone of stoic self-sacrifice, leaving the frustrated Ko-Ko to contemplate how much he would enjoy decapitating the big-headed Pooh-Bah.

Having been onstage a great deal in the first act, Ken was always grateful that he had a break before his first appearance in Act II. Most amateur performers treat the interval as a chance to soak up the congenial backstage atmosphere engendered by their eagerly-anticipated annual production, but professional principals usually prefer to use the time quietly to change costume and touch up make up, or simply to concentrate on the rest of their performance. Even at the end of his lengthy career with the D'Oyly Carte Ken was never complacent; taking the words and music for granted is a trap into which even the most experienced can fall and he made a point of going through his second act lines at the interval.

Act II of *The Mikado* shows another side of Pooh-Bah and Ken exploited this to the full. Having existed on a first act diet of superiority and sarcasm, the Lord High Everything Else displays other equally unattractive traits in the second part of the opera. Social climbing of the most nauseating type, abject terror at the prospect of being executed and concern over financial ruin gave Ken plenty of material to enlarge his characterisation.

Pooh-Bah's first entrance sees him in something of a panic having learned that The Mikado is nearing the city. Ken ran on from the back of the stage and delivered the line:

'The Mikado and his suite are approaching the city, and will be here in ten minutes.'

as if he had been running for some time, panting out the words with as much urgency as his breathlessness would allow. The need for an immediate execution to comply with the Emperor's orders being uppermost in his mind, he shows no sympathy for Ko-Ko's reluctance to decapitate the willing Nanki-Poo and Ken's:

'Chop it off, Ko-Ko! Chop it off!'

was said with much impatience. He stressed the second *'off'* so that the repeated instruction did not sound identical. He is aware that most versions of the libretto do not include *'Ko-Ko'* at this point, but he always said it and can only assume that he must have been told to put it in.

Prior to the line:

'Am I to understand that all of us high Officers of State are required to perjure ourselves to ensure your safety?'

Ken used the exchange about Ko-Ko's inability to kill anything to watch for The Mikado, looking offstage with great agitation. He stopped this abruptly as the irresistible urge to make some easy money overcame his fears and he said the line with more sarcasm than pomposity. His next line:

'Will the insult be cash down, or at a date?'

gave Ken the chance to press the advantage over Ko-Ko. Instead of asking a simple question, he said it in such a way as to leave no doubt that the latter option would not buy his co-operation. He chose to say the line:

'Well, it will be a useful discipline.'

not as an aside, but as a means for Pooh-Bah to again amuse himself at Ko-Ko's expense. By taking his time over '*well*', he made it seem as though Pooh-Bah is still thinking about the proposition when he has, of course, already made up his mind to accept the bribe. In his final line of the scene:

'Ha, Ha! Family Pride, how do you like that, my buck?'

Ken did not laugh aloud, but gave a chuckle of satisfaction at his own cleverness, the sneer on his face clearly stating that Pooh-Bah cares more about money than family honour. An interesting detail was his pronunciation of *'me buck'* as opposed to *'my buck'*.

When in the presence of The Mikado and Katisha, Pooh-Bah proves himself to be a social climber *par excellence*, but it never occurs to him that his efforts to impress are transparent to one and all. Ken established this sycophantic behaviour in his first line of the scene:

'I am the Coroner.'

During Ko-Ko's welcome of The Mikado he maintained his respectful bow until announcing himself with an ingratiating smile, clearly expecting The Mikado to recognise a person of great importance. He used the same tactic for the next line:

'They were all present, your Majesty. I counted them myself.'

when he again accompanied his self-importance with a sickly smile. Pooh-Bah persists with his obvious attempts to gain favour after the chorus have exited, but this time he tries to make an impression on Katisha, who has expressed her amazement at being jilted by Nanki-Poo. Ken said:

'I am surprised that he should have fled from one so lovely!'

with the utmost conviction, paying particular attention to *'lovely'*. He advises against playing the line to Ko-Ko and Pitti-Sing in order to get a laugh; the humour comes from Pooh-Bah's ridiculous attempt to flatter a middle-aged woman who, by her own admission, has a plain face. Pooh-Bah's next word:

'No.'

calls for good timing. Again, it is easy to fall into the 'cheap laugh' trap by playing the line to the others or to the audience. Without taking his eyes from Katisha, Ken paused for 3-4 seconds before saying it very quietly and sincerely. This approach always got a huge response and it demonstrates the importance of not underestimating the ability of an audience to appreciate subtlety. In response to her assertion that her face is unattractive, Ken swallowed hard before saying:

'It is.'

with genuine sincerity. However, by the time Katisha has described the delights of her left shoulder-blade and right elbow, Pooh-Bah has regained his usual over-confidence and Ken said:

'Allow me!'

with assurance, his presumption earning him a rebuke.

'My face is unattractive',
Ken with Patricia Leonard as Katisha

The next section of dialogue, which leads up to the quintet '*See how the Fates*', is quite straightforward. It shows Pooh-Bah to be as cowardly as his co-conspirators, the only difference between them and him being that his expressions of fright, remorse and fawning gratitude are delivered with inevitable superiority. This part of the scene belongs to The Mikado; as long as Pooh-Bah's interjections are in character, the performer need not do too much.

After The Mikado and Katisha have left the stage, Pooh-Bah, Ko-Ko and Pitti-Sing indulge in a bout of recrimination, each blaming the other for their predicament. Pooh-Bah is forced onto the defensive and resorts to his knowledge of fancy words in order to justify his overdone embellishments. Ken took the line:

'Merely corroborative detail, intended to give artistic verisimilitude to an otherwise bald and unconvincing narrative.'

quite slowly, taking care to be indignant without being incomprehensible. He was always aware that an audience needs time to take in unusual words. Having been attacked by the other two, Pooh-Bah retaliates with:

'But how about your big, right arm?'

and Ken said this to Ko-Ko in a nasty tone, the superiority in his voice suddenly replaced by spite. Having seen Katisha's formidable face, Pooh-Bah is greatly amused by the fact that Nanki-Poo is engaged to her against his will and also by the suggestion that Ko-Ko should marry her to resolve their dilemma. Ken used the lines:

'So does she.' and *'I am told that her right heel is much admired by connoisseurs.'*

to poke fun at the two unfortunate men. It was the only time in the opera that he allowed Pooh-Bah's sense of humour to be overt, gleefully making the most of their unenviable situations with obvious lack of sympathy.

Pooh-Bah has only three lines in the Act II Finale, but Ken made each one demonstrate the character's determination to impress The Mikado if it kills him – and it nearly does! Always wanting the last word, he is pompous to the end and Ken kept the overbearing tone going until Ko-Ko's angry intervention finally silenced him.

That he was more than successful as Pooh-Bah cannot be denied, yet Kenneth Sandford is modest enough to acknowledge that he tried hard, but might have done better. He looked fine in the part and he sang it well, but the dialogue gave him problems which, he believes, he only partially solved. Ideally, he would have liked to discuss with his fellow D'Oyly Carters how he might improve his interpretation. Ideally, he would have had access to a stage director with the ability to help him make the most of the words. As it was, he strived alone for 25 years to do justice to W. S. Gilbert's inspired dialogue and if his thoughts help other Pooh-Bahs to successfully take up the challenge, he has only one thing to say:

'I should be delighted.'

MAKE UP

In his early days with the company, Ken's make up for Pooh-Bah was based on the Kabuki style and resembled a mask. Over the years he modified this approach and his make up, as suggested below, became less stylised.

Ken's first job on arriving in his dressing room for a performance of *The Mikado*, was to take a bar of soap and apply a thick layer directly onto his eyebrows, allowing plenty of time for it to dry. He then put on his 'bald' wig. Using mainly number 5 greasepaint mixed with a touch of number 9, he covered with a very pale base, taking care to work the make up into the edge of the wig where it joined his forehead. Whenever provided with a new wig, he covered it with an even layer of the base he used on his face, carefully working it into the fabric representing skin. For this reason, it is important to always use the same colour on the face as on the front of the wig – this is much easier when using pancake as opposed to mixing greasepaint. Sometimes, as the wig got older, the fabric front stretched a little, so Ken used spirit gum just under the edge to keep it flat against his skin. The dried soap flattened and, effectively, blocked out his eyebrows ready for the Japanese-style brows. Using black pancake and a brush, he painted on upturned eyebrows, which started on top of his own before continuing in an upward sweep above the part blocked out by the soap. Again using black pancake, he drew thick eye lines which started in the corner below each eye, stopped at the middle of the lower lid and continued on the top lid in the shape of a narrow triangle which tapered off at the side of the eye. The eye lines work particularly well if they are parallel with the eyebrows. Finally, using a mixture of carmine and crimson lake greasepaint, he painted on a full mouth which turned down at the corners and then thoroughly powdered his handiwork.

Ken points out that his make up for Pooh-Bah was very much simpler at the end of his career than at the beginning, but the make up can be as stylised as the actor wishes, providing it fits in with the director's design. If he wants to go the whole hog, it is easy enough for a performer to find books about the Kabuki tradition and copy the patterns onto his face.

HORROR MOMENTS

It is not unusual for performers to have nightmares about finding themselves alone on stage when they should not be. Occasionally, such bad dreams become a reality and having to ad lib until those who are 'off' eventually arrive is a frightening experience. Such was the case during a performance of *The Mikado*, when John Reed was left to cover for the absence of Pooh-Bah and Pish-Tush in the scene prior to the *'cheap and chippy chopper'* trio late in Act I. With Pish-Tush nowhere to be seen, a frantic Ken decided that he must go on stage to help John until their absent colleague put in his appearance. He rushed on and told John that Pish-Tush was in possession of a letter form The Mikado and that he would be arriving at any moment. A grateful John then joined Ken in looking offstage, with both men making such suitable remarks as: 'I wonder what's keeping him?' and 'Oh, I expect he'll be here soon'. After what seemed to be a lifetime but was, in reality, only a minute or two of impromptu dialogue, Pish-Tush raced onto the stage and breathlessly said:

> *'I am a bearer of a letter from His Majesty the Mikado.'*

to which Ken smartly replied with no little sarcasm: 'Second Class, obviously.' The Pish-Tush, whose blushes I will spare, later confessed to having lost track of time and apologised profusely for nearly causing two heart attacks, but picking up the pieces of the scene after such an unsettling event was not easy.

Fortunately, such incidents are rare in the professional theatre but, however skillfully or amusingly they are negotiated, their memory lingers on in the minds of performers and audience alike.

HAPPY MOMENTS

Seldom given to flights of fancy, Ken nevertheless claims to have had an out-of-body experience in the middle of *The Mikado*. During a passage of dialogue in Act I, he suddenly found himself floating several feet above the stage watching his own performance. It would be easy to imagine such a strange sensation to be distressing but, oddly enough, Ken found it pleasurable. It seemed perfectly natural at the time and although it lasted for only a few moments, he enjoyed listening to his dialogue as others were hearing it and was quite impressed by his own acting. He rejects the suggestion of having been at the general anaesthetic again and assures me that, over the years, he experienced the phenomenon on several occasions.

A FINAL THOUGHT

Pooh-Bah is a larger-than-life character with more than his share of human failings, that much is clear. What is not clear, however, is why he behaves in such an obnoxious manner – Gilbert certainly gives us no clues. It is possible that he was poking fun at the perceived hypocrisy and snobbery of the aristocracy, but Ken believes that Pooh-Bah could just as easily be a self-important bureaucrat on any town or city council; the sort of corrupt official who takes on public office to serve himself rather than the people he represents and who considers himself superior because of his position of influence. Indeed, with this in mind, he often rehearsed the dialogue in his native Yorkshire accent and found that this exercise produced a feel for the character that he rarely achieved on the stage. The accent was, of course, irrelevant, merely helping him to get to the heart of the words, but he remains convinced that he was onto something significant and regrets not having the opportunity to pursue it further.

'Another insult'

Ken as King Paramount with his author standing behind him in the striped coat

CONCLUDING THE CHARACTERS

THIS chapter has been devoted to the eight characters which occupied most of Ken's working life during his distinguished career with the D'Oyly Carte Opera Company. It should not be forgotten, however, that he played two other roles; the previously-mentioned Sergeant of Police in The *Pirates of Penzance* and King Paramount in *Utopia Limited*.

Ken has made no secret of the fact that he was extremely uncomfortable playing The Sergeant, nor that he considered himself to be unsuited to the part. He feels, therefore, unable to offer any useful or constructive comment, save that a performer wanting to play it should be sure that they can sing the low notes and have a flair for slapstick comedy – advice which Ken bases on painful experience.

As far as King Paramount is concerned, Ken remembers so little about the handful of performances at London's Savoy Theatre and Royal Festival Hall during the company's centenary celebrations of 1975, that he feels in no position to give a detailed appraisal of the character's demands. He can only say that it requires physical, vocal and mental stamina if the artist is to give a good account of both himself and the role. Paramount is on the stage for much of the opera and Ken remembers feeling exhausted by the many dance routines he had to perform, some of which came in the middle of a solo or vocal ensemble. He thoroughly enjoyed the dialogue and recalls being struck by the difference between the gentle and very human King Paramount and the other King that he played, Hildebrand in *Princess Ida*. The former is King in name only. He is manipulated by two devious courtiers whose scams and comfortable lifestyle are threatened by his desire to improve the lot of his native people. The latter is a King of absolute power, whose subjects and advisers would not dream of questioning his decisions. It was this comparison that helped Ken to create a loveable and sympathetic Paramount; a man who is as simple and unsophisticated as Hildebrand is worldly-wise and cultured.

Although he dreaded having to apply and then remove so much very dark make up, Ken enjoyed the challenge of such a demanding, but rewarding role. He regrets that the D'Oyly Carte management saw fit to drop the production after so few performances and believes that it could have been played during London seasons, when provincial transport costs did not preclude its inclusion. *Utopia Limited* may not represent the very best of Gilbert and Sullivan, but it is worthy of more than curiosity value. If the standard bearer of the Savoy tradition had not neglected it, audiences might have come to appreciate it as he did.

Ken can boast that he has played a principal part in every one of the G&S operas – that is if you count a concert performance of *The Grand Duke* in which he sang Ludwig during the centenary season at the Savoy. It was certainly a great deal of hard work for one performance and he was delighted that he later had the opportunity of recording a role which he would have liked to play in full production. Of all the music that he has learned over the years, Ludwig's songs and ensembles proved the hardest for Ken to master. Every number seemed, to him, to be packed with difficult or obscure words, many of which buzzed around his head in the middle of the night. In particular, the frequently-cut song about Ancient Greece at the beginning of the second act gave him nightmares. He was only saved by the fact that his son's school had included Greek in its curriculum, leaving Anthony with the unenviable task of teaching his father how to pronounce the tongue-twisting words. Ken now looks back and laughs about having to learn King Paramount and Ludwig at the same time, glad that such toil is a thing of the past.

He has purposely avoided discussing his singing of the roles. Not because it interests him any less than his acting of them, but because it is almost impossible to describe a singing technique. Every singer is unique and likely to adapt the basic principles of voice training to suit their individual needs. Movements, gestures and facial expressions are things that we can see and clearly understand, but the singing voice is invisible and mysterious. Singing is a mental, more than a physical process and, as such, is difficult to define. Ten baritones may produce similar tone or word colour in ten different ways, but Ken believes that few of them could clearly explain how they produce the effect. It is a very personal matter and, for that reason, he sees no point in trying to describe his way of singing. He would say, however, that diction is extremely important; it is no use making a beautiful sound if the words cannot be understood. Acting does not end where singing begins; the principles that apply to interpretation of the spoken word generally apply to the sung word and, in both cases, imagination is the key to word colour. If Ken's singing has given pleasure over the past 42 years he is gratified – and hopeful that his many recordings of the Savoy Operas will continue to both entertain and instruct.

Ken is anxious to make it clear that interpretation is a matter of personal taste and opinion. Any thoughts or advice offered in the previous pages may be accepted as helpful, or rejected accordingly. His ideas are not the only ideas and his method one of many methods. If his experience serves to encourage deeper enquiry into the wonderful creations of W.S. Gilbert and Sir Arthur Sullivan and the stagecraft needed to do justice to their work, he will be content.

AFTER THE CARTE

'But our year is not so spent, and our days are not so faded'

When Ken awoke on the morning of February 28th 1982, he could be forgiven for feeling depressed. He was 58 years old, his 25-year career with the D'Oyly Carte Opera Company had ended the previous evening and, with the exception of a few concerts, he had no offers of work. In truth, he had no idea what he was going to do with the rest of his life. Had he been told that, 17 years later, he would still be actively involved in performing Gilbert and Sullivan, it is unlikely that he would have believed it. By nature a modest man, he did not realise, at such a low point, that his reputation was to make him much sought after, both in Britain and North America, for many years to come. Any thoughts he might have had about retirement were quickly forgotten as the invitations to appear in concerts, full productions, master classes and conferences gradually built up to the point where his plans to return to some serious painting went on the back burner once again.

Ken's free-lance career did not take off overnight and, in the first months of redundancy following the closure of the company, he was grateful that he had no major financial obligations that would have forced him to seek regular employment. He busied himself with jobs around the house and was surprised to find that he did not miss the D'Oyly Carte routine as much as he had feared – in fact, he thoroughly enjoyed the freedom of not having to go to work every evening. He was, however, looking forward to the forthcoming concert engagements in his diary and was particularly excited by an unexpected invitation to appear in a series of prestigious Gilbert and Sullivan Galas in Los Angeles that November. They were to be introduced and narrated by the American actor, William Conrad, who had recently played the title role in the Brent Walker video of *The Mikado*. The heavyweight television detective, Canon, proved to be great fun and told Ken that he had been surprised to be offered the part of The Mikado. Seemingly, the casting director had heard that he aspired to play in *Falstaff* and presumed him to mean *Verdi's Falstaff*!

There were Gilbert and Sullivan concerts nearer home, too. Before the company closed down, the management had promoted several concerts featuring both its principals and chorus, which continued, under the auspices of other promoters, after the D'Oyly Carte had given its last performance. Ken enjoyed these occasions, because they brought back together the colleagues whose friendship he valued, keeping him in touch with both them and the loyal fans who turned up at every venue. He also enjoyed the variety of the concert format, which allowed him the freedom to play excerpts from many of the operas without the bother of having to put on costume and make up. By the end of 1982, it became increasingly obvious that the promoters' main objective was to make profit from the concerts. This prompted a feeling amongst some of the membership that such profits would be better spent funding more engagements for the group, rather than going into the pocket of managers. This opinion was reinforced by a snowbound engagement at the Opera House in Buxton, when some of the artists were not paid for their services and there were murmurs that the concert group would fare better if it could be run by the performers themselves. A few of them, including Ken, discussed the matter seriously and came to the conclusion that such action was not beyond the bounds of possibility – any dates secured would be a welcome addition to those arranged by other organisations. A proposition to this effect was put to the group and the decision to go ahead with self-management was taken – the first step to the formation of a company with which Ken is still proud to be associated and which has given him enormous pleasure during its sixteen-year life.

Within a short time, a steering committee was elected to supervise the setting up of a formal company and secure dates for the group, the latter responsibility being allotted to Ken. This development was not welcomed by the person who had promoted many of the earlier concerts and, after several acrimonious exchanges, it became apparent that the former D'Oyly Carte performers would be best served by severing existing ties and looking after their own interests in the future. That they proved successful beyond their expectations is evidenced by the continuing appeal of the same group of artists who, on the threshold of a new millennium, fondly refer to themselves as 'The Antiques Roadshow'!

Once the momentous decision to go it alone had been taken, things happened quickly. Bookings for the group were made at theatres around the country; the setting up of a Company Limited By Guarantee (with charitable status) was moving ahead and, on the 11th of September 1983, the new company, G & S a la Carte Ltd., was officially launched to coincide with a concert at the Grand Theatre in Wolverhampton. Ken was one of five members elected to the board and was nominated as Managing Director, although responsibility for the running of the company was equally shared with the other directors. The new company quickly established itself as the leading Gilbert and Sullivan group in the concert field and received critical acclaim wherever it appeared. The unique format of semi-staged excerpts given by seven principals and up to 20 chorus accompanied by two pianos, was made possible because the company took only as much profit as was necessary to cover overheads. There were no shareholders to consider and the

Mr.K. Sandford, 13th June, 1983
128 Argyle Road,
London. W13

Dear Mr. Sandford,

Thank you so much for setting out your proposals regarding the establishment of a group of artists to provide concerts of Gilbert and Sullivan.

Your memorandum was considered by the Trustees who feel, broadly speaking, that they would like to help you in what we all regard as a worthwhile enterprise.

We thought, therefore, that we should put to you various proposals of a concrete nature as to how we might be of assistance.

These are as follows:

We would allow you to publicise your group as having the approval of the Trustees of the D'Oyly Carte Opera Trust. The exact wording you could use should perhaps be a matter of further discussion between us. It might for instance be appropriate for you to bill your concerts as "in association with the D'Oyly Carte Opera Trust".

We much appreciate your offer to devote the profits from each concert to the Trust and we do feel that it would not be unreasonable to ask you to guarantee a £100 fee per concert for the use of the name.

We would, of course, agree to assist you in any way we can with help and advice for any concert from either the Trustees or Mr. Truelove. The Friends of D'Oyly Carte would also be pleased to publicise your concerts through their newsletter.

We are most grateful to you for your offer to help with the sale of D'Oyly Carte records and souvenirs but we are not involved in any way with video.

Yours sincerely,

M. B. Radcliffe, Secretary, D'Oyly Carte Opera Trust

A COMIC SURPRISE

An evening of Gilbert & Sullivan, Ex-D'Oyly Carte Opera Company, Birmingham Hippodrome

Reports of the death of D'Oyly Carte have been greatly exaggerated. Last night – one year to the day after the late lamented company was forced to close – the Hippodrome staged a wake with a difference.

The afficionados who packed the theatre to hear a selection from 11 comic operettas as W. S. Gilbert and Arthur Sullivan had intended them were in for a surprise.

There were no costumes or scenery, and the set was like something out of Hinge and Bracket with potted plants, albeit with two grand pianos.

When the dinner-jacket chorus opened up with "If you want to know who we are" from *The Mikado* it looked like a Welsh male voice choir had come to town.

It was a drawing room concert atmosphere, but if the staging was different the much-loved music was the same as ever.

If only the Arts Council, which cut off the company's financial lifeline, had seen the antics of the ex-Savoyards, they would never have penned that notorious "tired and wooden" epitaph.

It was G & S as nobody has seen it interpreted before, but sung so magically that not even the purists could take offence.

D'Oyly Carte is not dead, just resting – and to prove it they'll be back at the Hippodrome on May 6.

CHRIS WALDER

Birmingham Evening Mail, 28 February 1983

directors received no payment for their work, the company's mandate being to secure engagements for its members.

In November of 1983, after lengthy negotiations with the Trustees of the D'Oyly Carte, the two companies entered into a formal agreement which gave permission for G & S a la Carte Ltd. to present itself as 'The Magic of D'Oyly Carte' until such time as the D'Oyly Carte Opera Company should be relaunched. This arrangement, whereby both parties benefited from the use of the famous name, proved highly successful and 'Magic' concerts went from strength to strength. From small provincial theatres and halls to the most prestigious venues in the country, the new company was always well received and the impact of the D'Oyly Carte's demise seemed to be softened by the performances given by the defunct company's familiar names. Ken's involvement, both as director and performer, gave him great satisfaction, although the running of the group meant a great deal of work for himself and his colleagues on the board. They held regular meetings in each others' homes, travelling between London and the Midlands on a monthly basis to deal with company business and forthcoming concerts. Such commitment was rewarded by the increasing number of dates they secured and the many favourable press reviews praising the group's fast-moving presentation, which broke new ground with slick choreography and imaginative staging.

The next few years saw 'The Magic of D'Oyly Carte' appearing with great success at London's Barbican and Royal Festival Halls, courtesy of the promoter, Raymond Gubbay, Birmingham's Hippodrome Theatre, Dublin's National Concert Hall and the Palace Theatre, Manchester, as well as at many other venues around the country. Several of the concerts were broadcast and the company made a brief return to full productions when it presented *The Yeomen of the Guard* at The Barbican, followed by *The Pirates of Penzance, H.M.S. Pinafore* and *The Mikado* at Bradford's Alhambra Theatre and The Theatre Royal, Nottingham in 1985, for which the D'Oyly Carte scenery was made available. Having kept the D'Oyly Carte name before the public with high-quality performances of Gilbert and Sullivan, it came as a blow when Ken received a letter from the D'Oyly Carte Trustees stating that G & S a la Carte Ltd. would no longer be allowed to use the famous name once the D'Oyly Carte Opera Company had re-opened in 1987. The news was not unexpected, but Ken and his fellow directors were left to ponder on the future of their own organisation in light of this development. If the new D'Oyly Carte should become hugely successful, it would probably mean the end of the road for 'Magic' concerts. The new company, however, proved to be a very different animal from its progenitor. Its touring schedule and repertory were limited and the new style of productions drew mixed reviews. Although some concerts were arranged for its principals, it became clear that they were no match for G & S a la Carte's established and well-respected presentations. After a quiet period, dates for the group began to come in once more and the directors, anxious to keep the 'Magic' element in the billing, chose 'The Magic of Gilbert & Sullivan' for future engagements.

It says a great deal about the talent of the performers and their lasting friendships that they are still performing together in 1999. Ken is amazed by the enduring appeal of the group and laughs as he recalls the directors' futile attempts to close down G & S a la Carte Ltd. It was becoming increasingly difficult to secure dates for the whole company and, mindful of the fact that the members were no longer spring chickens, the board reluctantly decided to recommend closure after a farewell performance sometime in 1997. Promoter, Raymond Gubbay, however, had other ideas and arranged 'Magic' concerts at The Barbican Hall in London, Birmingham's magnificent Symphony Hall, Manchester's impressive new Bridgewater Hall, The National Concert Hall in Glasgow and Liverpool's Philharmonic Hall. Accompanied by a full orchestra, the veteran Gilbert and Sullivan company delighted large and enthusiastic audiences and there seemed little point in winding up the company – particularly as the 'Magic' family loved getting together several times each year. As long as the public still wanted to see them, the board would postpone closure plans. That is the current state of affairs. With concerts planned to celebrate the millennium, 'The Magic of Gilbert & Sullivan' sails proudly on whilst the new D'Oyly Carte Opera Company has, ironically, all but disappeared. Looking back on those first tentative discussions about the performers running the concerts themselves, Ken is proud of what has been achieved by his colleagues and finds every 'Magic' concert not only a source of delight, but also a welcome reminder of the old days on tour. Whilst driving through Manchester en route to the Bridgewater Hall in 1998, he experienced a feeling of *deja vu* when he passed a shop sign which read 'Leech's Funeral Service'. Little wonder that he became a touch emotional – it seemed as though 40 years had stood still.

Ken was happily enjoying the best of both worlds; with plenty of time at home and enough 'Magic' dates to keep him professionally interested, semi-retirement suited him nicely. But, late in 1983, he received a phone call from Geoffrey Shovelton, one of the 'Magic' principal tenors, regarding a proposed Gilbert and Sullivan concert tour of North America. As it was to be for only two weeks, Ken decided that he would very much like to be included in the party to travel. Geoffrey had arranged the tour under the promotion of a first rate New York agency and Ken was keen to see how such a trip might differ from those he had undertaken with the D'Oyly Carte. It was to prove very different. The small group of five singers and a pianist flew to Boston on February 13th, 1984, to begin the first of 10 fascinating tours in which Ken took part during the following 12 years.

Gone were the days when luggage was handed over at the Savoy Hotel and loaded into buses to be collected on arrival at his destination. Such small-scale touring required, quite literally, a 'hands on' approach to travelling. Although the tours were extremely well organised, Ken and his former D'Oyly Carte colleagues had to handle heavy suitcases into hired vehicles and drive themselves to hotels and concert venues, sometimes travelling several hundred miles after a long flight. He was always amused by the idea of arriving in the U.S.A. aboard a huge jet aircraft, transferring to a six-seater plane to fly to some tiny airport in the middle of a field and then completing the journey squashed into a glorified van surrounded by the group's luggage - it was the sublime to the ridiculous! The itinerary for the first tour set the pattern of those to follow, with sometimes as many as 10 one-night engagements in as many days. The group's performances included appearances in Massachusetts, Rhode Island, New York, Detroit, Pennsylvania, Washington DC and North Carolina, the mix of small towns and large cities being a feature of the tours. From magnificent 3000-seat concert halls, to intimate small theatres, shopping malls and school gymnasia, the wandering minstrels brought their professional Gilbert and Sullivan expertise to enthusiastic audiences across America.

The Washington Post

Gilbert & Sullivan, Tried and True

Tuesday, October 23, 1984 – **The ticket of Gilbert & Sullivan was far more popular Sunday night at the the Natural History Building than Reagan-Bush or Mondale-Ferraro. Despite the competition from the presidential "debates", Baird Auditorium was filled to capacity with comic opera lovers who came to hear some of the principal members of the legendary but now extinct D'Oyly Carte Opera Company from London perform excerpts from the duo's work.**

The "Savoyards" spokesman, Geoffrey Shovelton, promised the enthusiastic listeners that "everyone will hear two or three of their favourites." The troupe, named after the Savoy Theatre (where Gilbert and Sullivan's operas were premiered), succeeded admirably in its goal. Shovelton was joined by a quartet of actor-singers, and accompanied by former conductor David Mackie on piano.

Scenes of spoken dialogue alternated with the famous "patter songs" from *Iolanthe*, *Yeoman of the Guard*, *The Mikado*, and other masterpieces. Shovelton announced the programme from the stage, describing the synopsis of each opera and sharing amusing anecdotes from D'Oyly Carte's distinguished history. The company gave its final performance two years ago.

Although the schedules were physically and mentally demanding, the lengthy journeys sometimes leaving little time to rest or get a meal, Ken enjoyed the challenge and marvelled at his own stamina. The tours took the singers from east to west and north to south of the vast North American continent and Ken made brief visits to many towns and cities in which the D'Oyly Carte could not have considered appearing. He had never previously been to Florida, Kansas, Texas or South Dakota and began to realise that life in small-town America bore little resemblance to the much more sophisticated lifestyle of the large cities in which he had appeared. This certainly provided him with a number of amusing anecdotes and, more than any other factor, brought home to him the complete contrast of this kind of tour to those he had experienced with the D'Oyly Carte. Many of the ten tours he undertook with Geoffrey and various of their colleagues included dates in the Bible Belt of America's Mid-West. On arriving in Springfield, Missouri in the February of 1988, the members of the group were informed that dancing on the stage was deemed, by the devout local inhabitants, to be unseemly and that even the simplest steps would be considered offensive. Ken thought that the concert organisers were joking, but the performers decided that if that was what the audience wanted, that was what the audience would get. Nothing had been mentioned about dialogue, so they included the appropriate spoken links into their musical items. The audience was dominated by the stony-faced elders of the local church, who sat, expressionless, in the centre of the auditorium. After *'Were I thy bride'*, Ken completed the excerpt from *Yeomen* with Shadbolt's lines about his numerous conquests. He realised that this was not going down too well after he had said:

'But, Lord, how she woo'd!'

when he felt an icy blast of disapproval from the house. By the time he had finished, the silence that replaced the usual laughter told Ken that the audience was most definitely not amused by such a display of debauchery, leaving him to wonder whether or not he should leave the Stage Door wearing a disguise.

As a lover of Western movies, Ken was enchanted by the idea of visiting Sioux Falls in Iowa. It proved to be a tiny settlement boasting a bank, a café and, to his astonishment, a magnificent concert hall. Seemingly, the local inhabitants prided themselves on their tradition of choral singing and had equipped themselves with a venue worthy of their talents. During the long hours spent driving through the Mid-West, they passed through many such small communities and he remembers the group stopping for refreshments at a drug store located on a dirt road miles from anywhere. The influx of five English people and a Scotsman, with their strange accents, gave the incredulous locals something to talk about for years, but left the thirsty travellers with the distinct impression that they had just landed from another planet!

On a few occasions, their journeys proved to be quite frightening. Having landed from the U.K. at Kansas City, the group collected the hired car and set off for their destination, Iola. A sudden violent storm made driving conditions treacherous and, with visibility reduced to a few yards, the weary performers got hopelessly lost. Having driven for what seemed like hours in torrential downpours, one of them spotted lights in the distance. More by luck than judgement, they had found Iola, but it had been an unnerving experience. At the start of the 1998 tour, they arrived in Buffalo in bitterly cold February weather. The following day was a rest day and it began to snow heavily. Before long, Ken was told that Buffalo was experiencing a 'white-out' and that he should not attempt to leave the hotel to do his shopping. He had heard that such ferocious blizzards could cause anyone foolhardy enough to venture outside in such weather to become totally disorientated. Ken, as usual, had to experience this for himself before he would believe it and set off for the local stores. Having got no further than 50 yards from the hotel, he realised that he had completely lost his bearings and tried to turn back. He struggled to retrace his steps but, in zero visibility, it was almost impossible to know in which direction he was heading. It was a very relieved Kenneth Sandford who finally groped his way into the hotel lobby. He believed. The following day, the group set off for Guelph in Ontario, driving north through New York State towards the Canadian border. The road conditions were atrocious and they passed many vehicles abandoned at the side of the road or buried in snowdrifts. However carefully they drove, there were many narrow escapes and the border officials told them that they were amazed that it had been possible to get through at all.

For the most part, their travels were tiring, but uneventful – a necessary part of the job. Ken welcomed the opportunity that such wide-ranging tours gave him to meet up with old friends from his American trips with the D'Oyly Carte. Whenever they played in Michigan or Illinois, he could be sure that Harry Benford, of Gilbert and Sullivan Lexicon fame, would come to the concert with his wife, Betty. Ken corresponded with them, but it was always nice to see them in person. When playing the group's regular date at the Natural History Museum in Washington, he was able to briefly catch up with friends of 20 years standing. Overall, he thoroughly enjoyed these hectic tours and, despite the demands of long journeys and one-night engagements, was glad to have experienced so much of the North American continent. Unfortunately, the New York agency responsible for the excellent organisation of their itineraries decided that the 1990 tour was to be the last. By 1993, Geoffrey had succeeded in persuading another agent to take up the reins, but Ken found the schedules and planning much less to his liking. After the 1996 tour, he was so exhausted on arrival home, that he reluctantly decided to make it his last. After all, he was 72 years old and should be taking things easy! Nevertheless, he looks back with great pleasure on the frantic days that took him around the United States of America in an inappropriately titled 'recreational vehicle'. He thought it unlikely that he would return . . .

Although most of Ken's career after the closure of the D'Oyly Carte involved concert work, he took part in a number of productions, both at home and in North America. During a dreary February morning in 1983, Ken was pottering about his home in Ealing when he received a telephone call. By 8-15 that evening he was appearing as Sir Despard Murgatroyd at the Garrick Playhouse in Altrincham, Cheshire. The Sale Gilbert and Sullivan Society's Despard had been taken ill and unless a replacement could be found, the production would have to be cancelled. Some artists might have considered it beneath their professional dignity to appear with amateurs, but Ken did not look at it that way. He had nothing else to do, it would be helping out the society and, above all, it was one of his favourite parts. He had a thoroughly enjoyable week.

'Tomorrow it may pour again'

In the early summer of 1985, Ken accepted an invitation to take part in an open-air production of *Iolanthe* at Gawsworth Hall in Cheshire. It was the beginning of an association that was to last for nine years. The owners of the beautiful 15th-century house presented an annual season of plays and musical events in the gardens of their home, with the audience picnicking Glyndebourne-style before the performance. Ken took part in three of their Gilbert and Sullivan productions before being asked to direct the 1988 production, *Princess Ida*. Reluctant to take on the responsibility of both directing and performing, he asked me to join him as co-director in a fruitful collaboration that spanned six productions. To say that staging a Gilbert and Sullivan opera on a, frequently, saturated lawn was fraught with perils is something of an understatement. With both the audience and orchestra under cover, performances were never cancelled however inclement the weather – and it often was. Whenever it rained, the performers donned transparent waterproofs and continued stoically, although singing in chilly, damp air was hardly good for the vocal chords. The daily ritual in the hall of watching the lunch-time weather forecast led to the development of rehearsing alternative stage business which avoided the artists having to sit on wet grass or chairs. This pragmatic approach led to the unforgettable sight of Patricia Leonard making her dignified entrance as The Duchess of Plaza Toro, in Act II of *The Gondoliers*, with a sheet of dry-cleaner's plastic protecting her elaborate, two-feet high, white court wig.

Aside from the weather, there were many practical difficulties associated with the Gawsworth productions, not the least of which was scenery. Whatever the opera being performed, the black and white half-timbered house could hardly be covered up or moved. This presented no problems for the setting of *Princess Ida* or *The Yeomen of the Guard*, but Venice or Titipu? Ken quickly came to the conclusion that a suggestion of the location was all that was needed; the audience would hardly be expecting a full set for an outdoor show. Blue and white-striped poles planted into the lawn for *Gondoliers*; scaffolding designed as mast rigging for *H.M.S. Pinafore* and portable tomb stones for *Pirates* were sufficient to set the scene. The size of the performing area presented problems with the timing of entrances and exits behind the natural hedge 'wings'. At 75 feet wide by 50 feet deep, it was a considerable area to cover, requiring both principals and chorus to allow plenty of time to get on and off. When Sullivan's introductory music was only a few bars long, it was necessary for the Musical Director to add repeats or extensions if the performers were to appear or disappear in good time. Another problem was in the lighting department. In early July, total darkness did not fall until the end of the show and it was difficult to capture the atmosphere of any scene set at night, but Ken has always believed that the audience's power of imagination should not be underestimated.

Having taken Gawsworth's unique staging requirements into account, the weather usually had the last word, leading to some memorably funny moments. Ken's particular favourites in the disaster department include the night when a very wet performance of *Patience* was invaded by a plague of frogs from the nearby lake. The slight hysteria amongst the ladies' chorus and evasive actions taken by principals trying to dance round them left the audience rolling with laughter, as the leaping amphibians upstaged everyone. He also remembers the inelegant skidding and numerous falls caused by the slippery conditions. During the opening chorus of *Iolanthe*, the fairies were struggling to control their feet during their dance sequences, much to the amusement of the audience. Eileen Jackson, playing Celia, turned this to hilarious advantage when she slid through a large puddle formed on the grass and ended up in a 'splits' position that she would, normally, have been unable to achieve. Undaunted by her embarrassing position, she assumed a theatrical pose with her arms triumphantly raised and received a tumultuous round of applause for her troubles.

During the last two years of his association with the Gawsworth Summer Opera, Ken's relationship with the owner of the house deteriorated rapidly. He never got over the fact that the said owner insisted that the second act of *Pirates* be interrupted so that he could appear in the middle of the policemen's routine for the audience to sing 'Happy Birthday' to him. He was also unhappy with the Musical Director, who invited his orchestra to join him in making music, before adding that he had no idea what that had to do with Gilbert and Sullivan. His final show at Gawsworth was *The Yeomen of the Guard* and Ken believes that our joint production was one of his finest achievements. He is rather sorry that he left with a sour taste in his mouth, because the colourful spectacle of Gilbert and Sullivan being performed against the stunning backdrop of the floodlit hall will remain with him always.

It was ironical that 'The Magic of D'Oyly Carte' ventured into its first fully-staged opera without him. In the August of 1985, whilst the company was presenting *Yeomen* at The Barbican in London, he was appearing with John Reed in a production of *The Gondoliers* for the famous Berkshire Choral Institute in Sheffield, Massachusetts. He was, naturally, disappointed to miss the chance of playing Wilfred Shadbolt once more, but he joined in the planning of the company's first full production with enthusiasm. Jon Ellison was to replace him, so he flew to Boston in good heart, his only concern being that he would have to wait to find out how *Yeomen* had fared. It was good to be teamed up with John again and any disappointment he may have felt at missing out on Shadbolt was soon forgotten as he looked forward to playing Don Alhambra, one of the roles he had missed in the three years since the demise of the D'Oyly Carte. He and John entered fully into the spirit of the week-long summer school, offering advice on stage technique and dialogue delivery to the less experienced performers and joining in the social activities with gusto. It was his first taste of coaching and he enjoyed it as much as performing.

Having been abroad during *Yeomen*, Ken was delighted to take part in the performances of *Pirates, Pinafore and Mikado* in Nottingham and Bradford in the autumn of 1985. He had not missed playing Pooh-Bah in the previous three years, but absence makes the heart grow fonder and he returned to it with enthusiasm. The fact that it was for their own company made all the difference and it was wonderful that the audiences seemed to welcome back the company as long-lost friends. He had not missed playing The Sergeant of Police for a quarter of a century, but with John Ayldon playing The Pirate King, it was a logical decision for Ken to take on The Sergeant once again. Nothing had changed; the low notes were as low as before and he was still not comfortable playing red-nose comedy, but the experience he had gained since his final performance of the role for the D'Oyly Carte in 1962 carried him through. Despite his misgivings, he relaxed and enjoyed a part that he had once loathed, particularly as Alan Spencer's routines were both challenging and amusing. The inclusion of *H.M.S. Pinafore* for the short season was a real bonus for Ken, giving him, at last, the chance to play Captain Corcoran – a challenge to which he rose splendidly, his singing of *'Fair Moon'*, in particular, drawing great praise.

After such a busy year in 1985, the following year was much quieter production-wise. He had Gawsworth in July, but nothing either side of it. He was quite philosophical about this and hoped to use the time to work on his paintings of scenes from D'Oyly Carte productions. That was when he received the unexpected invitation to direct *The Gondoliers* for the San Diego Gilbert and Sullivan Company. The idea of a few weeks of Californian sunshine appealing to him as much as his first opportunity to direct, he quickly made up his mind to accept. The production was an enormous success and Ken enjoyed every moment of the directing process, from the initial rough ideas for his concept, to the final detailed dialogue coaching and lighting design. He found it fascinating to spend the daytime putting his ideas on paper and then seeing them come to life during the evening rehearsal. It soon became obvious to him that coaching less experienced performers than himself was a great way to pass on the acting skills he had acquired in his 36 years on the professional stage and he delighted in watching the development of his protogees.

During the next few years, Ken's involvement in full productions was limited to his appearance as Private Willis for the Toronto Gilbert and Sullivan Society's *Iolanthe* in 1988 and the annual season at Gawsworth, when he was able to both perform and share directing responsibilities with myself. He welcomed the chance that this gave us to get away from the rigid stage business of the old D'Oyly

San Diego Union

Saturday, 21 June 1986

"GONDOLIERS" REVIVAL IS GILBERT AND SULLIVAN AT EVERYBODY'S BEST

Music Review "The Gondoliers" by David Gregson

The San Diego's Gilbert and Sullivan revival of this classic, which began its six-performance run last night at the Casa del Prado Theatre in Balboa Park, is absolutely the best thing this organisation has ever done. Under the brilliantly paced, stylistically immaculate direction of Kenneth Sandford, an actual veteran of Britain's famous, defunct D'Oyly Carte Company, our local group achieved heights of ensemble excellence rarely seen in amateur or semi-professional G & S troupes.

With its cast of unusually strong principals, its fine choral singing, its gorgeous 18th century costumes, its superb choreography and stage movement, its uniformly well-executed, carefully-measured diction, this "Gondoliers" is an authentic pleasure from beginning to end.

Like the Duke of Plaza-Toro, this production invites – nay demands – an audience.

Carte and take a fresh look at the presentation of the Savoy Operas. It was not that he was interested in modern, gimmicky Gilbert and Sullivan, but more that he wanted the characters and dramatic situations to be credible to modern audiences. He has always been convinced that it is possible to be true to the intentions and spirit of the authors whilst doing away with the restrictions imposed by the conventions of Victorian staging. He loved the creativity of principal rehearsals, the development of characterisations and scenes something he could only dream about when he and his former D'Oyly Carte colleagues were with the company. He loved, too, seeing choristers mostly used to being treated as human scenery develop into responsive and responsible actors, their contribution to the production, once released from the restraints of straight lines and semi-circles, of great significance. Ken found his status as co-director very useful when it came to casting *The Pirates of Penzance*. Not wishing to play the Sergeant again, he and John Ayldon swapped roles, so that Ken might have, for the first time, the pleasure of striding the stage as The Pirate King – a delightful change for him. He now misses those days spent discussing the possibilities of Gilbert's dialogue with like-minded professionals and the joys of creating original stage business for both principals and chorus. They were some of the most rewarding moments of his career.

In 1995, the second year of the Buxton International Gilbert and Sullivan Festival, Ken was invited to recreate his masterly Doctor Daly in my pro-am production of *The Sorcerer*, which featured former D'Oyly Carte stars backed by an amateur chorus. As previously mentioned, he was thrilled to play the part once more and was particularly interested to see how much was gained by the amateur performers appearing alongside their professional counterparts. He thoroughly enjoyed the ambience of the Festival, in which he gave talks and Master Classes, although he felt that what should have been a celebration of the performance of Gilbert and Sullivan by groups of varying ability was spoiled by the competitive element that set them against each other. The following year, *The Sorcerer* was to be repeated, alongside my production of *Ruddigore*. Ken was tickled pink by the prospect of playing Sir Despard Murgatroyd after a gap of 13 years and happily brushed the cobwebs from his still-shiny interpretation. Patricia Leonard was to play Mad Margaret, so he knew that he would be working with an imaginative partner and he gladly seized the opportunity to bring some fresh ideas to his characterisation. The festival organisers had decided to encourage further American participation by holding a week-long leg of the festival in Philadelphia and this was to include both operas. The prospect of a short trip to the U.S.A. appealed to Ken and an amazing coincidence was to ensure his pleasure. An acquaintance from California contacted him in Philadelphia to say that she knew the whereabouts of his D'Oyly Carte Sir Despard costume. She was a friend of the person who had purchased it at the company's sale of costumes in the 1980s and, as she was travelling to Philadelphia for the festival, would be willing to bring it with her if he wanted to wear it! Needless to say, putting on that costume (which still fitted him perfectly) felt wonderful and made it easy for him to drop immediately into the melodramatic and villainous character of old.

In 1997, with the charms of the festival fast wearing thin, Ken agreed to play Captain Corcoran in my production of *H.M.S. Pinafore*. With the American part of the festival stretched to include Berkeley, California as well as Philadelphia, before the season in Buxton, it was a busy summer. There is little doubt that he was delighted to play the role, particularly with Valerie Masterson playing Josephine and Gillian Knight as Little Buttercup, but he was beginning to feel increasingly disillusioned with the festival. Not even a happy return to San Francisco and a wonderful party at the home of Rob Gawthrop made up for the fact that the festival organisers treated him with barely-concealed frostiness. It is no surprise to him that he has not been asked to take part in subsequent festivals and he is saddened to feel that his experience was not valued by an organisation which, in his opinion, has no concept of a professional approach to the theatre. He has not appeared in full production since, but feels that if his performance of Captain Corcoran at the Opera House in Buxton proves to be his last in costume and make up, then it is one of which he is proud.

'The amateur tenor, whose vocal villainies all desire to shirk'

Ken's appearances in concerts and productions, as well as his sorties into directing, have kept him professionally busy since 1982, but he has increasingly enjoyed his association with the world of amateur Gilbert and Sullivan. This interest dates back to a trip in 1985, when he gave talks and Master Classes in Chicago and Ann Arbor, Michigan, as well as his participation in a symposium held in Toronto in 1987, where he gave a memorable talk about his work to a large and appreciative audience of amateur enthusiasts. His easy manner and willingness to chat about Gilbert and Sullivan endeared him to the delegates and led to an invitation to a similar event in West Chester, Pennsylvania in 1989. On that occasion, the symposium, called 'Basingstoke!', saw him giving expert advice on dialogue and acting techniques, as well as taking the part of King Paramount in a 30-minute piece which I had written to introduce the uninitiated to the delights of *Utopia Limited*. He loved these occasions for the joyous spirit engendered amongst the international family of amateur Gilbert and Sullivan buffs and the chance to meet friends old and new. Harry and Betty Benford were always at these events, but it was at the Toronto symposium where he first made the acquaintance of Gareth Jacobs and his wife, Elizabeth Thomson; the start of a friendship that has grown stronger over the years.

There have been, and still are, many other opportunities for Ken to encourage higher standards in amateur Gilbert and Sullivan productions. He particularly looks forward to the annual Gilbert and Sullivan week-end held at Morfa Nefyn in North Wales, where he and several of his D'Oyly Carte colleagues entertain and instruct in the warm and convivial atmosphere of a seaside hotel. He also enjoys supporting the many amateur operatic societies of which he is president or patron, always ready to give advice in a charming and self-effacing manner. He feels strongly that such contact is important, because with so few professional productions of the Savoy Operas, the perpetuity of these timeless works is in the hands of amateur companies and their, often, ageing membership. He regrets that the very word 'amateur' is synonymous with low standards and embarrassing church hall productions. In his experience, this misconception is far from the case, with many groups boasting both talent and the willingness to put on their yearly productions in expensive theatres. Ken believes that amateur performers are only as good or bad as the people instructing them; they have the potential to become fine performers if guided by producers and musical directors of theatrical pedigree. If Gilbert and Sullivan operettas are to survive in this country, they must be performed in such a way as to make them fun for young people – they are the future. This does not mean that every Gilbert and Sullivan production has to be up-dated, modernised and subjected to a rock beat, but producers have a responsibility to make their shows imaginative and full of interest for chorus and principals, both young and old. Without such imagination and vision, amateur performances of Gilbert and Sullivan will continue to be the subject of ill-informed and unkind comment. They deserve a better fate.

Aside from his professional interests, Ken's life seems to be as full and busy as it has ever been. The notion that getting to the age of 75 means a blissful existence of rest and relaxation does not apply in his case. Whoever wrote that script never had Kenneth Sandford in mind for the leading role! He enjoys life to the full and is seldom still for more than a few minutes at a time; he always has something to do, be it in the garden, at the piano or in his studio. It is surprising that a man who lived for 40 years in the bustle of London should take so easily to life in Market Drayton. He and Pauline became disillusioned with life in the increasingly-congested capital and began to look around the North Midlands for a suitable home, although they had no fixed ideas as to their eventual destination. It was the house, as much as the location, that attracted them and they moved to the delightful Shropshire town in 1988. The large bungalow, built on top of a three-car garage, has a pleasant, rural outlook and the steep, banked garden is most unusual, entailing plenty of work for Ken. He has converted part of the garage space into a large studio, where he is, at last, able to indulge his undying passion for oil painting. In truth, he loves the peace of country life and does not miss London at all. He makes regular visits to Buckinghamshire to see his son and two grandchildren, but does not see his daughter as much as he would like, as she works in Kenya, living with his other grandchild in Nairobi. He enjoys singing for local community groups and is amused by the fact that Market Drayton audiences are completely unimpressed by his theatrical credentials. So are the mighty humbled!

Ex-Serviceman sings the opera at the WI

Mucklestone

The monthly meeting of Mucklestone WI was held on October 7 at Knighton Village Hall.

President, Mrs. B. Whalley, presided and she was pleased to welcome Mrs. S. Cartwright as a new member of the institute.

Mrs. Whalley thanked all those who had helped to tidy the garden outside the church.

Eight members attended the autumn council meeting held at Ashley Village Hall, chaired by president Mrs. H. Madeley.

Kenneth Stamford told us of his life in the RAF and the subsequent opportunities he had to sing Carousel at Drury Lane before he finally became a member of the D'Oyly Carte.

He sang songs from Oklahoma, Carousel and HMS Pinafore.

The knee blanket was won by the Westlands WI and the Unusual battle was won by Maer.

Market Drayton Advertiser, October 1988

Kenneth Sandford has enjoyed a long and illustrious career in the theatre, but he still looks to the future. The year 2000 marks his 50th year in Show Business and he is thrilled that he will be able to celebrate this milestone in the company of his 'Magic of Gilbert & Sullivan' colleagues, as they come together for a series of concerts around the country. Perhaps the secret of his success lies in his belief that there is always more to learn. He is still working on his technique; practising every day, learning new songs and visiting his pianist once a week in an effort to improve his singing. Even though he no longer appears in full productions, he discusses the possibilities of Gilbert and Sullivan's immortal creations with the zeal of a convert, his enthusiasm and desire for self-improvement a perfect example of the true artist. He is a giant in his field and a role model for any professional performer, but he is also a modest, charming and ordinary man from Yorkshire and it is fitting that this book concludes with tributes from a few of the many people whose lives have been enriched by his talent. On behalf of the countless others, I echo the sentiments of Gareth Jacobs. Thanks Ken.

* * * * * * * *

As a youngster living in Golders Green, I was taken regularly to see shows at the Golders Green Hippodrome. The annual visits by the D'Oyly Carte Opera Company were firm favourites and I recall vividly Kenneth Sandford playing Private Willis, Grosvenor, the Grand Inquisitor and above all, Pooh-Bah. My "O" Level exams, the peak of my scholastic achievements, coincided with a two-week stint by the Company at Golders Green and I still recall clearly the joy of slipping into the ten shillings (50p) stalls to savour a couple of hours away from last minute cramming and another bout of exam nerves.

More than forty years on, I am proud and delighted to be working with Ken and and to know that he is still delighting audiences old and new with excerpts from the roles that he made so much his own. If there is such a thing as a true Savoyard, then Ken Sandford is exactly that, somebody who has devoted himself to bringing the wonderful, topsy-turvey world of Gilbert and Sullivan alive to the delight of audiences everywhere.

Raymond Gubbay

* * * * * * * *

To me, Ken on stage instantly means finesse and class. As an actor, he has never shown complacency and like all the best artistes, always searches for the best in himself to present, in turn, the best to his audience. I noticed immediately, when working with the "Magic of D'Oyly Carte", that it was the long-serving, experienced and brilliant Ken Sandford who not only asked for musical suggestions, help and advice but positively thrived on whatever contributions I could make . . . some of his younger colleagues not only lacked his talent, but also his generosity of spirit. I have spent much of my career in the musical theatre and to find an actor's brain at work in the Savoy Opera world is rare; add other exceptional qualities such as a fine voice and brilliant timing – and choose your own favourite moments from his characterisations; my personal memories will always include his exquisite Don Alhambra in *The Gondoliers.*

Ken helped me to understand why musical direction in the theatre must be word-based . . . now, I work always with that ideal in mind.

Kenneth Sandford was one of my first heroes; I feel privileged to have him as a colleague and friend . . . he is a true star in the Savoyard Galaxy.

David Steadman

* * * * * * * *

Kenneth Sandford was quite my favourite; very individual, and subtler in style than the often primary acting colours going on around him. He seemed to be able to make each of his eight or nine acting parts in the repertoire each uniquely different, and each one stayed in the memory.

Kenneth really showed me the way, both before and during my time at RADA, how it was possible to infuse any characterisation with depth and colour, and he was an enormous influence on me.

Michael Simkins, Actor

Betty and I have enjoyed seeing Ken Sandford in Savoy operas many times over many years. Our overriding impression of Ken is that whenever he is on stage he is doing his absolute best to do justice to Gilbert's words and Sullivan's music. He has never appeared in the least bit bored and he invariably demonstrates an admirable professional attitude toward his work.

The first time we met Ken face to face was in 1978 at a New York G & S Society reception for the D'Oyly Cartes. We could see at once that Ken was a major attraction to the fans, and he was the soul of patience with even the most pestiferous of them. He was a good listener, and the merry twinkle in his eye told of good humor and appreciation of others' wit.

In 1978 I was bold enough to send Bridget D'Oyly Carte a copy of my newly-published Gilbert & Sullivan Lexicon. She wrote a letter of thanks and graciously invited Betty and me to visit her next time we were in London. Shortly thereafter we were able to accept her invitation. Earlier in that week, however, we had travelled up to Birmingham to attend a D'Oyly Carte performance of *The Mikado* and were enjoying a meal with Ken. Of course we couldn't resist boasting to Ken that we were looking forward to joining Bridget for lunch at the Savoy. Ken responded enviously that, in his many years with the Company, he had never received such an invitation. That has always struck us as indicative of the Company's lack of managerial imagination.

In 1979 we learned that Ken, in addition to being a superlative singer and actor, was also a master painter. We immediately commissioned an oil painting. A year later, while in London, we took possession of the newly-finished work. It met our specification, showing Gilbert, Sullivan, and D'Oyly Carte at a rehearsal of *The Mikado* in the Savoy Theatre. Appropriately enough, we picked it up backstage after enjoying another of Ken's performances, The treasured painting now hangs in a place of honor (in a good light!) in our study.

Harry Benford

* * * * * * * *

You couldn't throw him. And I've tried.

I first interviewed Kenneth in 1975 in the early days of Birmingham's first, and still best, commercial radio station, BRMB, before it surrendered to mindless pop and prattle.

By our third encounter in 1977 we had established a good repartee and our annual chats became something we both enjoyed.

One of my favourite encounters was in 1980 when Kenneth was joined by John Ayldon and Yvette Davis for a two-hour Sunday night special. I was determined to ruffle the sanguine Sandford style, but I may as well not have bothered.

We discussed everything from landladies to faux pas, from parody to commercials, and he would not hesitate, flinch or become tetchy. Anybody who heard it will recall that he laughed a lot, but there was no rancour.

I saved my king hit until near the end. Birds Eye had decided that Captain Corcoran's famous song from *Pinafore* would be ideal for selling one of their marine derivatives. After all, it was out of copyright and would cost them nothing to steal.

Through his earphones came the hideous sounds of.

"I am the Captain of the Fish Fingers,

(You're Captain Birds Eye too.)

And be it understood they're very very good

And white cod through and through,"

And so on to the gut crunching finale:

"So shout hooray and give three cheers

For Captain Birds Eye and his fish fingers." (Repeat).

Throughout it all, Ken sat motionless. We had done it. Was he about to lose it?

Was he heck!

The microphone came back on to Kenneth's audible guffawing. I think it's rather fun," said Ken. "If it helps sell Bird's Eye products – fine. But it might also help to remind people of *Pinafore* – and in doing so give them the incentive to come along and see a show."

As to other productions, he was full of praise for the work of the amateurs in sustaining and supporting Gilbert and Sullivan. And the *Black Mikado*? He loved it and went to see it four times.

In a nutshell, this consummate professional was incapable of voicing an unkind or indiscreet word about anything. In private, he suffered fools not at all and could say his piece with ease, but when the red light was on or the curtain was up, nothing at all shook him.

Dr Ed Doolan MBE., BBC Radio WM

* * * * * * * *

Looking back on a long career and on the people who have been a strong influence and example to me, the name of Kenneth Sandford is up there with Donald Adams, Thomas Round and John Reed.

I joined the D'Oyly Carte hot out of Music College, when I felt in some way prepared for singing on the stage, but found in my fellow artists a wealth of experience and superb talent for dialogue, comedy and timing, for which I was totally unprepared.

Ken possesses a voice of exceptional quality of expression and tonal variety, which is seldom found elsewhere. We all wait, time after time, to hear his 'Fair moon to thee I sing', or Dr. Daly's aria, never tiring of experiencing that soaring effortlessness that is so much a part of his marvellous singing. But it is as a performer supreme in his craft, with a complete mastery of his art and a generosity of spirit to his fellow performers that I shall always fondly remember him and be influenced by him.

Valerie Masterson C.B.E.

* * * * * * * *

My wife Liz and I have had the good fortune to have known Ken since the eighties, but our friendship developed when he came to Toronto, where we were living at the time, as guest of the local Society where he played Private Willis in 1988. It was a tremendous coup for us, and to gaze, first hand, at the sheer professionalism and stage discipline of the consummate artist knowing his craft was a wonderful experience for us all.

As amateurs, we have never (well, hardly ever) missed an opportunity to see Ken perform, or to gain from his experience from master classes such as those he gave at Buxton at the G & S Festival. For us to appear in the same productions as Ken, again in the Festival in Buxton and the US, will be long-cherished experiences. His dialogue delivery and timing is acknowledged amongst the finest in the business, and he has always made a special effort to pass on this talent to us amateurs. For this, we will always be grateful.

In 1987, when Ken was a guest speaker at the Utopia '87 symposium in Toronto, I had the honour of introducing him. I followed the expected line by saying that we were now going to meet a veritable army of special guests from all walks of life. I then listed all of Ken's characters and introduced them all as 'Kenneth Sandford'. To countless amateurs everywhere, he is that and much, much more. To Liz and I he his also a dear friend. Thanks, Ken.

Gareth Jacobs